THE AMERICAN EXPLORATION AND TRAVEL SERIES

Hunting and Trading on the Great Plains
1859–1875

James R. Mead, 1900

HUNTING AND TRADING ON THE GREAT PLAINS, 1859-1875

BY JAMES R. MEAD

Edited by Schuyler Jones

Introduction by Ignace Mead Jones

UNIVERSITY OF OKLAHOMA PRESS : NORMAN AND LONDON

Library of Congress Cataloging-in-Publication Data

Mead, James R. (James Richard), b. 1836.
Hunting and trading on the Great Plains, 1859–1875.

(American exploration and travel series; v. 69)
Bibliography: p.
Includes index.
1. Mead, James R. (James Richard), b. 1836.
2. Pioneers—Kansas—Biography. 3. Pioneers—
Oklahoma—Biography. 4. Hunting—Kansas—History—
19th century. 5. Hunting—Oklahoma—History—19th
century. 6. Indians of North America—Kansas.
7. Indians of North America—Oklahoma. 8. Kansas—
History. 9. Oklahoma—History. I. Jones, Schuyler,
1930–   . II. Title. III. Series.
F686.M43A34   1986   978′.02′0924   86-4343
ISBN 0-8061-1894-6 (alk. paper)

The paper in this book meets the guidelines for permanence and durability of the Committee on Production Guidelines for Book Longevity of the Council on Library Resources, Inc.

My feelings on first setting foot on the soil of Kansas were various. We had a feeling of insecurity; thot we had left the land of law and order and got among outlaws and desperadoes. This feeling, however, wore away soon. I felt that I had entered a land where an important scene in my life's history was to be enacted out and perhaps my lot cast for life.—JRM on crossing the Missouri River, Tuesday, May 31, 1859.

Contents

Illustrations

Maps

Editor's Preface

READERS may be curious to know some of the background of this book, which was left unpublished for nearly one hundred years after it was written.

Sometime in the last decade of the nineteenth century, James R. Mead spent several days dictating to a stenographer an account of his early years on the plains. The resulting script ran to ninety-three pages of single-spaced typing and was entitled "Reminiscences of Frontier Life." It is not known just when Mr. Mead dictated this manuscript or when it was typed. The first page bears the line "(Written in 1888)" typed in below Mr. Mead's name, but questions about this date arise from evidence in the text itself.

In the second paragraph of page one Mr. Mead tells us that his father "still uses a gun occasionally at his advanced age of 85 years." Mr. Mead's father, the Reverend Enoch Mead, was born on September 2, 1809. Thus in 1888 he would have been seventy-nine, not eighty-five, years of age. And there is yet another problem here: Enoch Mead died on December 6, 1892, at the age of eighty-three. This error in the text is one of several on which I comment below. Other statements in the text point to either 1893 or 1894 as dates for at least part of the typescript. For example, on page 18 of the original typescript Mr. Mead, in recounting how he had processed buffalo hides and tallow, writes: "We would render out the tallow in our large kettle (that was in 1859. Yesterday, October 3rd, 1893, I used the same kettle to boil a quantity of linseed oil used in painting my buildings)." References in the last sections of the typescript to events that occurred in 1894 are further evidence of a date later than 1888. A careful examination of the text has led the editor to conclude that parts of it were probably dictated as early as 1890 and that the remainder was set down from time to time up to about 1895.

The present volume has been put together from two different categories of text: James R. Mead's unpublished manuscript "Reminiscences of Frontier Life" and his articles, speeches, and letters.

The "Reminiscences" form the core of the book and provide its structure. Since they were taken down in dictation and typed by a stenographer, it has not been thought necessary to reproduce exactly the spelling, punctuation, and paragraphing of the original, particularly as nothing indicates that JRM ever corrected the typescript. Besides the error about his father's age on the first page, the typed manuscript mentions a Kansas town called Wallace in two or three instances. And of course, there is a Wallace, Kansas, in western Wallace County near the Colorado border. But from JRM's notebooks we learn that the events he describes at Wallace actually took place near Wilson in Ellsworth County. There is no doubt about this, and yet Wallace remains unaltered in the "Reminiscences." Furthermore, the names of some of JRM's friends and associates were misspelled, and there were other minor errors, no doubt due to the stenographer's misunderstanding certain words or misreading her own notes. If JRM had read the typescript it seems reasonable to expect that such corrections might have been made.

In the interests of readability, the narrative has been reparagraphed, divided into chapters, and supplied with chapter headings. The main change has been to rearrange the sequence of events in the original narrative so that dated incidents for the most part now follow a chronological order. Other minor changes have consisted solely of the occasional breaking up of a particularly long sentence into two or three shorter ones, and in a very few instances the deletion of a repetitious word or phrase. Many of the footnotes are by JRM, as indicated. They have been lifted directly from his letters or other manuscripts wherever additional information has been found. Thus, although not intended by him to be footnotes, they serve the purpose, clarifying various points without altering his meaning. The remainder of the footnotes contain, for the most part, information that is not derived from JRM's own writings, and the editor takes full responsibility for any inaccuracies they may contain.

The second source of material, as mentioned, has been his published articles. Some of these, notably "The Saline River Country in 1859," contain material that overlaps with certain incidents described in the "Reminiscences." In every case the published version provides greater detail, and I have unhesitatingly transferred all such information to the present work. In doing so, nothing has been rewritten. Virtually every sentence in the account published here remains as JRM wrote it. In some cases an article provides an entire episode not found in the "Reminiscences," and here too I have freely borrowed text, so that the present volume is as complete a record of JRM's experiences as possible. Careful consideration was given to the problem of whether or not to cite and cross-reference the source of each such addition to the original text of the "Reminiscences." In the end it was decided that to do so would burden the text with tedious footnotes without any substantial advantages.

Mr. Mead's manuscript is a primary source of information about the places, the people, and the events he describes. Some may find it tempting to dissect his narrative, footnoting every fact and commenting on each observation. However, it was not the editor's intention to go further than the identification of people and places. In some instances it has not been possible to pin down each place mentioned, and a few of the people named have not been traced. The editor has also occasionally given in to the temptation of constructing an unnecessary footnote, but every effort has been made to adhere to the principle outlined above.

James R. Mead took the time to dictate this text mainly because of the repeated urgings and encouragement of Mr. Charles Payne of Wichita. For some of JRM's other writings we are indebted to Mr. George W. Martin, Secretary of the Kansas State Historical Society, Topeka. On November 8, 1908, JRM wrote to Mr. Martin to say, "I am thankful that through your influence I was induced to put in permanent form some of my own experiences and observations of the early days, which I otherwise might have neglected to do" (letter in the files of the Kansas State Historical Society, Topeka).

Although pleased to have these experiences on paper, JRM does not seem to have entertained the idea of seeing them in book form. For some years he had been writing occasional articles for the *Kansas State Historical Society Collections*, the *Transactions of the Kansas Academy of Science*, and various newspapers, but when the typescript of the "Reminiscences" was finished, it was laid aside in JRM's home at 433 Wabash Avenue in Wichita, and no effort was made to find a publisher. Together with other manuscripts, notes, letters, photographs, and books, it has been with the family in Wichita ever since. Throughout this book references are made to these letters, photographs, and other documents, which are described as being in the Mead Collection, Wichita. All the materials are in the private collection of Mr. Mead's daughter, Ignace Fern Mead (Mrs. Schuyler Jones Jr.).

The editor felt that the title "Reminiscences of Frontier Life," although entirely appropriate, was perhaps ill suited to a volume intended for a wide audience, and from JRM's own writings he considered using another, "Indian Summer," which is a recurring phrase both in JRM's narrative and in his letters home. Indian Summer was a season of the year that JRM found exhilarating, and the period of his youthful adventures on the plains was a kind of Indian summer in American history—at least for the Plains Indians on the unfenced prairies among the great buffalo herds. James R. Mead lived through the winters that marked their end and always looked back on that Indian summer of his life with great longing. But the publishers, in their turn, decided that the title "Indian Summer" might limit sales among those unfamiliar with the book's subject, and we have taken instead what I intended to be the subtitle: *Hunting and Trading on the Great Plains, 1859–1875.*

SCHUYLER JONES

Oxford, England

Acknowledgments

SEVERAL individuals and institutions have helped in various ways in the preparation of this book. The Kansas State Historical Society of Topeka has supplied information, copies of letters, and photographs; Mr. Peter Narracott of Oxford has spent many hours in studio and darkroom to copy and print the illustrations; Miss Margaret Loveless, Chief Cartographer of the School of Geography, Oxford, has prepared all but one of the maps; Mr. William C. Ellington, Jr., Wichita City Historian and Head of the Local History Section of the Wichita Public Library, has prepared the drawing of the Mead house at 433 Wabash Avenue and has clarified several historical points; Schuyler Jones, Jr., has expedited the process of collecting information, assembling text and illustrations at every stage, and has carried out a good deal of the research for the footnotes. Other persons and institutions who generously gave their time to assist in one way and another are Robert Puckett, Director of the Wichita-Sedgwick County Historical Museum Association; Dr. H. Craig Miner, Professor of History at Wichita State University; Susan Miner of the Wichita-Sedgwick County Historical Museum Association; Dr. John Rydjord of Wichita State University; Stan Harder of the Old Cowtown Museum, Historic Wichita, Sedgwick County, Inc.; Stan Adams of the Wichita-Sedgwick County Historical Museum Association; Dorothy Starr of Towanda; Ione Graybill of Newton; Mr. and Mrs. John Cottingham of Newton; Frank Good of the *Wichita Eagle and Beacon*; Allan Skinner of

Anchorage Alaska; Gail Carpenter; Edna Marie Lee, Editor of *Kanhistique*, Ellsworth, Kansas; Linn Peterson, City Clerk of McPherson, Kansas; Earlene Marston of Gypsum, Kansas; Carrie Jacobson Ash of Gypsum, Kansas; Mr. M. B. Vanarsdale of Wichita; and the Travel and Research Grants Committee of the Board of the Faculty of Anthropology and Geography, University of Oxford.

I.M.J.

S.J.

Hunting and Trading on the Great Plains
1859–1875

Introduction

BY IGNACE MEAD JONES

THE following account of one man's life and experiences in Kansas in the days when it was still a territory and during its early years as a state is separated from the present by only a few decades, yet the sharp contrast between Kansas in the 1850s and 1860s and the Kansas we know today makes it seem remote. The story is told by James R. Mead, who went to Kansas as a young man in 1859 and made his home there for the rest of his life.

The same spirit of adventure, the restlessness, and the desire for a new and better life which prompted young Mead to go west had encouraged his father to leave New England in 1837 for the wilderness of Iowa. Enoch Mead, father of James R. Mead, was born in Greenwich, Connecticut, on September 2, 1809, on a homestead his ancestors had purchased from the Indians. An incident which occurred on that homestead during the Revolutionary War gives it a place in history that is still remembered.

Enoch's grandfather, General Ebenezer Mead, was standing in front of his house in time to witness General Israel Putnam make his famous dash on horseback to escape British troops down a rocky precipice which is still known as Putnam Hill. The pursuing British horsemen, arriving at the brink of the hill some moments later, reined in sharply and, seeing Putnam galloping away below them, naturally concluded that he had ridden his horse down the

3

The Reverend Enoch Mead. Mead Collection, Wichita.

steep stone steps in front of them. But Putnam, who knew the area well, had swerved to the left and ridden down a path hidden among the bushes which paralleled the steps. As the American general raced away, the British opened fire, and Putnam turned in his saddle shouting, "God cuss ye; when I catch ye I'll hang ye to the next tree."[1] Later that day he and his Stamford regiment did capture thirty-eight British soldiers, but if they were hung, history does not record it.

During his boyhood Enoch Mead lived on this Greenwich farm which had been in his family for seven generations, and he spent his leisure time boating, fishing, swimming, and hunting on Long Island Sound. When he was fourteen he entered the classical school in Stamford. Encouraged by one of his instructors, a Yale graduate, he later applied for admission to that college, passed the entrance examinations in 1826, and graduated in 1830 in a class of seventy. In the autumn of 1830 he entered the Theological Seminary at Auburn, New York, and was ordained a Presbyterian minister three years later. He first served at Lockport, New York, and for a time thought of going west as a missionary. But in 1834 he accepted a call from the Congregational Church of New Haven, Vermont, to be its pastor.

Enoch Mead remained in New Haven until May, 1837, when, partly to escape the severe Vermont winters, he decided to fulfill his desire to go west. With no particular destination in mind he travelled by way of Philadelphia, Pittsburgh, the Ohio River, and the Mississippi to Alton, Illinois. From there he went up the Illinois River to Peoria and then on to Knoxville, Illinois, which at that time marked the end of organized public transport systems. From Knoxville he walked alone through new country marked by few roads or bridges until he reached Rock Island. Here he crossed the Mississippi to the frontier village of Davenport, then consisting of perhaps half a dozen families. Upon learning that the county seat of Rockingham was a larger place only four miles away, he went on and found a village of several hundred people. As a minister he received a warm welcome and was urged to settle, for, as local citizens told him, "The Sabbath has not yet crossed the Mississippi."

Enoch Mead decided to stay and soon had organized a Presbyterian Church and started a village school. After teaching for one term in this school, he returned to Vermont for his family. In 1835 he had married Mary Emmes James of Middlebury, Vermont, and on May 3, 1836, their son James Richard Mead was born. Now, in a

1. Some of these details of Enoch Mead's life and family are recorded in the *History of Scott County, Iowa*, (Chicago, 1882), pp. 1232–35. Other information has come from original diaries and letters in the Mead Collection, Wichita.

covered spring wagon, the little family travelled 1,200 miles over primitive roads and trails, camping out or staying overnight at farm houses, to reach their new home on the banks of the Mississippi in Iowa.[2]

Within a few years Rockingham, having lost the county seat to the fast growing and more advantageously situated Davenport, began a swift decline. Its Presbyterian Church struggled to compete with the Metropolitan Church in Davenport, and Enoch Mead soon found himself without a congregation. He became an itinerant preacher, travelling as far as a hundred miles to hold services in some remote hamlet. During his last year of such work he travelled over three thousand miles on horseback to reach distant settlements served by no other minister.

At best, such activities paid little, and Enoch supported his family by farming. Soon after arriving in Iowa he had purchased land lying between Davenport and Rockingham overlooking the Mississippi River. Part of his homestead was lowland, which he farmed, and part was hilly and covered with fine timber. It was in these hills and woods that young James spent as much time as possible, hunting, studying nature, roaming at will, fascinated by life in the open.

James and his younger sister, Elizabeth, received much of their early schooling from their parents, and life on this frontier farm was made intellectually stimulating by frequent family trips into Davenport for lectures, musicals, church services, parties, and visits to friends. In his diary young James occasionally described these excursions:

Feb. 13, 1854. Ploughed up the hill. I intend to follow some better trade than this. Went to town to hear Dr. Judd lecture on anatomy. He delivered a very instructive lecture, "Be careful of your Health."

Feb. 14. Worked in the morning up the hill. Went to lecture in the evening with Elizabeth.

On another evening, discouraged after a hard, cold day working on the farm, he wrote: "March 18th. I have resolved not to follow farming for a living. I am going to try to get a station on the railroad. It is the kind of work that suits me."

On March 20, 1854, James, then in his seventeenth year, attended a literary banquet in Davenport at LeClaire Hall. The ad-

2. Ibid.

Mary Emmes James Mead. Mead Collection, Wichita.

mission fee, which included supper, was seventy-five cents. Of this he wrote:

John Dillon delivered an oration which was well worth hearing. Then we had some splendid music by the band and then we went into the other room to supper, which was not very good. There was plenty of ice cream, but it was sour. They had negro waiters who did the thing up right. Miss Sylvester was there but I was too bashful to ask her company. I believe she would have went with me. They had a good many off handed speeches, some of them first rate. I did nothing but listen. I resolved this night that after this I will bend all my energies to get an education. It is everything. What a difference being somebody and being a nobody. I mean to go to college next winter and study with all my might. If I can only board in town. I can learn almost everything. It is now two o'clock a.m. and I am still writing. James Mead.[3]

James did go to college the following winter, though it was not his first experience of formal schooling. Six years earlier he had attended Iowa College in Davenport as a preparatory student. In the 1849–50 catalogue he is listed as a Latin scholar. He was then fourteen years old. This college catalogue also lists the main subjects taught: Greek, Latin, and English. "English" was apparently interpreted rather broadly, for under recommended texts we find the following: McGuffey's fourth *Reader,* Macauley's *History of England,* Will's *Grammar,* Colburn's *Mental Arithmetic,* Davie's *Arithmetic,* Morse's *Geography,* Olmstead's *Natural Philosophy,* Stillman's *Chemistry,* Davie's *Surveying,* and Day's *Algebra.* Some of James R. Mead's school books survive in the Mead Collection, Wichita, among them Morse's *Geography* of 1849, in which Kansas is shown as "Indian Territory," extending from the Missouri River to the Continental Divide and north to the forty-second degree of latitude. The territory included Long's Peak and James Peak, now known as Pike's Peak, which was originally named after Dr. Edwin James, the official botanist and geologist on Long's 1820 expedition to the Rocky Mountains. On July 13 and 14, 1820, Dr. James, accompanied by one or two other members of the expedition, successfully completed what is believed to be the first ascent of this mountain. Dr. James was an uncle of James R. Mead's mother, and young James once heard an account of the climb from the man himself.

The tuition at Iowa College was five dollars for the thirteen-week term, three terms making a complete academic year. Room and board for students could be had "with good families for $1.50 per week, exclusive of washing." It is not known how long James

3. The original diary is in the Mead Collection, Wichita.

*Elizabeth Mead, Mary E. Mead, and James R. Mead, about 1848.
Mead Collection, Wichita.*

Mead attended this preparatory school, but from his diary of 1854
we know he had at least one year of college. We also learn that the
first term he studied Latin, algebra, geography, penmanship, com-
position, and declamation. In the second term he took geology,
surveying, and algebra. On April 4, 1855, he wrote: "This is the
last day I shall be here. My school days for this year and perhaps
forever, are over."

In that same year, at the age of nineteen, he got a job in Davenport. In his diary for June 24, 1855, he wrote that he was "engaged
in what is known as the McKarty Mill." He continues: "My reasons
for leaving the farm and coming to town were, 1st, the superior
advantages I would here possess for mental improvement such as
attending lectures, meetings, and also the opportunity I would have

for observing the manners and customs of the people and, 2nd, I hoped to better myself in a pecuniary point of view. Whether this latter expectation will be realized remains to be seen."[4] In August, 1855, he wrote to his mother, who was on a visit to New England with Elizabeth, to say, "I hope you will give yourself no uneasiness about my getting into bad company, for in the first place I have not the inclination and next I have no time for anything but business."[5]

From letters which James later wrote to his father, it seems clear that Enoch Mead, together with a man named Smith, had invested a substantial sum of money in a sawmill and that Mead, Smith, & Co., subsequently went bankrupt. The debts thereby incurred haunted the family for years and may have been one of the main reasons why James decided to seek his fortune elsewhere.

In October, 1856, James made a trip to his father's old home in Greenwich, Connecticut, and visited his father's brother Theodore, who was still living on the family homestead at the foot of Putnam Hill. On this trip James spent some time in New York, where he heard Henry Ward Beecher preach. Of this he wrote: ". . . his sermon surpassed my most sanguine expectations. The house was crowded to its utmost capacity. Before the sermon he baptized sixteen babies." While in New York, James visited several "galleries of paintings" and P. T. Barnum's Museum, where he was especially impressed with Tom Thumb and the little carriage and horses given to him by Queen Victoria.[6]

James Mead enjoyed these travels greatly. The sight of new country delighted him, and his letters home are full of enthusiastic observations. This taste for travel never left him, and in later years, in addition to his adventures in Kansas and Indian Territory, he travelled to Colorado, Minnesota, Montana, California, Washington State, Alaska, Texas, New Mexico, Florida, Cuba, and Washington, D.C.

In 1857, James wrote a characteristic note of mild irritation to his mother on the farm urging, "I wish you would hurry up my coat and pants along as fast as possible, as I have nothing to wear." In a letter dated February 7, 1858, to his father, who was visiting his brother Theodore in Greenwich, James wrote from Davenport: ". . . the weather is mild and changeable. Saturday we had a slight

4. Original letter in the Mead Collection, Wichita.
5. Ibid.
6. From information in original letters in the Mead Collection, Wichita.

fall of snow. As I write it looks as though we might have more. The roads are getting pretty good, though I am afraid they will thaw out in a few days. The ferry boat still runs, though the [Mississippi] river is full of heavy ice. . . . Elizabeth is getting along finely with her poem. . . . I shall return to the mill in the morning early. . . . I am going down to the island in a few days to put that wood in better shape. It will be impossible to get it over this winter. The Cabin I think had better remain where it is for the benefit of any adventurer who may chance to need its shelter."[7]

The Colorado gold rush of 1858 was undoubtedly a major influence in James R. Mead's life. He did not participate in it, though he certainly thought of doing so, but perhaps more than anything else, it turned his thoughts westward and he was soon longing to see the Great Plains of America. He planned his journey with characteristic thoroughness and determination, and on May 4, 1859, the day following his twenty-third birthday, he headed west with a team, a wagon, a horse, and a few companions. He was later to write to his father, "Of one thing you can rest assured, I can take care of myself."

The present volume is James R. Mead's own story of his life and adventures in Kansas from 1859 to 1875, with a final chapter from the mid-1890s. Dictated for the most part some thirty-five or forty years after the events described, the narrative is mainly concerned with those incidents which Mr. Mead remembered with the greatest interest. It is clear that as he grew older he found his own successes in politics and business less and less interesting, while at the same time his early adventures with the Indians and buffalo hunting had passed into history. He was acutely aware then that he had been part of something that was gone forever, and this knowledge caused him to record that earlier part of his life.

It is important to view Mead's book in this light, for in it he says almost nothing about the Civil War, the founding of Wichita and its early history, his real estate and railroad enterprises, his periods of office in the Kansas state legislature and the state Senate, or any other activities for which he is known in Kansas history. Perhaps he felt that such things were already a matter of record, while his earlier adventures were for the most part known only to himself, his family, and a few friends.

7. Original letter in the Mead Collection, Wichita.

James R. Mead, about 1855. Mead Collection, Wichita.

In this Introduction I have sketched James R. Mead's early years to the spring of 1859. Since his own narrative relates the events of the next fifteen years and more, it is appropriate to broaden the context of his account by taking up another side of his life, beginning in 1869.

In that year James R. Mead sold his Towanda ranch and moved to

Wichita. The energy and enthusiasm he had formerly devoted to hunting, exploring, and trading with the Indians was now directed to building a city. In the previous year, while a member of the Kansas Senate,[8] Mead, with the assistance of Governor Samuel J. Crawford, D. S. Munger, W. W. Lawrence, and others, organized and promoted a Wichita Land and Town Company. The townsite at the junction of the Big and Little Arkansas rivers was, however, within the bounds of the Osage Trust Lands. The Homestead Act of 1862 did not apply to trust lands, nor were preemption claims recognized on such lands. These restrictions made the Wichita site less attractive for settlement and other development, particularly as they also inhibited railway expansion.[9] Nevertheless, the Wichita Town organizers directed Munger to take a claim near the junction of the Big and Little Arkansas rivers, and in fact, both Mead and Munger staked claims on the Wichita site in 1868, though they were not able to file on them until later; Munger in 1869 and Mead in 1870. Others soon followed.

When the question of a name for the new settlement arose several were suggested, among them Beecher and Hamilton, but Mead held out for the name Wichita, arguing, as John Rydjord has recounted, that it already had that name: "It is known far and wide as the Wichita Town for the Indians who lived here."[10] Governor Crawford was inclined to adopt the name Hamilton, but Mead, supported by Wilhelm ("Dutch Bill") Greiffenstein, backed the Indian name and "may therefore be given the chief credit for naming Wichita."[11]

During the 1870s the town founders, J. R. Mead, D. S. Munger, N. A. English, "William" Greiffenstein, and William Mathewson, were busy encouraging immigration, developing the townsite, promoting the cattle trade, establishing banks, luring railroad companies, encouraging newspapers, and building bridges, sawmills, grain mills, hotels, and fine homes. In 1870 all these men, with the exception of Munger, who was nearly sixty, were quite young.

8. In 1864, JRM was elected from Butler County to the Kansas House of Representatives. In 1868 he was elected to the state Senate for the district comprising Morris, Chase, Marion, and Butler counties, plus all the unorganized territory on the west to the state line, which was then largely unpopulated but has since been organized into some thirty-five counties.
9. See MINER, 24–25.
10. See RYDJORD, p. 173.
11. Ibid.

Mead was the youngest at thirty-four, English and Mathewson were forty, and Greiffenstein was forty-one. They had courage, vision, enthusiasm, and daring. They believed in themselves, the future of Kansas, and above all, in the town they had established.

On July 29, 1870, Mead filed his 160-acre claim at the United States Land Office at Humboldt, Kansas, paying $1.25 an acre. This quarter section extended from Douglas to Central, and from Broadway (originally named Texas Street and then Lawrence) to Washington. This was the beginning of a decade in which Mead achieved success, suffered severe losses, and embarked on new enterprises, including the cattle trade, farming, banking, selling real estate, and acquiring interest in a toll bridge, a grain mill, and a brick plant. Finally, he went off to Colorado to try gold and silver mining in the Rockies.

In 1870, Mead wrote to his parents to say, "we have at last reduced our Rail Road matters to a certainty and will have the cars running here in six months." However, the certainty of 1870 failed to materialize into an 1871 reality, for the Santa Fe Company decided not to extend its rails south from Newton, Kansas. When this news reached them, the town leaders held a hurried conference and on June 2, 1871, Mead telegraphed T. J. Peter, superintendent of the Santa Fe, asking, "Upon what terms will you build a branch of your road to Wichita?"

The reply came three days later. "In answer to yours of the 2nd, will say if your people will organize a local company and vote $200,000 of county bonds, I will build a railroad to Wichita within six months."[12]

Seventeen days later the Wichita and South Western Railroad was incorporated with Mead as president and Henry C. Sluss, an attorney, as secretary. On August 11, although not without a spirited fight, the necessary bonds were voted. On May 16, 1872, the first train pulled into Wichita.

The Wichita leaders were good friends and fellow town promoters, but there was keen rivalry among them. Each did his utmost to entice business to his part of town. The following quote is from an article Bliss Isley wrote for the Wichita *Beacon* on July 11, 1926:

12. LONG, p. 30. Numerous documents relating to the Wichita and Southwestern Railroad Company, as well as correspondence with the Santa Fe Railroad Company are in the Mead Collection, Wichita.

"William Greiffenstein was shrewd, but there was another man who also had traded with the Indians in Wichita before the coming of the white man, who was every bit as shrewd as Greiffenstein. . . . This man was J. R. Mead. He owned a quarter-section east of Lawrence between Douglas and Central. Mr. Mead was not so advantageously situated as Munger and Greiffenstein since they owned Main Street and he was east of Lawrence, but he determined to turn this to his own advantage and made a new Main Street. . . . Mr. Mead organized a railroad company, the Wichita and Southwestern, and this company built a railroad from Newton to Wichita, which was later sold to the Santa Fe. Mr. Mead, being President of the road, laid rails across his own farm and built a depot on what is now Douglas Ave.

"He determined to make Douglas Avenue another Main Street. In fact, he intended to make it more main than even Main itself and so he laid it out 114 feet wide. It was the first avenue in the southwest and it ran from the new depot to Lawrence. Greiffenstein realized here was a thoroughfare he had to recognize, and so he replatted the south line of his sub-division, laying out a Douglas Avenue along his own property and surveying lots to face on the new street, Douglas."

Thus was Douglas Avenue born. It may be that Mead's neighbour N. A. English, who owned the 160 acres immediately south of his, was annoyed by Mead's gesture in giving land for half of the new avenue to the city. In any case, Mead in the end paid English and W. B. Smith (who had purchased a small frontage from English) for their half of Douglas, from Broadway to Washington. English received five lots in Mead's addition, worth $500, plus "Lot No. 2 on Douglas Ave., J. R. Mead's Addition and the Building thereon."[13] Smith was paid thirty dollars. Then the entire 114-foot-wide right-of-way was given by Mead to Wichita as a public thoroughfare "forever."[14] This was that part of Douglas Avenue which runs from Broadway to Washington.

Banking was another enterprise Mead undertook in the early years of Wichita. To quote L. S. Naftzer: "The Wichita Bank was really the first legitimate bank establishment and was opened for

13. Lot No. 2, Mead's Addition, is the third 25-foot lot on Douglas Avenue, now part of the Fourth National Bank complex.
14. Original documents in the Mead Collection, Wichita.

business in the spring of 1872 by J. C. Fraker, President, J. R. Mead, Vice-President, and A. H. Gossard, Cashier, and was located in the most credible frame building in the town at that time. [It] remained in that location until the spring of 1873 when it was chartered as the First National Bank of Wichita."[15]

Mead invested heavily in the bank, and his parents and sister also bought stock. Times were good, with settlers arriving daily and new businesses springing up. Although Mead had sold his Towanda ranch, he still had his trading post and post office there, and business continued under the management of Timothy C. Peet. From Towanda, Mead freighted supplies to the Indian Territory, where one of his best customers was his friend William Mathewson, who was a licensed government trader at the Kiowa and Comanche agency six miles from Fort Sill.

Mathewson, with the help of his capable wife, Elizabeth, sold supplies to the Indians in return for furs and hides. From Mead's ledgers we find that in the eleven months from January 4 to November 25, 1873, Mathewson's account with him was in excess of $26,000. The Mathewsons paid with buffalo robes and hides, wolf and bear skins, and sometimes by drafts.[16]

In 1861, James R. Mead had married Miss Agnes Barcome of Montreal, Quebec, and she had shared his frontier homes at Saline River, Salina, and Towanda. But on April 17, 1869, she died in her twenty-eighth year, from complications following the birth of her second son, J. William. Mead's sister, Elizabeth, travelled from the Mead home at Rockingham, Iowa, to Towanda and a few weeks later returned east with the infant William. Despite all her care and attention the baby died at the Mead farm in Iowa on August 10 of that same year.[17]

When Agnes died, Mrs. Mathewson, who was a close friend of the Meads, took the other children—James Lucas, known as Bun-

15. BENTLEY 1: 95.

16. JRM's diaries, letters, and trading-post ledgers are in the Mead Collection, Wichita.

17. Elizabeth Mead's letter to her brother telling of the death of William is in the Mead Collection, Wichita. In March, 1880, the body of Agnes Mead was moved from Towanda to Davenport, Iowa. The reinterment of Agnes and J. William took place on March 30, 1880, in the presence of Enoch Mead, Mary Mead, and Elizabeth Mead. That same evening Lizzie wrote to her brother to say, "Mother and son are reunited at last." Mead Collection, Wichita.

Elizabeth ("Lizzie") Mead, sister of James R. Mead. Mead Collection, Wichita.

nie;[18] Elizabeth Agnes; and Mary Elenora, or Mamie—and cared for them at her home in Topeka. Later, from Fort Sill in Indian Ter-

18. James L. Mead always signed his personal letters Bunnie, but his father often spelled it Bunny.

ritory, Mrs. Mathewson often wrote to Mead of business matters, and sometimes her letters were more personal. One poignant line in her letter of December 29, 1871, reads: "I hope you all spent a plesant Christmas. Tell Bunny he must write me and let me know what Santy Clause brought him and Mamie. I didn't get anything brought to me. I suppose no one thinks enough of me to give me a Christmas present."[19]

In Wichita, Mead's freight wagons and mule teams were often stationed at his homeplace on Central Avenue, and there were lively times when a large wagon train arrived or departed heavily laden with supplies for the Indian Territory. Broadway then was a narrow muddy road, and the noise and confusion of a long train of wagons pulled by teams of straining mules created a good deal of excitement, especially among the children.

In 1872, Mead helped persuade his good friend Col. Marsh Murdock to sell his successful newspaper in Burlingame, Kansas, and come to the thriving little town of Wichita to start a newspaper. When Syl Duncan brought Murdock's printing press from the end of the rail line at Newton to Wichita, he stopped overnight at Mead's place. The first issue of the *Wichita City Eagle* came off the press on April 14, 1872, and it was still coming off the presses in 1986, more than 113 years later.

Along with his freighting, Mead conducted a good deal of cattle business, making frequent buying trips to Texas, where he purchased cattle and had them driven to the railhead at Wichita. Things looked good for Mead in 1872. He purchased more bank stock, went on a hunting trip with his son Bunnie and several friends, and travelled to Washington, D.C., on business. There he met General Grant, Charles Sumner, and other notables of the day. During that same summer he shipped 930 buffalo robes to Philadelphia and calculated that he might get seven or eight thousand dollars for the sixty-five he had left.[20] Trains were by this time running regularly to Wichita, and the depot built on his land had been completed.

J. R. Mead's first home at the Central Avenue location was a modest frame house, but in September, 1872, he began the construction of Wichita's first red-brick mansion. One of its novel fea-

19. Original letter in the Mead Collection, Wichita.
20. Ibid.

tures was a zinc-lined bathtub. A few years later he added a greenhouse to the building.

In 1873, Mead married Lucy Inman. She was Mrs. William Mathewson's sister and had become Mead's housekeeper when Mrs. Mathewson was no longer able to care for the children. In that same year Kansas experienced wind and dust storms in March and April, followed by good rains in May, and a plague of grasshoppers in August.[21] The Wichita Bank was chartered as the First National Bank of Wichita and moved to its new brick building on the northeast corner of First and Main, with J. R. Mead as vice-president.

In the latter part of September, 1873, there was a general bank panic, and Mead wrote that the banks in the West, including the First National, "have shut up their funds and aren't paying out currency, but certifying checks." Mead wrote his parents that the bank had $200,000 out in bills, and nearly as much in deposits but only $20,000 in currency.[22] Fortunately, by the middle of October everything had calmed down and financial affairs were back to normal.

In 1873, Mead bought for $10,000 controlling interest in the El Paso (Derby, Kansas) Toll Bridge across the Arkansas River. This was a move to protect his investment in the Wichita Toll Bridge, as there was talk of making the El Paso a free bridge. The following year Mead had hopes that Congress would uphold his $7,500 claim against the government for supplies he had furnished the Kaw Indians in 1867. The money was to come out of the proceeds of the sale of Kaw Indian land in Kansas. His bill had passed the House, and he hoped it would pass the Senate, but the money was never paid.

During the summer of 1874, Mead travelled to New York to bid on some government contracts, but was unsuccessful. Back home, in spite of the drought and the grasshoppers, the corn and wheat crops were good, farms were selling well, and improvements were being made on them. Wheat was selling at one dollar a bushel.

The failure of the First National Bank of Wichita in 1876 was a severe blow to Mead and to the town. The bank examiners found

21. A much more serious plague of grasshoppers descended on Kansas in August, 1874. See MINER, 89–96.
22. Original letter in the Mead Collection, Wichita.

James R. Mead's house at 433 Wabash Avenue, Wichita, which was his home from 1893 to 1910. Drawing by William C. Ellington, Jr.

W. ELLINGTON '70

that the president, J. C. Fraker, had embezzled thousands of dollars of the bank's funds. Brought to trial in Leavenworth, Fraker threw himself on the mercy of the court, claiming that he had made bad loans to cattle men and farmers to see them through hard times, but had taken nothing for himself. The court thought otherwise. He was convicted and sentenced to five years' imprisonment at the federal penitentiary in Jefferson City, Missouri. To repay bank depositors, Mead made his capital available and sold much of his property. It is recorded that not a cent was lost by any depositor.[23]

In 1879, Mead, who had never quite forgotten his youthful dream of digging for gold in the mountains, decided to try his luck at mining in Colorado. His first efforts were centered near Alpine, fifty miles from Leadville, where he had mining claims adjacent to The Tilden, a producing mine. He was confident that he would find an extension of this rich lode in his sector. On March 20, 1879, he wrote that he felt "sanguine of citing Tilden lode," but by May 5 he had changed his mind and wrote that he was "satisfied we cannot find the Tilden."[24]

Discouraged by this failure, he moved his mining operations to the Tin Cup mining district in Gunnison County and worked in that region well into 1881. His mining claims located on West Gold Hill comprised El Capitan, Chelsea, C.Z., Amhurst, Champion, Park, and Deer Park. Prospects seemed favorable. F. M. Hausling of the assaying firm of Hausling and Burn of Virginia City, Colorado,[25] wrote: "I prophesy a future for the El Capitan Lode property unprecedented in the history of mining in Colorado, for the union of two such large veins of high grade mineral as the 'Iron Bonnet' and 'El Capitan' will prove a property of enormous wealth."[26]

As it turned out, this was overly optimistic. In 1881, Mead offered El Capitan for sale for $50,000, and it finally sold in 1883 for $25,000.[27]

Back in Wichita, Mead devoted his time to his farms south of town, to the cattle business, and to his Wichita town property. In

23. Altogether, Fraker's misdeeds cost JRM something in excess of $25,000.
24. From original diaries and letters in the Mead Collection, Wichita.
25. Virginia City later became Tin Cup.
26. Original letter in the Mead Collection, Wichita.
27. From JRM's diaries, letters, and mining papers in the Mead Collection, Wichita.

the early eighties Wichita continued to grow and prosper at a reasonable rate, and by the spring of 1885 business was booming. Eastern money flowed into the city, new additions were platted and sold far from the city center, new buildings sprang up, prospects were bright, and the financial mood was optimistically speculative. Pushed to unstable heights by outside speculators, the boom went too far. In 1887, Marsh Murdock, editor of the *Wichita Eagle*, published an editorial entitled "Call a Halt," of which one effect was to discourage wild speculation by outside investors and promote more sober expansion. At first J. R. Mead was not greatly affected by the drop in land prices that followed. In September of that year he wrote his sister to say that "times are not as booming as they were last spring, but we are doing much more building than ever before and growing rapidly."[28]

In the spring of 1888, Mead and two friends, George Travis and William H. Hackney, purchased gold and silver mining property near Rimini, Montana, north of Helena. Their holdings comprised about 500 acres. Incorporated as the Travis Mining Company, this partnership continued into the 1890s. Mead spent four summers working and overseeing the mines, and although he was disappointed in the quantities of the minerals found, he did eventually profit from the sale of the mine.

Wichita was still suffering from the collapse of the boom when Mead wrote to his parents on October 10, 1890, that "the boom has ruined nearly every one here and the drought and hot winds this year has prevented immigration coming in."[29]

Lucy Inman Mead died in 1894 after twenty-one years of marriage. She and James R. Mead had no children. In 1896, Mead married for the third time. His bride was Fern Hoover and he brought her to the home he had purchased in 1893 at 433 North Wabash, across from William Mathewson's property—the land known for years in Wichita as Mathewson's Pasture. In a letter to his sister he wrote, "Fern and I are well and living very happily. More so to me than at any time since Agnes' death. Through her influence we have both joined the Presbyterian Church. Fern is active in Church work. I have joined the sons of the War of the American Revolution."[30]

28. Original letter in the Mead Collection, Wichita.
29. Ibid.
30. Fern Hoover was the daughter of Martin Hoover and Loreta Siebert Hoover. She

Mead's son Bunnie (James L.) was now living in Chicago, where he had successfully founded a bicycle factory which later became one of the largest in the country, manufacturing Ranger bicycles. Always interested in Wichita and its success, he now had the capital to invest in the city at a time when most investors were reluctant to buy. Acting on the advice and property selection of his father, Bunnie Mead purchased twenty-two Wichita buildings in the 1890s and early 1900s. These are scattered throughout the main business district on Douglas Avenue, North Market, North Main, and First Street. Except for some sites taken by urban renewal, nearly all of this property remains in the James L. Mead estate. Bunnie Mead's Wichita property was managed by J. R. Mead right up to the time of his father's death in 1910.

Mead and Fern travelled a great deal. They visited Alaska, sailed to Cuba, went on a six-week camping and sightseeing trip in Yellowstone Park, and made frequent trips to Chicago and Davenport. They spent part of some winters in Galveston and New Orleans. Two daughters were born to them, Ignace and Loreta.

That J. R. Mead was a skillful business man is abundantly clear; what his own account of his early life on the plains and his letters home does not reveal are his intellectual interests. Those are shown, to some extent at least, by his private library and his published papers. He was keenly interested in geology, ethnology, archaeology, and history and must have been among the very first to undertake archaeological excavations in Kansas. He was also interested in natural history and, in addition to his ethnographic and archaeological collections, the house in Wichita contained his collection of *Mollusca*. In his later years he carried on an extensive correspondence with and supplied specimens to botanists, geologists, and other specialists. One of his acquaintances was Carl Akeley, the naturalist.

---

was born on November 14, probably in 1878, near Des Moines, Iowa. Her family moved to western Kansas sometime in the 1880s and took up farming in Lane County southwest of Beeler. Dighton was not far away and was their main supply point. The Hoovers lived in a dugout, faced hard times, and came near to starvation. They were eventually driven out by drought and moved to Wichita. Martin Hoover worked in the construction business for a time and later became a policeman. JRM met Fern when he visited the Hoover home to see her father. Martin Hoover later died in Texas. Fern's mother, Loreta, moved to Perry in Indian Territory, where she spent the remainder of her days. Fern married Hunter Jordan of Wichita in 1914 and used the name Fern Mead Jordan afterwards. She died on October 31, 1959, in Topeka, Kansas.

Fern Hoover Mead. Mead Collection, Wichita.

James L. ("Bunnie") Mead. From a photograph taken on September 23, 1901. Mead Collection, Wichita.

Also during the latter part of his life, Mead was invited to make numerous speeches about early days in Kansas and he wrote several articles for scientific publications. In 1888 he was elected president of the Kansas Academy of Science. He was a life member of the Kansas State Historical Society and its president in 1907. Although normally a quiet man, he became animated and talkative when in a group of kindred spirits. Many notable friends visited

*James R. Mead, Ignace Mead, Loreta Mead, and Fern Mead at 433
Wabash Avenue, Wichita. From a photograph taken by Bunnie Mead on
May 15, 1907. Mead Collection, Wichita.*

Ignace Mead in about 1906, with part of James R. Mead's ethnographic collection at 433 Wabash Avenue, Wichita. Mead Collection, Wichita.

Biographical Summary of the Life of James R. Mead

1836   Born at New Haven, Vermont, to the Reverend Enoch
            Mead and Mary Emmes James Mead.
1839   Family moves from New England to Rockingham, Iowa, in
            Scott County, near Davenport, Iowa.
1849–51   Attends Iowa College, Davenport, Iowa.
1852–53   Works on father's farm south of Davenport.
1854–55   Employed at McKarty's lumber mill in Davenport.
1856   Travels to New York and New England.
1857–58   Works at McKarty's lumber mill.
1859   Travels across Iowa and Missouri to Kansas Territory;
            stakes a claim at Burlingame; travels west on Santa Fe
            Trail; meets Col. William Bent. First buffalo hunt. Estab-
            lishes Saline Ranch. Begins trading with Indians.
1860–61   Hunting along the Saline, Smoky Hill, and Solomon rivers.
            Appointed sheriff of Saline County. Freights hides and furs
            to Leavenworth. Explores territory to the west.
1861   Marries Agnes Barcome on December 1. Is captured by
            Sioux warriors.
1862   Builds home in Salina, Kansas. Expands hunting and trad-
            ing business. Is captured by Confederates during Salina
            Raid on September 19.
1863   Moves to Towanda, Kansas, on the White Water River;
            builds home, trading post, and post office. Visits the Ar-
            kansas Valley. Son James Lucas ("Bunnie") Mead born in

Rockingham, Iowa, January 13. Trades with the Wichita Indians in the valley of the Little Arkansas. Travels south into Indian Territory.

1864   Establishes trading post between the Little and Big Arkansas rivers. Is elected to the Kansas House of Representatives from Butler County. Daughter Elizabeth Agnes born at Towanda, August 9.

1865   Establishes trading post on the Ninnescah River near site of Clearwater, Kansas. Meets Satanta, war chief of the Kiowas; Heap of Bears, chief of the Arapahoes; and Black Kettle of the Southern Cheyennes. Represents the Wichita Indians at the Treaty of the Little Arkansas. Meets Kit Carson.

1866   Establishes trading post at Round Pond Creek on the Chisholm Trail in Indian Territory. Applies to Col. J. H. Leavenworth at Fort Zarah, Kansas, for a license to trade with the Kiowa and Comanche Indians. Daughter Mary Elenora born at Towanda on October 31.

1867   Obtains license to trade with the Osage Indians at their camp west of the Arkansas River. Cholera epidemic in Kansas.

1868   Travels in Indian Territory; is captured by Cheyenne war party. Together with Governor Samuel J. Crawford and others incorporates a new town at the junction of the Big and Little Arkansas rivers, which Mead names Wichita. Stakes out 160-acre claim on the Wichita site. Elected Republican senator for the Fifteenth District of Kansas.

1869   Appointed chairman of the Ways and Means Committee of the Kansas State Senate. Son J. William Mead born at Towanda on March 29. Wife Agnes dies at Towanda on April 17. Son J. William dies at Rockingham on August 10.

1870   Sells Towanda ranch. Employs Timothy C. Peet to run trading post and post office at Towanda. Moves to Wichita. Builds frame house on Wichita claim. Is appointed chairman of the Joint Ways and Means Committee of the Kansas House and Senate. Gives Episcopal Church 150-by-140-foot plot of land on Wichita site. Is appointed United States marshal's deputy for Kansas's Butler, Sedgwick, Sumner, and Cowley counties.

1871   Organizes Wichita and Southwestern Rail Road and becomes its president. Together with three other "horsemen," turns Texas cattle herds and economic prosperity toward Wichita. Lays out Wichita's Douglas Avenue, making it 114 feet wide. Travels to Philadelphia. Invests in first bridge built across the Arkansas River. Freights supplies to William Mathewson at the Kiowa and Comanche Agency near Fort Sill in Indian Territory. Is appointed director of the Topeka and Southwestern Railway Co. Guides Santa Fe Railroad surveyors south to Medicine Lodge.

1872   Becomes vice-president of the Wichita Bank. Travels to Washington, D.C.; meets General Grant. Goes on last buffalo hunt. Sees first train arrive in Wichita. Starts building Wichita's first mansion. Persuades Col. Marshall M. Murdock to leave Burlingame, Kansas, and come to Wichita to start a daily newspaper.

1873   Marries Mrs. William Mathewson's sister, Lucy Inman. Buys controlling interest in the toll bridge at El Paso (Derby), Kansas. The Wichita Bank becomes the First National Bank of Wichita.

1874   Buys sufficient land to give Douglas Avenue from Broadway (Lawrence) to Washington to the city of Wichita as a public thoroughfare. Travels to New York to bid on government contracts. Goes into the cattle business.

1875   Travels to Texas on cattle business. Sees Wichita property values drop.

1876   First National Bank of Wichita goes into the hands of the receiver; President J. C. Fraker accused and convicted of embezzlement.

1877   Sells property to repay bank depositors; all customers' losses made good.

1879   Mining in Gunnison County, Colorado, in Alpine and Tin Cup.

1880   Mining in Colorado.

1881   Mining in Colorado and farming south of Wichita.

1882   Mining in Colorado. Is elected vice-president of the Kansas Academy of Sciences. Reelected president of the Old Settlers Association.

1883   Sells El Capitan mine on West Gold Hill in Tin Cup, Colorado. Wichita business improving.

1894   Wife, Lucy Inman Mead, dies on February 28. Travels down the Chisholm Trail on the Rock Island Railroad.

1895   Meets Fern Hoover. Travels with son Bunnie to Galveston, Fort Worth, and Houston.

1896   Marries Fern Hoover.

1897   Joins First Presbyterian Church and Sons of the American Revolution.
1898   Travels to Chicago and Davenport. Manages Bunnie Mead's Wichita property investments.
1899   Extended camping trip to Yellowstone Park with Fern.
1900   Mother dies at Davenport on Decemaber 11. Continues farming, but spends increasing time managing son's real estate investments in Wichita. Becomes a Mason.
1901   Travels to California, the Pacific Northwest, and Alaska with Fern.
1902   Daughter Ignace born in Wichita on April 20.
1904   Visits St. Louis Worlds Fair. Travels to Chicago and Davenport. Daughter Loreta born in Wichita.
1906   Addresses Kansas State Historical Society on September 27.
1907   President of the Kansas State Historical Society.
1908   Travels to Florida and Cuba with Fern and the children, including Bunnie and his family.
1909   Managing Bunnie Mead's real estate interests in Wichita.
1910   Dies at his home at 433 North Wabash Avenue, Wichita, on March 31, in his seventy-fourth year.

Hunting and Trading on the Great Plains
1859–1875

James R. Mead, about 1859. Mead Collection, Wichita.

CHAPTER 1

From the Mississippi to the Great Plains

What I write now I will try to have correct as my memory serves me and just as I would tell the story to an old plainsman, without any attempt at literary excellence. —JRM

I WAS BORN in New England, but the home of my youth was on the banks of the Mississippi River near the city of Davenport, Iowa. Arriving there before the land was surveyed by the government, I early learned to use a rifle, and the woods were full of game. My father, while a professional man, was also an enthusiastic sportsman. He was a good shot and among the best swimmers, skaters, and boatmen in Yale College while a student there. He still uses a gun occasionally at his advanced age of 85 years.[1]

From my ancestors I inherited the love of nature, the free life of the forest and plains, and a fondness for hunting. My surroundings when a boy were exceedingly well adapted to these tastes. My father owned an extensive tract of timber and prairie land on the banks of the Mississippi River just opposite the mouth of Rock River.[2] The islands in the river, as well as the swamp lands bordering it

1. The "85 years" is an error, probably made by JRM's secretary in taking dictation or in typing. The Reverend Enoch Mead, JRM's father, was born in Greenwich, Connecticut, on September 2, 1809, and he died on December 6, 1892, at Rockingham, Iowa, at the age of eighty-three. That this error passed uncorrected would seem to indicate that JRM did not read the manuscript after it was typed.

2. Rockingham, Iowa.

1. *Mead's route from the Mississippi River to the Missouri, 1859*

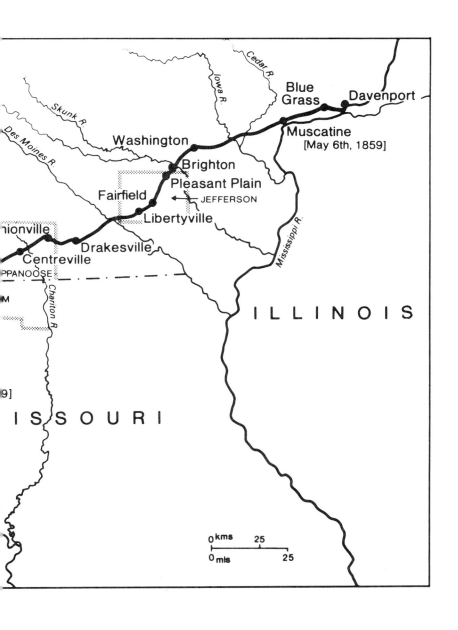

Cedar R.

Iowa R.

Skunk R.

Des Moines R.

Blue
Grass

Davenport

Washington

Muscatine
[May 6th, 1859]

Brighton

Pleasant Plain

Fairfield

JEFFERSON

Libertyville

nionville

Drakesville

Centreville

PPANOOSE

M

Chariton R.

Mississippi R.

I L L I N O I S

9]

I S S O U R I

0 kms   25

0 mls   25

and also the heavy timber were full of game, as were the timbered
bluffs on the Iowa side. I became proficient in capturing the various beasts and birds which abounded in the country. Turkeys and
pigeons were then very numerous in the fall of the year, and there
were prairie chickens by tens of thousands, quail innumerable, and
a few deer. Raccoons were plentiful in the woods, and many a night
I have spent in the fall hunting them with my dogs. I was very lithe
and active and could climb a tree almost as nimbly as a squirrel.

Amid such surroundings I grew to manhood. The dream of my
youth was to see the buffalo and other noble game in their native
wilds. Kansas was at that time first in men's minds in our neighborhood, occasioned in part by a visit from General James H. Lane,
who had set the land aflame by his majestic presence and forceful
eloquence as he depicted the woes and beauty of "bleeding Kansas."[3] When I became of age the long wished-for opportunity came.
In the spring of 1859 I organized a little company of neighborhood
boys and rigged up a couple of ox teams. I had a fine riding horse
and had made to order two rifles as fine as skilled workmen and
money could produce. We took clothing, a little money for convenience, and plenty of grit. Stocked up with enough provisions to
last us six months, we "lit out" for the great plains—as happy and
careless a set of young fellows as ever left their homes for the first
time to go into the wilderness.[4]

We crossed the states of Iowa and Missouri and edified the inhabitants of the latter by singing patriotic songs. One of them began with the verse:

3. General James H. Lane (1814–66) was known as the "Liberator of Kansas." In
1855 he helped to set up a Free State Constitution at Topeka. When the U.S. Senate
refused to admit Kansas under this constitution, Lane made antislavery speeches in
neighboring states, urging men to migrate to Kansas to vote for a free state. In June,
1856, when the Missouri River was closed to Free State immigration, Lane opened up a
new route through Iowa and Nebraska. The Lane Trail began at Iowa City, passed west
across southern Iowa, crossed the Missouri River opposite Nebraska City, and then
turned south into Kansas, ending at Topeka. In 1861, Lane led the Kansas Brigade
against Gen. Sterling Price in Missouri. After the Civil War, Lane lost political support
in Kansas by working for President Johnson's Reconstruction Party. He committed suicide in 1866. William Esley Connelley, "The Lane Trail," KSHC 13 (1914): 268–79.

4. From JRM's "Journal of Incidents and Events occurring During an Excursion to
the Rocky Mountains," we know that he set out on May 4, 1859—the day after his
twenty-third birthday. This same manuscript also enables us to trace his route from the
Mississippi to the Missouri. The original journal is in the Mead Collection, Wichita.

We come to rear a wall of men
'Round Freedom's Southern line
And plant beside the cottonwood
The rugged Northern pine.

It was a rather risky business, considering the feelings then existing, but we came through without trouble. At evening when in camp on some timbered creek we could hear the pheasants drumming in the thickets and it was music in our ears.

After twenty-seven days, without accident or incident of particular note, living off the fat of the land, buying eggs at three cents per dozen, our two cows which we had brought along furnishing an abundance of milk, we reached the Missouri River at Weston where there was a horse ferry boat. There we crossed on Tuesday, the thirty-first of May, 1859, and came down to Leavenworth.[5] After looking over the town and fort we drove out to a little creek eight or ten miles in the country. When we had been there about a week the young men who had come with me got homesick and wanted to see their mammas. They decided to go back, so we divided the teams and the rest of the plunder we had with us. They took the backtrack for home to settle down on their ancestral estates. I was much too delighted with the new and beautiful country to think of returning and set out to see something more of it.

From the city of Leavenworth there was a big wagon trail extending to the historic city of Lawrence. It pursued nearly a direct course between the two places, paying no attention to anything but the best route and safest crossing of the Grasshopper,[6] Big and Little Stranger, and other streams with suggestive names. The beautiful scenery was varied by flocks of gaily feathered Carolina Parakeets,[7] chattering in the tree tops, while gaudily attired Dela-

5. In a letter home dated Leavenworth, Kansas, Thursday, June 2, 1859, JRM wrote: "Leavenworth City is a *very* stirring place. Is growing very fast. Will make a large place some day not far distant." Original letter in the Mead Collection, Wichita. In view of JRM's lifelong interest in ethnography, it is interesting to note that his arrival in Kansas Territory coincided—almost to the day—with that of Lewis Henry Morgan, who was to become famous for his pioneering anthropological work on North American Indian kinship systems. See MORGAN, 25.

6. Now known as the Delaware River.

7. The only parrot that was native to the United States. The last recorded sighting of a Carolina parakeet was in Florida in the 1920s. They had a yellowish green body, a long pointed tail, and an orange-yellow head. In the first half of the nineteenth century they

wares rode tough little ponies, or loafed about John Sarcoxie's log cabins.[8]

At Lawrence we crossed the Kaw by a primitive rope ferry; the huge windmill on the north end of Mount Oread was yet to be built.[9] Having made the acquaintance of other travellers, we went in company up the Kansas River to Lecompton, the Territorial Capital. There was the U.S. Land Office and settlers were flocking to "file" or "prove up." Ely Moore[10] sat at his desk signing "declaratory statements," and Robert S. Stevens,[11] the projector and builder of the M. K. & T. R. R., occupied a 12×14 unpainted board office, reaping a rich reward of dollars making out "filing papers," "final proofs," and pleading contest cases. "Money to Loan or Prove Up" was the device on many a little board building, the customary interest being half the land. Verily the money-lender has been with us since Territorial days.[12]

Lecompton was also the headquarters of the pro-slavery authorities who hoped to make Kansas a slave state. The location had before that time been an Indian trading post of considerable note. Lecompton occupied one of the most beautiful sites I ever saw, but died with the cause it was established to promote.[13]

---

ranged from North Dakota and New York south to Texas and Florida and were common in forest areas of the Mississippi and Missouri valleys. See AUSTIN, 147.

8. John Sarcoxie, the son of a Delaware chief, lived at the Delaware trading post on the Kansas River. Sarcoxie, Missouri is named after his father. See BARRY, 142.

9. Construction of the windmill was begun in 1863 and was only partly finished when Quantrill and the border ruffians burned the town on August 21 of that year, destroying the mill along with most other buildings. The windmill was rebuilt and completed in 1864. Mt. Oread, where the original town was settled on July 31, 1854, was so named after the Mt. Oread School in Worcester, Massachusetts. Lawrence itself got its name from Amos A. Lawrence of Boston, a man who was active in encouraging antislavery people to emigrate to Kansas. See BLACKMAR 2: 112–13.

10. Ely Moore was a government Indian agent, appointed special agent of the Five Confederated Tribes of Indians in 1853. His agency was at Miami Mission on the Osage River, about 10 miles southeast of present-day Osawatomie in Miami County. In 1856, Moore established the first Territorial Land Office at Lecompton. Ely Moore, Jr., *KSHC* 12(1911–12): 338, and Albert R. Greene, *KSHC* 8(1903–1904): 3.

11. About the time that JRM first arrived in Lawrence in the spring of 1859, Robert S. Stevens was, among other business matters, setting up the Lawrence Bank in partnership with Governor Robinson and Robert Morrow. Later Stevens bought them out and became sole owner. George W. Martin, *KSHC* 12(1911–12): 368.

12. Writing home from Lecompton on July 9, 1859, JRM provides this view of Lawrence, Kansas: "Lawrence is a tremendous place for a young one. . . . It has a fine location . . . lots of pretty girls and fast women, and is overrun with rats." Original letter in the Mead Collection, Wichita.

13. JRM's first impressions of Lecompton were different. In a letter home dated

The trail which I at this time followed continued on to Tecumseh, an old Indian trading post, where lived Thomas N. Stinson,[14] and on to Topeka, a muddy little town on a hill.[15] We tried boating corn down the Kaw River from Topeka, Lecompton, and Lawrence to McAlpine's warehouse at Wyandotte,[16] for government use, 500 sacks each load. Boating was not a success that summer; too little water, too many sand-bars; but I did meet two Delaware Indians who had been Frémont's guides to California, and got much valuable information of the plains and mountains.[17]

Thence turning southwest, we reached the Wakarusa at a rocky ford, where dwelt the urbane, diplomatic Chester Thomas,[18] who spent an evening in our camp to our great delight. The wagon trail then took us to Burlingame, where were the Schuyler mansion[19] and I. B. Titus' toll bridge.

I spent part of that summer in looking over the eastern part of the Territory. Staking out a piece of land at Burlingame, I made an attempt to break up eighty acres of prairie, but the sun and wind dried the ground till it was hard as a grindstone. I became dis-

---

Lecompton, June 13, 1859, he wrote, "Lecompton is a small place with a poor location, never can be much." Original letter in the Mead Collection, Wichita. The proslavery constitution of Kansas had been adopted at Lecompton in 1857.

14. Col. Thomas N. Stinson had been put in charge of a government trading post established for the Potawatomis at Uniontown, about fourteen miles west of Topeka. In 1852, Stinson established Tecumseh, Kansas, and did much to develop the town. BLACKMAR 2: 684 and *KSHC* 13: 371.

15. In a letter home dated Lecompton, Kansas, July 10, 1859, JRM wrote: "Topeka will probably be the capital of the Territory and around it are some fine chances to invest. I know one farm of 160 acres, 9 miles from Topeka, half timber, 75 acres fenced, 30 or 40 broke, two houses on it, a fine creek running through the timber with lots of fish in it, and plenty of rock and coal in the banks, all for $600. Good prairie can be got alongside for $3 an acre." Original letter in the Mead Collection, Wichita.

16. Wyandotte, now Kansas City, Kansas, had its origins in the 1842 federal government decision to give certain members of the Wyandotte tribe a section of land each from public lands on the west bank of the Missouri River. The remainder of the tribe were persuaded to leave their settlements and move to a reservation at the mouth of the Kaw or Kansas River. Their village became known as Wyandotte. In 1858, John McAlpine and James Washington built a flour mill and a sawmill at Wyandotte. *KSHC* 12: 54 and 90–91.

17. John Charles Frémont (1813–90), famed explorer of the West.

18. The Honorable Chester Thomas was born on July 18, 1810, at Troy, Pennsylvania. In 1858 he moved to Kansas to farm in Shawnee County. In 1859 he was elected to the Territorial Council to represent Shawnee, Osage, and Lyon counties. In 1861, President Lincoln appointed him special postal agent for the Western Territories, which included Nebraska, Dakota, Colorado, Utah, and New Mexico. See the Kansas volume of the *U.S. Biographical Dictionary* (1879).

19. Home of Burlingame's first mayor, Phillip C. Schuyler.

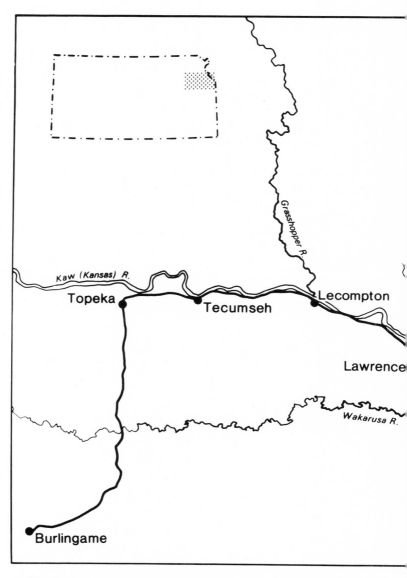

2. *The Trail from Leavenworth to Burlingame, Kansas,*
via Lawrence and Topeka

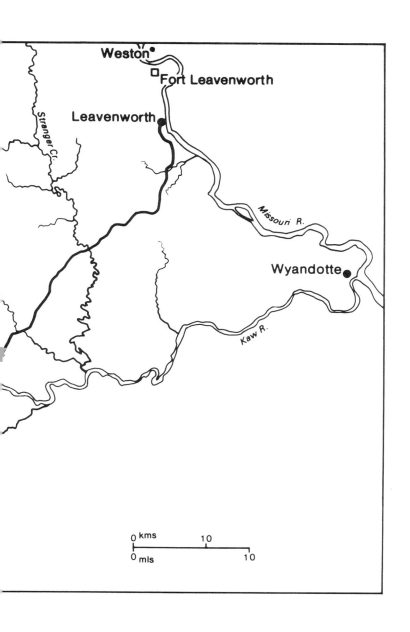

Weston

Fort Leavenworth

Leavenworth

Stranger Cr.

Missouri R.

Wyandotte

Kaw R.

0 kms   10
0 mls   10

gusted with honest endeavor and quit, retiring to the hospitable home of that genial frontiersman I. B. Titus on the banks of Switzler Creek at Burlingame.[20] Here I assisted him in sitting on his porch beside the great Santa Fe Trail, watching the dusty trains drag their slow lengths along with a rattling fire of popping whips, mingled with strange oaths in mixed Mexican and frontier jargon. Col. Titus owned the toll bridge across the creek at the Santa Fe crossing. The bridge probably cost a hundred dollars; it was built of logs cut from trees growing on the banks of the stream. In the summer he used to take in a toll of $20 or $30 or more each day. So Kansas had its redeeming qualities even then.

Col. Titus had an interesting family, was a good friend, and everybody liked him. While I was at the house enjoying his hospitality I made the acquaintance of Miss Agnes Barcome—the young lady who afterwards became my wife.[21] I had a fine riding horse, and she also had a very fine animal, and we enjoyed many happy hours riding about the village and visiting with friends.[22]

The great Santa Fe Trail connected people of diverse race and language, separated by hundreds of miles of savage wilderness. This huge trail, 60 to 100 feet wide, was worn smooth and solid by constant travel of ponderous wagons carrying 8,000 to 10,000 pounds each. Sometimes three wagons trailed together; from 10 to 30 constituting a train; drawn by eight, sixteen, or twenty oxen or mules each; coming in from New Mexico loaded with wool, hides, robes, or silver, returning with almost everything used by man, woman, or child. The drivers were known as "bull whackers" or "mule skinners," mostly semi-Indian, half-civilized, faithful, pa-

20. I. B. Titus staked out a claim on the south bank of Switzler Creek as early as 1854—one year before the little town of Council City was started. Titus had a house and a blacksmith forge on his claim, to which he added a toll bridge to carry Santa Fe Trail traffic over the creek. Switzler Creek was named after a man who was run over and killed by a wagon while descending the eastern bank of the stream at the old Santa Fe crossing. In 1857 the name Council City was changed to Burlingame in honor of Anson Burlingame, later U.S. Minister to China. See ANDREAS, 698 and 1529; *KSHC* 17: 375; BLACKMAR 1: 255–56.

21. Agnes Barcome was born in Montreal, Canada, in April, 1841. She married James R. Mead in Burlingame, Kansas, on December 1, 1861.

22. In a letter home dated Tecumseh, Kansas, August 13, 1859, JRM gives this description of Burlingame: "Burlingame contains sixty houses, ten or more of them two story cut stone, one large two story hotel, several smaller ones, a good sawmill and grist mill. A large stone flouring mill is about half done. . . . There is a stone church going up." Original letter in the Mead Collection, Wichita.

tient, brown-skinned, with hair of jet hanging on their shoulders, wielding lashes with such skill as to cut a rattlesnake's head off at 20 feet, or cut through the tough hide of a refractory ox. The popping of their whips on entering a town or at a bad crossing sounded like the rapid discharge of firearms. So well had the route of this trail been chosen, that no considerable hill or unsafe ford occurred in its more than 400 miles through Kansas, while convenient camping places, with fuel, water, and grass—three essentials—were found at convenient distances.

In that delightful summer I found good people and friends everywhere. The beauties of the Kansas climate and scenery and the wonderful life and activity on the old Santa Fe Trail constantly increased my interest, and I became more anxious than ever to see something of the buffalo on the great plains. The warm blood of youth longs for adventure. Here was an opportunity. My impatient rifles longed to show their mettle. Later they had their fill, for to my shame be it recorded that they laid low 2,000 buffalo, and other of God's creatures in proportion, during some years of service.

So in the fall of that year, on the first of September, 1859, I organized a hunting party of young men, of whom D. R. Kilbourn was one, with six or seven teams. On the fifth of October we started west on the Santa Fe Trail, crossing Dragoon, Log Chain, and Rock Creeks to Council Grove,[23] which at that time was the western boundary of civilization. Then on across Diamond Springs,[24] Cottonwood, Little and Big, and Running Turkey creeks to a little wayside trading-house south of the big bend of the Smoky Hill, called a ranch, as all such places on the plains were then called. Any camping place on the Santa Fe Trail was as good a point for business as

23. On July 17, 1825, a Santa Fe Road Surveying and Marking Expedition, consisting of 40 men, 57 horses and mules, and 7 baggage wagons, left Fort Osage near present-day Independence, Missouri. Reaching the Neosho River in the second week of August, they held council with the chiefs of the Great and Little Osage Indians under the famous Council Oak, in a fine grove of trees since known as Council Grove. Here a treaty was made for the right-of-way over the plains, and $500 in gold and $300 in merchandise was paid to the Indians. BARRY, 122; and *KSHC* 14: 794–804.

24. A well-known camping place on the Santa Fe Trail, because of the great abundance of clear, cold water that gushed out near the head of Otter Creek (now known as Diamond Creek). Here too was timber and grazing, and in time the camping place became a staging post with several stone buildings and a corral. Originally known as Jones Spring, it was renamed Diamond of the Plains by members of the 1825 Santa Fe Road Surveying and Marking Expedition. *KSHC* 14: 794–804; and BARRY, 142.

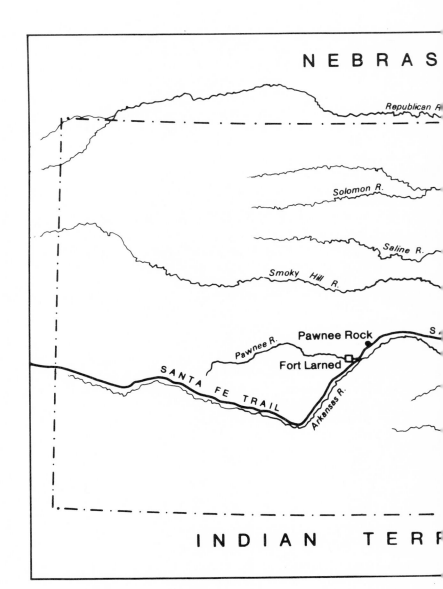

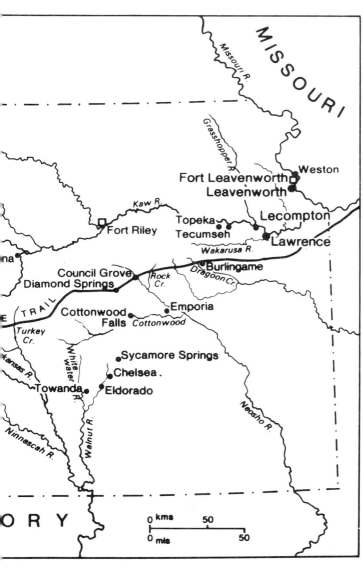

MISSOURI

Missouri R.

Grasshopper R.

Kaw R.

Fort Riley

Topeka
Tecumseh

Fort Leavenworth
Leavenworth

Weston

Lecompton

Lawrence

Wakarusa R.

na

Council Grove
Diamond Springs

Rock
Cr.

Dragoon Cr.

Burlingame

E

TRAIL

Turkey
Cr.

Cottonwood
Falls

Cottonwood

Emporia

Sycamore Springs

Chelsea

Towanda

Eldorado

White Water

Walnut R.

Neosho R.

Ninnescah R.

O R Y

0 kms 50
0 mls 50

3. Kansas and the Santa Fe Trail

the main street of a town. Along the trail we met long trains of wagons; they usually drove twenty miles a day or less, as water and camping places required. Some of these trains were loaded high with the coarse wool from New Mexico.

It was a custom in those days along the trail to entertain the "tenderfoot" with wonderful stories of life on the plains. One story that I recall was of a young fellow just out from the east who inquired of an old plainsman returning from the Santa Fe if there were any rattlesnakes on the plains.

"Lot's of 'em," replied the plainsman.

"How big are they?" asked the newcomer.

"I don't know," came the answer. "I have seen them stretched across the trail with their heads in the grass on one side and their tails hid in the grass on the other, but I couldn't tell you how long they were."

In many places the Santa Fe Trail was 100 feet wide, worn smooth and hard by the broad wheels of countless wagons, each drawn by four to eight spans of mules or oxen, with a loose herd driven behind containing the sore-footed, lame, given-out, and extra animals. They were called the "cavayard."

Among others we met Colonel Bent, with a train-load of buffalo robes and furs from his fort up the Arkansas.[25] Some of these trains were accompanied by merchants from Santa Fe riding in carriages and carrying large amounts of specie. As one ox train was passing, loaded with wool, we stopped at the side of the trail to view the uncouth caravan; men, teams, and wagons covered with dust. The immense wagons which were used in those days could carry in bulk as much as a railway car and these wagons were loaded to the top of the bows with wool. Underneath each wagon a net was swung, made of hides or sacks sewed together, filled with buffalo-chips for fuel, or sometimes a log of driftwood was swing-

25. Col. William Bent, together with his older brother Charles Bent and Ceran St. Vrain, built a large fort on the Arkansas River in southeast Colorado in 1833. From this base they conducted a small trading empire that stretched from Texas to Wyoming and from the Rocky Mountains into Kansas. Subsequently, the Indian Wars of 1847 disrupted this trade, and cholera spread over the plains. In 1849, William Bent, now the only survivor of four brothers, moved out of the fort and burned it to the ground. Four years later he built a new stone fort at Big Timbers, 38 miles downstream. This was his headquarters at the time he first met JRM. See GRINNELL [1], "Bent's Old Fort and Its Builders," *KSHC* 15(1922): 28–91.

ing underneath, with cooking utensils and rawhide ropes hung along the sides.

I walked out to the train to get a closer view and, to my astonishment, the first driver I noticed was a young man named George McGranahan who was raised on a little farm back in the woods near my father's home in Iowa. We had spent many happy days hunting and roaming the woods together in our boyhood. I had lost trace of him and here he was, just coming in from Santa Fe, neither he nor I knowing that the other was on the plains. Within a few years he owned a wagon train of his own.

We usually travelled about twenty miles a day or until we reached a convenient creek for camp where we could find timber and an abundance of pure water and grass for our animals. At the Turkey Creek crossing nearly due south of the big bend of the Smoky Hill River we were told that there were plenty of buffalo a short distance back from the Trail, north or south. We turned north and struck off across the prairie in that direction. The plains seemed boundless; not a tree or bush was in sight. The ground lay in long, rolling swells, always higher ground bounded the horizon in the distance.

During the morning I noticed a number of big gray wolves which had been killed by strychnine put out by hunters, and some carcasses of buffalo. Toward noon as we approached the divide between the Arkansas and the Smoky Hill Rivers, we observed in the distance what appeared to be a belt of timber extending along the horizon in each direction as far as we could see. As we approached nearer we saw that it was a vast herd of buffalo grazing—to our imagination the most entrancing sight the universe afforded—and such a sight as the eye of man can never again behold.

After getting among them, quite a number of inexperienced young men of the party took their guns in feverish excitement and started out on foot for the glory of killing the first buffalo. The popping of their guns continued for the next two hours as we drove slowly along. Later they came straggling in, exhausted with running and empty-handed, declaring that lead would not kill a buffalo; that they had shot fifty times and had not, apparently, "fazed" one of them. One man assured me that "a buffalo could pack twenty pounds of lead." I saw that it was useless to attempt to get up to the buffalo on that open prairie and, in the company of such inexperienced enthusiasts, did not attempt it. So we drove on until evening and camped at the head of a creek running north to the Smoky Hill River.

It was that glorious, exhilarating season of the year known as Indian Summer—as beautiful in the land of the Indian and buffalo as among the hills of New England. There were buffalo on all sides of us and mingled with them were groups of antelope grazing or playing over the hills. It was the most beautiful scene I ever beheld: an abundance of game on every side, quietly feeding or reposing in the sunshine, and at home as the Great Creator placed them before the advent of that merciless exterminator, so-called civilized man.

To the north of our camp, standing in the great bend of the river to which they gave their name, were groups of isolated buttes known among all plainsmen and Indians as the "Smoky Hills." As we first saw them through the haze peculiar to the fall of the year, their name seemed most appropriate.

The next afternoon there came to our camp a lone man, an unarmed stranger on foot in search of help. He told us that he and his brother had gone out with a wagon and two yoke of oxen to spend the winter hunting on the Saline River. Arriving at a difficult crossing on the Saline, they were delayed, having to cross their outfit on a bridge made by felling trees. Their oxen died of Texas or Spanish Fever as they had nearly reached their destination; leaving them in the wild buffalo country afoot with no animals or any way of travelling, on the bank of a miry river, and no help within fifty miles, so far as they knew. One man had stayed behind and the other had started for the Santa Fe Trail to get help.

This was my first introduction to the vicissitudes and accidents common to those who tempt fortune in the wilderness, of which I experienced my full share in succeeding years. We invited him to stay with us and the next morning, in company with our visitor, who had some experience in buffalo hunting, I set out to have a quiet little hunt away from our too enthusiastic companions.

After going some distance from camp we noticed a small herd of buffalo lying down on a slope of a ravine. By following up the ravine we found it an easy matter to approach within seventy-five yards of them. Here we cautiously raised our heads over the bank and studied them as they lay in the warm sunshine. They were unconscious of our presence until we showed ourselves, and then they all got up and stood looking at us.

My companion showed me where to aim in order to strike a vital spot and, following his direction, I sighted and pulled the trigger. All the buffalo ran about a hundred yards, then stopped to see what had made the noise. After a moment the one I had shot at tumbled over dead. One was all I cared to get, so we scared the others off and went up to the dead bull to look him over. We admired his huge size, his ponderous shaggy head, and glossy black robe.

At first I was very much afraid of buffalo, as I had read such terrible stories of their ferocity when wounded that I could hardly be induced to go within shooting distance of them. I afterwards found, however, that they were entirely harmless unless wounded and approached too closely.

We took the tongue of this buffalo and some of the tenderloin, and then started back to camp. Before reaching camp I succeeded in killing another big bull—a very fine one—and so we arrived in camp loaded with choice meat and with two short black tails as evidence of our success and skill. We found that the other fellows whom we had left in camp had also gone out, but none of them had hunted buffalo before, and as a result they had practically made a failure of it. They had found two old bulls that were so aged that they could hardly get up—and bulls in those days usually lived until they died of old age—and all began firing at a distance, gradually crawling closer until they had shot about twenty pounds of lead at them (the hill behind the buffalo would make a good lead mine sometime in the future), finally getting the bulls securely dead. They then cut off some of the meat, and when we arrived they were trying to cook it. They had heard of hump steak, but did not know in what part of the animal it grew, so they had taken a piece from the top of the hump, which is just about the toughest piece of meat imaginable. When taken from such ancient bulls as the two our valorous companions had shot and put in the pan to fry, such a steak would curl up and crawl around, and the aroma of ancient bull that filled the air was anything but appetizing. The meat I brought in proved to be sweet, tender, and delicious. And we retired to our blankets to dream of fairyland.

We soon discovered that there were no buffalo in that vicinity except bulls, and I would remark here that it is a very common thing for a large section of the country to be covered with buffalo which are exclusively bulls—most of them past their prime. They travel in advance of the cows and go in great herds by themselves, while the cows and young animals stay back on the range. The outer edge of a great herd will also frequently be composed entirely of bulls. I have travelled a whole day through country covered with buffalo, cutting across their course, and failed to see a cow or young animal from dawn to sunset. This occurs in their Spring migration North; the bulls, travelling more rapidly, leave the cows and young stock far in the rear.

So we decided to go further into the buffalo range and find better animals. The next morning we hitched up and drove down to and across the river into camp at the foot of the great buttes from which the Smoky Hill River derives its name. These buttes, known to all the Indians of the plains of Kansas, have been noted landmarks for trappers, hunters, and explorers, as well as Indians, from time immemorial. Around these buttes are mounds and burial places and ancient camp remains showing this to have been a favorite resort for the prehistoric people who once inhabited this valley. An Archaeologist, in excavating an old camp, found part of a chain armor—perhaps a relic of Coronado's expedition.

In the great bend of the Smoky Hill we found buffalo cows and calves and young animals in great abundance—thousands of them all over the country. There were also many other varieties of game. Every day we saw groups of antelope and an occasional deer.

Along the timbered streams were plenty of wild turkeys, but we hardly noticed them. There was too much game and when we had an abundance of choice buffalo meat we had no desire for any other. We never tired of it, though it was our principal food the year round. It seemed to take the place of all other food—a perfect ration. Our meals usually consisted of buffalo meat in unlimited quantity, bread in the form of "flap jacks" fried in buffalo fat, and plenty of coffee, with sugar to sweeten it, drunk out of a new tin cup.

After loading the teams with the choicest meat I was approached by the visitor who had come to our camp. He wanted me to go back and help him out of the difficulties in which he and his brother found themselves. I laid the matter before my companions and they advised me very strongly not to do it. They pointed out that he was a total stranger and might be an outlaw sent out by some band of robbers and thieves; we knew nothing at all about him, and for me to take my team and outfit—which was of considerable value—and go with him into an unknown country, entirely uninhabited, would be too great a risk. But I was so delighted with the country and its wealth of animal life, that I was glad to find an excuse to remain. So with their consent, as they had plenty of teams and did not require any assistance from me, but against their advice, I decided to go with this stranger.

CHAPTER 2

Hunter's Paradise

EARLY the next morning we struck off across the buttes in a northerly direction toward the Saline River. During our drive that day we passed through what might be termed a hunter's paradise. The whole country had the appearance of a well-kept park belonging to some English nobleman. The grass was eaten down close by the buffalo and paths ran in every direction. The country was well watered by pure streams fringed by belts of timber and the high buttes were clothed with grass to their summits. From these heights a view of broad valleys and rolling hills could be obtained for fifteen or twenty miles in every direction, and the whole country was dotted over with herds of buffalo lying down in the sunshine, taking their ease or grazing upon the short nutritious grass which covered the earth like a carpet.

Here and there scattered among the buffalo were herds of antelope feeding, playing, travelling about, and adding variety to the landscape. The only disturbing element in this apparent Eden was the presence of large numbers of great grey wolves, ready to devour the dead or crippled animals or the weak or straggling ones. If they failed to find these, they were able and willing to pull down and kill the biggest and strongest cow or bull—yet they never molested man. Trotting round the herds was the cunning and crafty coyote— a picker-up of unconsidered trifles, entirely harmless, fond of scraps of rawhide, a freshly oiled boot, an unlucky rabbit, or a crippled bird—all are equally accepted.

By travelling briskly all day we came to the banks of the Saline River and to the camp of the man who was with me. There we found his brother and a dog alone like a shipwrecked sailor on an uninhabited island in an almost unknown country, and liable at any time to be discovered by bands of Indians. A horde of hungry wolves had discovered the camp. The nights were a pandemonium of fighting, snarling, and howling as they devoured the dead oxen within fifty feet of the tent. Nothing was left but the large bones, and the terrified man and dog supposed their time would come next. Judging by their howling that night I imagined there must have been a thousand wolves in the vicinity. A little later I gathered in the pelts of these same wolves.

Next day we took their wagon apart and, together with its contents, floated everything across the river on logs. Their goods were stored in a tent on the north bank of the river within a mile of where they proposed to build a cabin and remain throughout the winter.

There had been a great flood in the Saline Valley in 1858 and the river bottoms were covered with a large growth of sunflowers, which had grown to a height of about ten feet. Through these the buffalo had made their trails and in riding along them on horseback I met several huge buffalo bulls who were within a rod of me before I could see them—much to our mutual surprise. Along the bluff was a line of drift, showing that the valley had been covered six feet deep with water. This line of drift extended far up the river, and the valley above where the town of Lincoln now stands must have been covered, judging from the drift, ten to fifteen feet deep, occasioned by the bluffs on either side and the thick timber forming a gorge.

I moved the party up to their chosen camping ground—a beautiful location—and they suggested that I should stay with them and hunt during the Autumn, or longer if I should see fit. The opportunities for hunting and sport were so excellent that I accepted their offer and we went to work to build cabins for our use and corrals and stables for our animals.

We also made a pasture by putting a fence one hundred yards in length across the entrance to a bend of the river, where the banks were so steep that cattle could not cross. The Saline River was very muddy, which is the case with many salt streams, and could only be crossed in a few places. We put our cattle in this enclosure and completed our cabins, which did not take long as timber was very abundant. We found that we had one of the most sightly places on the river, just where the river turned south from the northern bluff it had been following, leaving a wide bottom looking east which gave us a view down the valley for five or six miles. Behind the cabin was a heavy growth of big timber which entirely protected us from the north and west winds and afforded a most beautiful site for a camp.[1]

Having completed comfortable winter quarters, which became known as Mead's Ranch, I set out to explore the country. So far we had seen no one. Riding down the river fifteen or twenty miles, I found a lone squatter named Shipple,[2] who had a ferry across the river on the trail leading from Fort Riley to Fort Larned, and, a couple of miles further southwest on the Smoky, a little town of a dozen or more houses, called Salina.

Here I met some excellent people. Col. William A. Phillips,

1. Regarding the exact location of Mead's Ranch, JRM later wrote, "This camp was on the eastern curve of the Saline just west of the present town of Culver, in Ottawa County." In 1908 a Mrs. Emily Haines wrote an article entitled "Early Days in Ottawa County (*KSHS* 10(1907–1908), in which among other things she stated: "The Tripps had come into possession of a two-roomed, well-built cabin, built by Jas. R. Mead, and purchased of him on his removal to Butler County in 1863." Secretary George Martin of the Kansas State Historical Society wrote to JRM to check this point and received the following information, dated Wichita, Kansas, August 2, 1908: "Yes, I built that hewed-log house and fireplace, also cabins, corrals, etc. The premises described was my ranch, a mile or two east of the present town of Tescott, and about fifteen miles west of Salina. It was at that time the most suitable, beautiful and sheltered site on the Saline River. In the fall of 1859 I had built an ordinary log cabin, corral, etc., and that was my hunting headquarters, being in the midst of the buffalo and other game. The next year I built a hewed-log house of one-half stories, shingle roof, split in the nearby timber, of oak. The floors were of lumber hauled from Junction City or farther west. With my own hands I built a large fireplace and chimney of stone laid in adobe mortar. In December, 1861, I married and took my wife to the ranch, also brought up a family to live in the cabin for company and to aid in our work. In the fall of 1862 the Indians became so threatening, scouting and war parties of the Cheyennes bothering us, that we moved to Salina for safety, and in the spring of 1863 I sold the ranch to a Mr. Tripp" (Kansas State Historical Society, Topeka).

2. Two brothers, John Schipple and Goothardt Schipple, settled in what was to be the Salina area in March, 1858. In November, 1861, Goothardt Schipple was elected county commissioner. In that same election JRM was elected county surveyor. See BLACKMAR 2:637.

founder of the town;[3] H. L. Jones and his estimable wife, who kept a very comfortable hotel;[4] Alexander M. Campbell had a store and post-office;[5] two brothers, Robert H. Bishop and Rev. William Bishop, were there.[6] The surrounding country was a buffalo range. Between Salina and Fort Larned were two hunters' ranches; the Farris brothers, Henry and Irwin on Elm Creek,[7] and D. H. Page and Joseph Lemon at the crossing of the Smoky,[8] both on the Fort

3. William Addison Phillips, founder of Salina, was born in Paisley, Scotland. He arrived in the United States with his parents in 1839, and they settled on a farm near Sparta, Illinois. W. A. Phillips studied law and was admitted to the bar at the age of twenty-one. He married Margaret C. Spilman on June 9, 1854, and settled in Lawrence, Kansas, that same year. Colonel Phillips was an outspoken antislavery man, and through his work as a correspondent for the *New York Tribune* he did much to further the Free State interests of many Kansas settlers. From 1873 to 1879, Colonel Phillips was a member of the U.S. Congress. *KSHC* 5: 100–113 and BLACKMAR 2: 634–35.

4. In 1858, W. A. Phillips built the first hotel in Salina, using pine lumber hauled overland from the Missouri River. Later he sold the hotel to H. L. Jones. Mrs. Jones ran the hotel while Mr. Jones ran a general store. In 1861, H. L. Jones was elected to the Kansas legislature. ANDREAS, 698.

5. Together with W. A. Phillips, Alexander C. Spilman, and James Muir, Alexander M. Campbell was a pioneer settler and a founder of Salina, Kansas. Born in Renfrewshire, Scotland, on August 12, 1835, he emigrated to the United States with his family in 1848. They settled in Randolph County, Illinois. In 1853 the family moved to Clinton County, Missouri, and in 1856 to Kansas, where they settled in Lawrence. In 1858, A. M. Campbell accompanied W. A. Phillips and James Muir to the Saline River country to select a site for a new town, Salina. In October of that year Alexander Campbell married Christina A. Phillips, sister of W. A. Phillips, in Riley City. Campbell became deputy sheriff of Douglas County and was an ardent antislavery man. He engaged in farming, the Indian trade, and did some trapping. He was appointed postmaster of Salina in 1861. After 1858 he lived the remainder of his life in Salina. On March 31, 1906, in a letter to JRM, Alexander Spilman wrote: "Campbell is ripening into old age, together with his estimable wife, at Salina. He is one of the best and truest men I ever knew." See note 4, MEAD [14], *KSHC* 9: 11–12.

6. The Bishop brothers were from Whitburn, Linlithgow, Scotland. The family emigrated to the United States in 1834. William Bishop graduated from Illinois College at Jacksonville in 1847 and went on to Princeton to study theology. After holding two academic posts as professor of Greek language and literature, he moved to Kansas to become pastor of the Presbyterian Church at Lawrence. He became a prominent figure both in the church and in education in Kansas. He died in Salina on June 4, 1900. Robert H. Bishop, like his brother a graduate of Illinois College, settled near Salina in 1860 and took up farming. He was clerk of Saline County and deputy registrar of deeds. In 1863 he became a member of the Kansas legislature and in 1874 a justice of the peace. See notes 5 and 6, MEAD [14], *KSHC* 9: 12.

7. Henry and Irwin Farris were among the second group of settlers in Ellsworth County. The Elm Creek mentioned by JRM is now known as Clear Creek. The Farris brothers established their camp there on September 20, 1860—about a year after JRM established his ranch on the Saline. See note 7, MEAD [14], *KSHC* 9: 12.

8. Both JRM and the Kansas State Historical Society give the name Joseph Lemon,

Larned trail. I afterwards found these men to be good fellows and excellent hunters.[9]

Colonel Phillips offered me one-sixteenth of the town site and a vacant claim adjoining, if I would locate there and help build up the town.[10] I was out for sport and adventure, not for town building. I replied that I already owned all of the Saline country for a hundred miles west, with a million head of livestock, and that was enough.

Returning to the ranch with two men I had picked up, we now devoted our time to hunting, in which we were quite successful, as buffalo were very plentiful in the immediate vicinity, as well as antelope and other game. There were hundreds of turkeys along the timbered streams which were easily killed, and the woods were full of fox squirrels. The river and its tributary streams were alive with beaver and otter, and in the brush along the river were an abundance of quail, but we paid little attention to small game, as we had no use for it. There were also numerous prairie chickens of two varieties; the ordinary ruffled grouse of Iowa and Illinois, and another bird, not so large, which was called the pin tail chicken.

After hunting in this place for a short time we became curious to know what lay further up the river. The Saline River at that time was unexplored, and there were no names for the tributaries on the north side; so for convenience I named them, and by those

---

but ANDREAS, 811, records it as Joseph Lehman. In any case, D. H. Page and his companion had a hunting ranch about four miles west of that owned by the Farris brothers. Both were on the road leading from Fort Riley to Fort Larned. Page and Lemon (or Lehman) were among the first settlers in Ellsworth County and occupied their ranch from 1860 to 1863. Fort Ellsworth was later built on their ranch site, and later still, Fort Harker was built nearby. Joe Lemon was rated an expert hunter and had the reputation of being a man who could take care of himself and his companions under all circumstances. Note 8, MEAD [14], *KSHC* 9:12.

9. Regarding other neighbors, JRM wrote home to his parents on December 25, 1859, from Saline River to say, "There are a few settlers 15 miles below us, mostly Dutch, and I think a good deal of them in general as settlers, for they are generaly industrious and honest, while the other settlers on the border are (if all accounts are true) a most precocious set of rascals who make it a point to study everybodies business (but their own) and have a habit of borrowing horses and cattle of a dark night without consulting the owner" (Mead Collection, Wichita). JRM may be using the term Dutch to describe Germans.

10. When JRM first arrived in Salina, the little town had only recently celebrated its first birthday. The original town company was composed of W. A. Phillips, A. M. Campbell, James Muir, Robert Crawford, and A. C. Spilman. It was Alexander Spilman who suggested the name Salina, pointing out that the whole area was already known as the Saline River Country.

names they are still known. It was a country practically unknown, as it was very seldom visited by hunters, and by no one else except Indians. So one morning we hitched up our team and started up the river to see what the unknown might have in store for us. After following an Indian trail for about fifteen miles, we came to a beautiful tributary stream with fine timber along the water course and full of beaver dams. We named that Beaver Creek. Here I noticed that the ground was almost covered with the peculiar droppings of some animal I had not previously observed. These droppings had the appearance of round bullets and I came to the conclusion that they must be those of the elk.

While we were getting our supper, I told the boys I would like to go to the top of the hill which shut off our view of the valley, and take a look. Taking my gun I climbed up and looked over. There, spread out before me, was a great valley extending towards the west, and coming down through the sunflowers I saw a herd of animals which at first sight I took to be horses. But as they came closer I discovered that they were all the same color and some of them had immense antlers on their heads. I realized they must be elk, although I had not seen a wild elk until that moment.[11]

At once I decided to use my best endeavors to get one or two of them and, running back to camp, I told the two men that there was a herd of elk coming down the valley and that if they would stay in camp and let me go alone I would get some of them. One of my companions guessed that they were a drove of Indian ponies coming down to water and that we were about to get into a wild Indian camp. I replied that I had never seen herds either of ponies or horses that were all of the same color and having big heads of antlers.

Taking my gun, I hurried down into the thick undergrowth near the river. After a few moments I heard the brush cracking as the

---

11. These were wapiti (*Cervus canadensis*). Wyndham-Quin, Fourth Earl of Dunraven, has written the following humorous explanation: "The wapiti is a splendid beast, the handsomest by far of all the deer tribe. He is called an elk in the States—Why, I do not know; for the European elk is identical with the American moose, and a moose and a wapiti are not the least alike. But I presume the wapiti is called by the Americans an elk for the same reason that they call thrushes robins, and grouse partridges. The reason, I dare say, is a good one, but I do not know what it is. The wapiti . . . is exactly like the European red deer—only about twice as large—carries magnificent antlers, and is altogether a glorious animal." WYNDHAM-QUIN, 46–47.

elk came tramping through the timber. Clearly they would pass near where I was standing, so I waited and presently saw the band, with an enormous buck in the lead, passing about twenty yards in front of me. Drawing a bead right back of his shoulder, I pulled the trigger, but the mainspring of my rifle was weak, and the gun failed to fire.

Just behind the leader were two fine bucks walking abreast. I raised the hammer and shot at the nearest one, and the elk behind him dropped dead in his tracks, while the other went on, the bullet having passed clear through both of them.

When the herd had moved on I walked up to have a look at the dead elk. Suddenly I heard my two companions, whose curiosity had tempted them to follow me, shouting loudly.

"Why don't you shoot?" they yelled. "Look at them!"

They were too excited to think of the guns they held in their hands. I turned and there was the whole herd standing about one hundred yards away. It was a funny sight. Both men were calling to me to shoot and yet they stood with their own rifles in their hands, entranced by their first view of noble elk.

Dropping a loose ball into my gun, which was a muzzle-loader, I shot again, not paying much attention to where I was shooting. The elk ran a short distance and then turned and came back very near to the same place. I loaded my rifle hastily and fired another shot. They ran a short distance and stopped again among the big trees. Each time I shot they would run a little way and then make a circle to come back facing me, but getting a little further away each time. I shot four or five times in that way, putting loose balls down the barrel without using a patch in my hurry.

The elk finally concluded they had satisfied their curiosity and went off over a hill, and as they went I noticed two bucks and a doe staggering along as if badly wounded. After they had disappeared over the rise I walked to the top and about a quarter of a mile away I could see a cow standing; she had stopped as if wounded. I watched for a few minutes, and presently she lay down, so I went back to join the others, suggesting that we would let the elk lie there awhile, fearing that if we approached her at once she might get up and run and we would lose her; while if we left her alone, she would die where she was. After waiting about half an hour we went to her and found that she was nearly dead, and was so weak she could not get up. We soon had her hide off and the meat in quarters. I found that my bullet had entered her flank and, ranging forward, had gone through the center of her heart and then stopped on striking a rib. I found the bullet loose inside of the cavity near the heart. She had lived half an hour after being shot in this manner.

We soon dressed the cow and also the fine buck which I had killed. In dressing the buck I found that the bullet had gone through back of the shoulder and had just touched the point of the little projecting bones of the vertebrae. Probably the nervous shock had knocked him down. He had apparently dropped stone dead in his tracks, and yet he might have got up if I had not cut his throat, as there was no wound that was necessarily immediately fatal, as far as I could see. A bullet passing through such an animal's body does not always kill it.

Out of the fat inside of these elk I rendered out about a bucket full of pure tallow, as white as mutton suet, which we used for cooking purposes and found it to be most excellent. We took the quarters of these two elk to the camp and hung them up in the trees to cool. Since it was frosty weather they kept very nicely. I thought that I had never eaten sweeter meat in my life. I did not follow the herd to secure the other wounded animals as I should have done. I have no doubt two of them died within a short distance. I was then quite inexperienced and highly elated with my success.

On the next small creek were evidences of war. Scattered about were broken pots, kettles, pans, and camp equipage; some of them with bullet holes through them. Probably a small hunting party of Delawares had been surprised and driven out by the Cheyennes, who were jealous of this, their country. What they did not choose to carry away they had destroyed. A good deal of meat and skins were lying about. In walking along the bank of the timbered creek my foot struck the end of a chain extending into the ground. On digging down we found a nest of heavy new camp kettles, such as Indians use, cached. I gave the name of Battle Creek to this stream.

The Delaware Indians were the bravest men and the best trappers, and the most honorable and intelligent Indians that I ever became acquainted with. I saw them frequently, as they came up the

John Sarcoxie, right, with friends Charles Journeycake, left, and Isaac Journeycake. Kansas State Historical Society, Topeka.

river trapping in the fall and spring. One of them—John Sarcoxie, who was the son of the Chief of the Delaware Tribe—initiated me into the mysteries and secrets of beaver trapping and, among other things, the making of "Beaver Medicine." This is a scent which they prepare from various aromatic barks and spices mixed with castor beans. They put a pinch of the mixture in a split stick which they place in the bank of the stream above the trap. Any beaver passing up or down the stream is attracted to the scent and will swim to it and most likely get his foot in the trap.

It is not a usual thing for Indians to reveal their secrets to white men, but John Sarcoxie seemed to have no hesitancy in giving them to me. He also taught me how to trap beavers under the ice by driving green poles into the stream. The beavers would come to gnaw the bark off the green cottonwood poles and could be caught in a trap set in the bed of the stream.

The Kansas beavers made their homes in the banks of streams, as the ground is easily burrowed into. A beaver makes the entrance to his burrow under water, with a tunnel leading up to his sleeping apartments near the surface of the bank. In mountainous country, where the ground is rocky, they cannot burrow in this way and so build mounds out in the water, the same as muskrats in Kansas. They are exclusively vegetarians, subsisting on the leaves and tender twigs of willows and the bark of cottonwood, willow, and a few other trees and shrubs. They sleep in the daytime and work at night.

From the creek where we killed our elk we travelled up the river for about ten miles and found a large branch of the Saline River coming in from the northwest. In Salina I had been directed to a young man named Alexander C. Spilman for information.[12] He had

12. Alexander C. Spilman was born on October 5, 1837, in Yazoo City, Mississippi. His father was Dr. James F. Spilman of Mississippi, and his mother was Margaret Caraway of Tennessee. Alexander Spilman left Michigan University after one year to go to Kansas. He arrived in Lawrence in August, 1857. In 1858 he joined W. A. Phillips (his brother-in-law) and others to found Salina. In 1859 he surveyed the townsite and was a member of the board of commissioners to organize Saline County. At the outbreak of the Civil War he enlisted in Company F of the Sixth Kansas Cavalry, serving as sergeant. Later he was made captain of Company B, Third Regiment of the Indian Brigade. In 1866 he married Mary Amanda Kennison. He was representative for Saline County in the state legislature of 1867. In 1870 he moved to McPherson and took up farming. He later served three terms as probate judge of McPherson County and two terms as mayor of McPherson. See note 9, MEAD [14], *KSHC* 9:12–13.

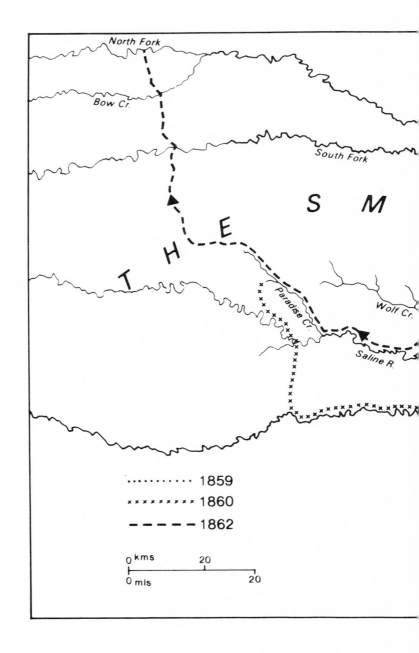

North Fork

Bow Cr.

South Fork

S   M

T   H   E

Paradise Cr.

Wolf Cr.

Saline R.

·············· 1859
×××××××× 1860
— — — — 1862

0 kms   20
0 mls   20

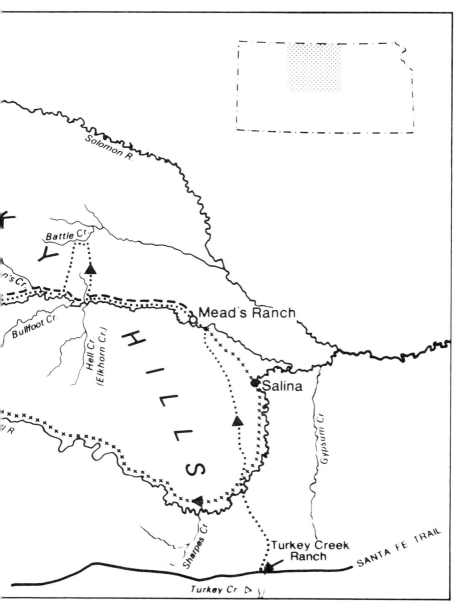

4. *The Solomon, Saline, and Smoky Hill country*

been up the Saline to a large tributary which he described as very miry near its mouth. Late that evening we approached a large tributary stream, and in the darkness drove into a salt marsh. I remarked that we had found Spilman's creek. We called it Spilman's Creek, from that time, and others adopted our name. When the U.S. Surveyors mapped the country they also adopted that name,[13] just as they did for other streams in the country which I had named, and these names they now bear on the maps. The names I gave were usually suggested by some circumstance connected with their discovery. They had no names at that time, and some of them were entirely unknown. I had gone further west than other hunters.

As we drove into a grove of timber to camp, a flock of turkeys happened to be roosting overhead, and one of the men fired a number of shots at them in quick succession. In the morning we found that a camp of Pawnees with horses, in a thicket within 200 yards, had left in such haste in the night as to leave some of their camp equipage.

On this large stream was abundant game and, in the thickets, shelters made of fallen wood where small parties of Indians stopped overnight while on predatory expeditions. No large camp sites were seen. Continuing on up the river we came to another large stream, which, from the large number of wolves we killed there, I named Wolf Creek, as it now appears on the map. On this creek I found the remains of two Indians, the flesh eaten by animals and ravens. Stuck fast in the bones were about thirty iron arrow points. Our verdict was, thieving Pawnees, overtaken by Cheyennes, evidently a large party, as each warrior shoots an arrow into a fallen enemy and those they cannot pull out remain, except the shaft, which is pulled off. Periodically the Cheyenne warriors spread out like a net and sweep over the rolling country of hills, streams, and valleys between the Solomon and the Saline, in eager search of these detested raiding parties, and sometimes their quest is not in vain, as these skeletons bore witness.

In a few days we loaded our teams with meat and hides and returned to our camp or "ranch," as we called it. In those days every isolated trading or hunting establishment was called a ranch. Shortly after our return, there came settlers out hunting from the eastern

13. The government surveyors spelled the name Spillman.

Alexander Caraway Spilman. Courtesy Linn Peterson, McPherson, Kansas.

part of the Territory. Hearing of us, they came up the river hoping to get loads of meat, but being ignorant of the habits of the buffalo, they had poor success in killing them. Sometimes they would spend a whole day trying to kill one buffalo which might prove worthless. As I was there for sport and enjoyment of the wide open spaces, I had plenty of time to devote to that purpose. I would go out with some of these parties and get a load of meat for them in the course of half a day, or, sometimes, in an hour's time. I helped to skin the animals and load up the wagons, and sent them home rejoicing.

There was an abundance of game in every direction from our camp and frequently they came within gun shot of our buildings. On one occasion I killed a buffalo from the cabin door. On another occasion I shot 27 buffalo out of a herd on the slope of a hill near our camp, which in those days was considered a very extraordinary achievement. But in later years I frequently made this an every-day occurrence if I chose to do so.

In those early days I was but an amateur on the plains and knew but little compared to what I learned in later years of experience. And yet I was quite successful as a hunter, partly because I was trained to rifle shooting in my boyhood, and partly because I had the finest rifles that could be made at the time, and was expert in their use.

In 1859 I was a beardless boy of slight build, but the fame of my success as a hunter gave me quite a reputation among settlers in the eastern part of the Territory. Stories travelled down river with each load of meat I provided and no doubt these stories became magnified and embellished at each successive camping ground. A result of this was that from time to time a wagon team would roll in and two or three six footers with long hair, bushy beards, and Kentucky squirrel rifles would inquire about the noted hunter of the Saline.

"Is this Mead's Ranch?" they would ask.

When I replied that my name was Mead, they would look me up and down.

"We'd like to see your father," they would say. "We have heard a great deal about him."

It was amusing to see the look of astonishment on their faces when I told them that I was the man they were looking for.

CHAPTER 3

Winter on the Plains: Hunting and Trading

In that same fall of 1859 the Kansas Indians, commonly known as the Kaw Indians, who were the original inhabitants of eastern Kansas, came up the Saline and Smoky Hill rivers from their reservation at Council Grove on their annual autumn hunt, as they had done from time immemorial. Chief Shingawassa and his band camped in the heavy timber immediately back of our ranch, and they constantly asked us to trade with them. They were able to supply themselves with a great abundance of meat, but they lacked coffee, sugar, flour, and tobacco, of which they were fond.

After trading with them until we had parted with a considerable portion of the provisions we had set aside for the winter, getting in exchange the furs they had collected in the neighborhood, I concluded it would be not only a matter of necessity but a good stroke of business to get a stock of goods and do some trading with them during the winter. So I loaded up what few furs and hides we had and started a man down to Leavenworth—250 miles—which was the nearest supply point in Kansas. At that time there was not a foot of railway in the territory, and we were dependent upon the Missouri River for our supplies.

A few days after the team had started on its way to the river, I saddled my pony and rode through to Leavenworth and went to the

wholesale grocery of Morehead and Ryan,[1] and told them I wanted
to buy some groceries but just then I did not have any ready money
with me. They asked me where I had bought goods before and
what I wanted to do with them. I replied that I had bought no goods
in Kansas, but I wanted to take them out on the plains and trade
with the Indians. After asking me a few more questions they told
me to drive up my wagons and load what I wanted. I said that I had
but one wagon, and did not want a very large amount of goods in
that. The team came and I loaded four hundred dollars worth of
goods consisting of coffee, sugar, flour, and tobacco—all staple articles with the Indians—and started our wagon on its way back.

In payment for my goods I gave a note without security, due in
thirty days. I thought it was the cheekiest piece of business I
had ever done in my life, being an inexperienced boy and a total
stranger. Completing my business, I rode through to the ranch in
about three days, where I found the whole face of the earth covered with buffalo going South on their annual fall migration.

With the two teams and men on the ranch we went to shooting
buffalo and taking their hides and tallow. Before the team which
was on its way back from Leavenworth had arrived, I had more
than sufficient to load it. I continued hunting for about two weeks
more and at the end of that time I was able to load another heavy
freight wagon. Both wagons then started back to Leavenworth,
consigned to Morehead & Ryan. They arrived there on the last day
of grace of the note I had given. Mr. Morehead sold the loads in
the wagons to W. C. Lobenstein[2] for eight hundred dollars, paid my
note, and loaded up the wagons with all the goods they could haul
back. From that time on my credit was unquestioned.

I had designed to spend the winter hunting, but now found myself an Indian trader. There were a great many Indians in the vicinity and my time was largely occupied by trading with them, and in
going to camps at a distance. I traded for wolf, beaver, and all kinds
of fur found on the plains, so that in the course of the winter I had

1. Messrs C. R. Morehead & Co. occupied Lot 3 in Block 3 of Leavenworth.
ANDREAS, 420.

2. W. C. Lobenstein had a three-story brick building at the southeast corner of Third
and Cherokee streets in Leavenworth, which was for years the largest commercial
building in the city. He bought and sold leather goods, buffalo hides and robes, and furs.
See JOHNSTON, p. 38.

established an Indian trading post of some considerable importance and obtained several thousand dollars worth of furs.

During the winter season, sandwiched in along between our trading expeditions, we used to take an occasional hunt for the sport it afforded. We found it also a very profitable business killing the big gray wolves which lived with the buffalo and travelled with them, and also the coyotes, which were numerous and seemed to live in the vicinity, not following the buffalo in their migrations as the gray wolves did.

Our method of killing wolves was to shoot down two or three old bull buffaloes in different places apart from each other, and usually at some considerable distance from our camp. We would let the buffalo lie one night in order to attract the wolves. The next night, just before dusk, we would go and scatter poisoned bait about the carcasses, each bait containing about one thirtieth part of a dram of strychnine. The reason we put our baits out after sunset was on account of thousands of ravens that seemed to live with the buffalo, and which were confined exclusively to the country occupied by them. They would come back and pick up the baits if put out before dark, so that instead of killing wolves, we would find we had a whole field of ravens killed.

We also found it necessary to go out early to get our wolves next morning, as the ravens and sometimes eagles would come shortly after sunrise and tear holes in their flanks and damage their skins. After the wolves were skinned we would allow the carcasses to lie where they were, and the ravens in eating their stomachs and intestines would also eat the partially digested baits. This would kill them, and the prairie about the carcasses would soon be dotted with the glossy, shining bodies of the defunct ravens, with an occasional bald eagle among them.

These ravens were much handsomer than the ordinary crow, larger and with a different voice, far more musical, full of antics and fun. They would circle around us, apparently talking to us in their language, which I could not very well understand. While flying in sport they would turn over on their backs and glide swiftly in that position for a rod or two, and then turn over and resume their natural flight. Their power of smell was great. I have frequently killed a buffalo out of sight in a ravine five or six miles North of the Saline River when a strong wind was blowing from the North, and in a few minutes I would see the ravens coming up from the river, flying close to the ground. They had scented the carcass five or six miles away.

Along in the winter, after the buffalo became scarce, these ravens, roosting along the streams in thousands, would eat the flesh of the hundreds of wolves which we had skinned and left lying around over the prairie. This meat would in time kill them, and they would drop from their roosts along the banks of the streams until the ground would be covered with them, and thousands of them would be found on the prairie dead.

These ravens did not nest in that section of the country—at least I never saw their nests in my travels. The buffalo, the gray wolves, and the ravens—companions in life—mingled their bones when swift destruction overtook them. The buffalo were killed by the bullets of the hunters, the wolves were killed with strychnine for their furs, and the ravens died from eating the poisoned carcasses of both, so that they all became practically extinct at about the same time. The prairie dogs also disappeared over the larger part of the buffalo range, but they died from natural causes, as they are not able to live in a country which is not tramped bare and eaten down close to the ground by animals. In other words, wherever the buffalo ceased to eat, the prairie grass and the rank grass grew up, and the prairie dogs perished. Occasionally a colony located on hard pan, where the coarser grass does not grow, survives.

During my first winter on the plains an old hunter with a team and outfit came to my camp. He was a man who had spent most of his life on the plains and in the mountains; a strong, resolute, rugged, and experienced man. He went up the river after a load of meat and in a few days was brought back with his skull fractured and his thigh torn open, and in a badly bruised condition. He said that he had shot a big bull buffalo and that it had dropped. Seeing the backs of other buffalo over the ridge beyond the bull, he reloaded his rifle and very carelessly started to run to the top of the ridge without paying attention to the wounded bull. The bull immediately charged him, and he ran down into a little rocky ravine. There the bull quickly overtook him, caught his horn in the man's thigh, tearing it open and throwing him headlong down the ravine, fracturing his skull. His companions found him lying insensible, with the dead bull near him. It had evidently fallen dead as it struck the man with its horns, all of which shows that the oldest and most experienced hunter will sometimes become careless. We took care of this man at the ranch, dressing his wounds as well as we could, until he was sufficiently recovered to travel to his home.

In this manner, dividing our time between hunting, trading, and enjoying ourselves generally, the winter passed away. We had very comfortable buildings with big, fine fireplaces, and an abundance of robes and furs for our bedding, the finest meat on earth to eat and the choicest of its kind, together with all the surroundings that any sportsman could wish for.[3] There was apparently nothing lacking, except the ability to properly appreciate the exceptional opportunities afforded of studying nature as it came from the hand of the great Creator.

When the early Spring of the year finally came, I decided to vary our hunting by trying what the river might produce. So I looked up some fishing tackle, and went down the river. I found the stream to be full of what we call in Kansas the silver or channel catfish—as fine a fish as lives. We could catch them, weighing from one to five pounds, about as fast as we could throw the baited hook into the stream. There was apparently no limit to the amount we might catch if so disposed.

I also noticed a great many porcupines coming out of their holes where they had hibernated during the winter. They would climb up in the elm trees and eat the young buds. They were queer animals, and different from all other wild animals in that they would never try to get out of your way; you could walk right up to them. As far as I could see, their food was exclusively the buds of trees. The European porcupine has quills a foot or more in length, while the American variety—we called them hedge hogs—has them about four inches long. The Indians used these quills to decorate their

3. In a letter home dated Saline Ranch, December 25, 1859, JRM gave a more detailed description of one building at the ranch: "We have some fears of the wild Copperheads which come down here in the summer. You have probably read of their doings on the Santa Fe Road. We are makeing arrangements to give them a warm reception if they should take a notion to trouble us. We are building a bullet-proof block house, fire proof on top, and shall have a well inside. We shall live and keep our valueables in it. I think Government will give them such a drubbing next summer as they never had before" (Mead Collection, Wichita). Before the Civil War the term Copperhead was used as a derogatory term to describe ruffians and bandits. Since JRM is writing in 1859, we assume he is using it in that sense rather than in the political sense that it was to acquire during the Civil War.

robes, and there is such a thing known as a porcupine robe, in which the ornamentation on the flesh side is made with the quills of the porcupine.[4]

The story that the porcupine throws its quills when attacked is a myth. They strike a violent blow sideways with their tails when disturbed, and dogs frequently suffer. On one occasion a porcupine drove its quills into the walnut stock of my rifle. These quills have a faculty of working deeper into the flesh as the barbs on them point backwards.

Skunks were plentiful, not only in the timber, but also out on the prairies. The Indians killed large numbers of them and saved the skins, which were of considerable value; and they also ate them and considered them choice meat. In talking with an Indian about this, he told me that there were a great many things that the white man did not know, and one of them was that the meat of the skunk was as good as any game animal on the plains.

The strong scent of the skunk comes from a volatile oil contained in two sacs near the tail, and which will burn with a green light, blazing as readily as kerosene oil. The Indians' way to dress a skunk, after taking out his scent bags, is to throw him into the fire to singe the hair off, by which means the unpleasant odor is destroyed. After singeing the hair, they wash and scrape him and he then looks as nice as a little young pig. Then dress him and cut his head off, spread him apart with sticks, and set him before a fire to roast, adding salt and pepper. When he is thoroughly cooked in that manner, it is said there is no finer meat anywhere, with no suspicion of scent about it. If any scent got on the clothing, it very soon passed off; the wind and dry air of the plains seemed to take it away so that it would not be noticed. In one consignment I sent seven hundred of their skins to market, afterwards to grace the shoulders of someone's darling in Europe or America.

There was another little animal on the plains which was quite interesting. That was the wood rat. It is entirely distinct from the rat of civilization, and also quite different from the mountain rat. These

4. Porcupine quills, dyed in a variety of colors and sorted according to size, were widely used by North American Indians to decorate hide clothing. As contact with white traders increased, the use of quills declined, as they were replaced by imported beads. See STRIBLING and DRIVER. Driver incorrectly states that the porcupine did not exist on the Great Plains and that Plains Indians had to obtain quills by trade.

wood rats usually made their homes in hollow logs in the timber, or in a cleft of rock. On top of this they would pile sticks, bark, and buffalo chips so that the whole thing would resemble a hay cock. There would frequently be a wagonload or more in one nest. I remember camping alone one night in a canyon where there was an abundance of timber and lots of these rats. When I went back into camp I threw my saddle and bridle on the ground as I usually did, and in the morning I found there was nothing left of my bridle but the iron bits, and all the loose lariats and straps I had were missing, cut up and carried off by the rats.

In the course of that first winter, the prairie chickens would come into the timber about the ranch every day and sit in the trees. We could shoot at them without going any distance from camp, if we felt like it, and without disturbing them very much, as they were not alarmed by the report of a gun. I noticed among the prairie chickens some of a lighter color and a little smaller than the others. I shot some of these and found they were a variety of chicken new to me. We called them pin tails, as their tail feathers were of unequal length. The meat of the breast was dark, while the thighs and legs were white. The breasts were speckled something like a guinea fowl. I concluded that I had found a new variety of prairie chicken, as I had not read up on ornithology at that time.[5]

There were some very fine fox squirrels living in the timber round the camp, subsisting principally on acorns. They were easily killed. Quails were plentiful all along the streams, but we never bothered them.[6] They were such small game that we did not think them worth our attention. In fact, we were troubled with an embarrassment of riches in the way of game and meat. With an abundance of buffalo we cared for little else. We experimented with cooking most of the animals we killed, and found coon and badger

5. This was the lesser prairie hen, *Tympanuchus pallidicinctus*, found only in parts of Kansas and West Texas.

6. On December 30, 1898, at the 31st Annual Meeting of the Kansas Academy of Science, held in Topeka, JRM read a paper entitled "Were Quails Native to Kansas?" from which we learn that he is referring to the bob white, *Colinus virginianus*, which he describes as "the same as I had killed in hundreds in Iowa and Illinois, but smaller . . . they were not numerous; a covey here and there. Half a dozen coveys might be seen in a day's tramp along the Saline or Smoky Hill or their branches." He also observes that "Bob White rapidly increased with the settlement of the country." *Transactions of the Kansas Academy of Science* 16: 277–78.

very good if properly dressed and prepared. Beaver tasted too much like the bark on which they subsist, while prairie dogs—which are not dogs at all but a kind of marmot or squirrel—are most excellent when fat and young, and their oil is very good for guns and gun locks, never gumming and only congealing in freezing weather.

The Indians in our neighborhood during the winter hunted buffalo almost exclusively on horse-back, and they used the bow and arrow as their ancestors had done before them—probably as long ago as when Noah planted his vineyard. Some few of them had rifles and they would go out into the hills where they could get close to them and shoot a few with their guns, but their dependence was on the bow, which they said was always loaded.

The Indians had great success in hunting raccoons. Their method of hunting them was to follow along the river and examine the trees for the scratchings made by the claws of the animal in climbing it. When they found such a tree, as they often did, they would cut and trim a small tree, leaving the limbs projecting a foot or more, in such a way as to make a ladder. They would lean this ladder against the big tree and climb up. They had small axes which they got from the traders, and if the tree was hollow they would chop holes in it or in the limbs, and poke the coons out or kill them in the hole. All the Indians had dogs which were about half wolf. They were very good coon dogs, but no account for anything else, except to eat in an emergency. Many of the large elm trees were hollow and had hollow roots and limbs, and thus the coons had many chances of escape. So they were not exterminated, though large numbers of them were killed.

Together with the Spring grass, the buffalo, which had mostly left late in the Autumn for their winter range in the Indian Territory, Texas, and the staked plains,[7] came back to us again. The first of them came from the North, which would seem peculiar, but many of the buffalo wintered in the broken country on the Solomon River and they came South to find the grass.

Soon the country was covered again with buffalo, antelope, and other migratory game, including ducks, geese, and swans. These

7. The Llano Estacado is a high plateau extending from west-central Texas north through the panhandle and west into eastern New Mexico.

birds settled down on ponds of water along the bottom land adjacent to the river. The Snow Goose came in great numbers and they would seek patches of an early grass called wild rye, until acres were covered and the earth looked like a field of snow.

In the course of that winter the Indian women were continually telling us that as soon as the grass came in the Spring and their ponies got fat and strong, the wild Indians on the plains—especially the Cheyennes—in whose country we were located and who were very jealous of the encroachments of the settlers, proposed making a raid down the Smoky Hill, the Saline, the Solomon, and the Republican Rivers simultaneously, and were going to clean out and scalp every settler they could find. These statements were reiterated so constantly by those who were our friends among the Indians, as well as others, that we believed it to be true, knowing the disposition of the wild Indians.

CHAPTER 4

Hunting Buffalo in Kansas Territory

IN the Spring of 1860 we loaded up our various belongings and went down into the settlements of Kansas and spent the summer. The summer of 1860 was very dry and in the fall the buffalo, in going south, crowded down along the eastern border of their range in order to get grass. There had been few buffalo in the country that summer, and the grass was fine. In the fall the first wave of returning buffalo stopped in the valley and had a regular play spell in the tall grass and weeds. They were almost as tame as domestic cattle; fat and fine. They kept coming until the valley was full before they crossed the river. In a week's time nearly all the grass in the country was eaten off close to the ground. Then, for the next three weeks, there was a steady wave of buffalo passing on to the south, day and night. The unceasing roar continued and, when their myriads had passed, the surface of the earth was worn like a road cut into innumerable parallel paths. Three weeks later I went forty miles west, and found vast herds of buffalo still passing south.

In the fall we returned to resume our hunting and trading on the plains, starting out early during the extremely hot weather. We thought it would be a fine thing to have some dogs to take with us, as we had none and there was such a great abundance of meat for them to subsist on. They would be company for us, if nothing else, and possibly protection. So whenever we met a man with one or more dogs on the road, or passed a farm house at which there were dogs, we asked them if they had any dogs to spare, and frequently found they had a surplus. By the time we got to our ranch, we had a retinue of ten or fifteen dogs of various sorts and degrees of excellence—a sort of job lot. But the record-breaking thing about it was that the heat was so intense that several of those dogs died from heat, although we were driving at a very moderate rate. To show the extremes of temperature on the plains, some of that same lot of dogs froze to death on a hunt that winter, notwithstanding the fact that they had all the meat and other food they could possibly eat.

On arriving at our ranch we found it occupied by a number of Italians. They had a great deal of baggage, and in some manner incomprehensible to us and for some purpose which we never could ascertain, had found their way far beyond the bounds of settlement or civilization. We informed them that the buildings belonged to us and were our property, and that we had come to take possession and carry on our business of hunting and trading. They told us that they had found the place abandoned, that they had moved in and taken possession, and that they proposed to stay there and were not going to get out.

We remained there *in statu quo* for a number of days on the verge of hostility. I then concluded that I would try and scare them out, as all other means had failed. So I went down to the nearest settlement—the little town of Salina—which, by the way, happened to be in another county, and there consulted with my friends as to what was best to do under the circumstances. Finally one of them, who knew a little about legal forms, drew up a writ of ejectment in true frontier style, but without any legal authority, and appointed me a deputy to serve it on the parties and notify them to get out forthwith or they would suffer all the pains and penalties as provided by the laws of the U.S.

Returning to camp with my documents, I duly served them on the Italians and they, having a wholesome fear of the law, which to them was an unknown quantity, capitulated at once and vacated the premises, much to our satisfaction. Two of the Italians proposed to stay with me and assist me in hunting, for such compensation as I chose to give them, their principal interest in life apparently being to get plenty to eat and a place to stay. The other man and his wife moved back into the settlement and finally brought up in Topeka where, to the astonishment of everybody, he bought out a business establishment and paid for it in British gold. His name was da Costa.

A few days later I took my two Italians on a little hunt about a mile from camp where I shot a number of buffalo cows.[1] Turning one upon its back, I split the hide down the legs and lengthwise of the body, and started them in to skinning the animal. I then went to work on some others lying nearby. After taking the skin off two cows, I walked over to see how my two Italians were progressing. They had skinned down one side of the cow—which is about a fair illustration of the difference between a green hand and an experienced plainsman.

Another time I told them to take the tongue out of a bull I had killed, lying near by. After about half an hour, seeing that they had met with some difficulty, I walked over and found that they had pried the buffalo bull's mouth open, wedged it with a rock, and were trying to get the tongue out from between his teeth. Taking it in the proper manner from under the jaw, I could remove it in ten seconds.

Camp life in our isolated home on the ranch was very pleasant. We put up some buildings and started in to cure a great quantity of buffalo meat that winter, imagining we could make money handling that. We were impressed with the thought that our willful waste would make a woeful want, and therefore we started in the very laudable design of saving all of the buffalo possible.[2] I saved the hides by pegging them out on the ground. To do this we hauled the green hides to our camp, wherever that might be, with a wagon. There we selected a smooth piece of ground in a sunny situation and proceeded to peg them out by cutting about twenty-four small holes in the edge of the skin and driving a little peg through each into the ground, stretching the hide into its proper shape equally

1. From a diary entry written by JRM on October 3, 1860, we learn the names of his companions at Saline Ranch: "Our force consists of Mr. Thompson, Ed Thomas, Wash Cavender, Jo and Banyola—two Italians—and myself, 6 in all." The diary is in the Mead Collection, Wichita.

2. Despite this observation, made some forty years after the event, JRM apparently had not foreseen the swift end of the buffalo. On September 23, 1860, he wrote home from Salina to say: "There is no danger of them all being killed for some time to come, not a bit. They are like the locusts of Egypt." And yet only twelve years later there was scarcely a buffalo to be found anywhere in Kansas. JRM's letter is in the Mead Collection, Wichita.

in every direction, and to its fullest possible size. In three or four days it would be dry and smooth as a shingle and as tight drawn between the pegs as a drum head. It could then be taken up, or might remain without harm where it was for a considerable time; and when taken up they could be folded together and piled up with almost as much regularity as a pile of large planks. This was necessary as we hauled them about two hundred miles to market, and it was important to have them lie smooth and close together on the wagon.

I also undertook to save the long curly hair from the buffalo head, and I did save several hundred pounds. But, failing to find a market for it, I took a quantity of it to a hair curling establishment and had it renovated and curled and made into a very large and splendid mattress, which I sent as a present to my father.

From all the young buffalos that were in good condition, we took the hams and loins and hump steaks—the best parts—to our ranch and salted them slightly, put them in great piles, and allowed them to remain in the building for a few days. We then hung them in a large smoke-house that we had constructed and smoked them until sufficiently cured. In this manner we cured a great many tons of meat, but we found that there was no market for it and the cost of transportation to the Missouri River was a great obstacle in the way. So we found that the curing of meat as a business was a failure.

We also tried our hand at curing buffalo tongues, of which we had hundreds from our own hunting and also in trading with the Indians.[3] We had learned that an Indian-cured buffalo tongue was one of the choicest delicacies we had eaten, and we flattered ourselves that we could cure our own buffalo tongues and have them all the year round in great abundance. So we proposed to put them in a pickle of brine for a short time and then afterwards hang them up in the chimney which we had built for the purpose, thinking that the smoke and heat would cure them. This, however, we found to be a mistake. The Indians watched us while we were experimenting and, shaking their heads said, "Heap no good." We came to the conclusion that they knew a good deal more about it than we did, and that their opinion of our method was correct. We afterwards

3. "Cured buffalo tongues had a market value of $1.00 each in 1858."—JRM.

found out how the Indians themselves cured the tongues. They would first boil them until well done, then split them in two and make a hole in the small end of each half. They then hung them up and smoked them a little without any heat, and let them dry in that condition. When dried in this manner they were the choicest of all meat that a mortal on the plains ever had—at least we thought so—and were the best possible provision for a hasty trip on horseback.

We also saved a large number of beautiful buffalo horns, but could find no market for them, so they were allowed to lie on the ground and go to waste. In the course of our experiments we thought we would engage in the manufacture of neat's-foot oil, which is made from the hooves and feet of domestic cattle. So I collected about a barrel full of buffalo feet, took off the skin and washed them carefully, then chopped the hooves and feet in pieces with an ax on a block, and put them in a large iron kettle we had and proceeded to boil them out and manufacture oil. But we found to our surprise that there was no oil of any consequence in a buffalo foot, and that instead of oil we had made a kettle of nice "calves foot jelly." which we found good eating, but the Indians came along and pronounced it "heap no good."

About the only thing we did make a success of out of the carcass of the buffalo was the hides and tallow. We could render tallow out and put it into "bales," which we made by constructing a frame of round sticks just the width of the wagon bed, 18 inches high, and three feet long. Then, taking a cow's hide without any hole in it and stretching it while green over this frame and lashing it together at the top and letting it dry in the sun, it became as tight as a drum, and if struck sounded a great deal like one. We would render out the tallow in our large kettle and when it was cool, pour it into these skin boxes until they were full. The boxes, or bales as we called them, each held about 500 pounds. In that form it would keep for a long time, could be transported any distance, and was always a cash merchantable article of commerce.[4]

The hides could also be kept for a reasonable length of time if care was exercised in keeping them dry and in excluding the moths, which were very destructive in the summer time. On one occasion I had eighteen hundred hides on hand which were damaged to the

4. "In 1859 this tallow was worth 10 to 12½ cts. per pound. It makes beautiful candles."—JRM.

extent of a dollar apiece by the moths. In speaking of hides, I do not mean the dressed robe; these moths fed exclusively on hides. When full-grown they are about an inch in length and very destructive. I never saw that variety of moth on buffalo skin. They work on the fur side, greatly damaging the skin for the purpose for which it is used. Most of these hides were taken to eastern markets and used for covering government saddle trees, as they made the best cover of any hide known and at much less cost than beef hides. This was during the Civil War. In the summer time it was necessary to remove the hide soon after the animal was killed or the hot sun would spoil it.

There was one method of curing buffalo meat which proved a great success. I took the hams of some fine fat heifers and young cows in the fall and, taking out the bone, left the ham entire. These I packed in barrels, putting a very little salt in each ham and around it, until the barrels were full, then putting a heavy stone on it. The barrels were filled so full that what little brine was formed ran over the top, the weights pressing the meat down. In this way the meat kept perfectly throughout the winter without any further care, and we had the most delicious steaks cut off those hams. One slice or cut could fill a frying pan full of the finest meat I ever ate. We saved four or five barrels of meat in that way for home consumption, which we used during the winter.

We found by experience that the Indians knew vastly more about handling the products of the buffalo than we did, as they had been in that business since long before Columbus sailed into the unknown western seas. Their method of curing meat was to cut it into long strips and weave it into a large mat. They would then make a framework of willows three or four feet high, and spread the mats of braided buffalo meat over these frames. Underneath this they would build a small fire which would slowly roast and dry the meat until it was beautifully cooked. They would then fold it into squares the size of their leather "bales," which they made for that purpose of prepared raw-hides, and press the meat in until the "bales" were tightly packed. Then they would pour tallow into all the crevices, making a solid mass. This meat would keep for a year perfectly good, and was ready to eat without any further preparation at any time, and was most excellent food.

The Indians also saved a great quantity of tallow which they put into "bales" in the same manner. Sometimes during the heat of summer, the Indians would cut the buffalo meat into thin strips which they would spread on platforms of poles built up from the ground, and let it dry in the sun and wind until it was thoroughly cured, making what would be called "jerked beef" or "jerked buffalo." This method was always a success on the dry, arid plains.

The Indians utilized every part of the buffalo. It furnished them with almost everything necessary to their subsistence and comfort. From the skins they made robes which were their winter clothing. From the great sinew which supports the head, they make their bow strings and the thread with which they sew all their skins and clothing, and all other uses for which we use twine or thread. From the horns they made large spoons and other useful articles. Its flesh was their principal food. From the summer hides they made their lodges, by removing the hair and tanning the skins after the manner of tanning a buckskin. It took the hides of thirty cows, i.e., buffalo cows, to make an ordinary lodge, while the big lodge of the chief would sometimes require twice or three times that number. The Indians also made their lariats of buffalo hide, and used it in the manufacture of their saddles, moccasins, leggings, and all other uses for which we need leather.

The usual method I adopted for killing buffalo, and that which proved the most successful and satisfactory, was to hunt them on foot. When I wished to go on a hunt, I would harness a team and take with me two men and a saddle pony. A camp kit, provisions and blankets, my rifle, and a good butcher knife apiece completed the outfit. I would then travel in the direction in which I supposed the buffalo to be—usually a day or two days' drive to the West of our "ranch"—and on coming in sight of herds would establish a temporary camp. Then, taking advantage of some sheltered ravine, and approaching them as near as possible on horse back without being observed, I would picket my pony and allow him to graze while I crawled forward, taking advantage of the inequalities of the ground to approach sometimes within fifty yards, often two or three times that distance. Selecting one which appeared to be a leader of the herd, I would shoot it, usually aiming low down just at the back edge of the shoulder, ranging a little forward. The heart of the buffalo lies low down, nearly at the bottom of the brisket, and three-fourths of the distance from the hump down to the brisket of the animal. A shot at that point is necessarily fatal in a moment or two. If I succeeded in killing the animal I shot at—which I usually did—the others would crowd round it or stand waiting for it to get up and lead them, apparently not apprehending any danger, and not understanding the reason their leader stopped. After two or three are shot, they pay no further attention to the gun, and if so disposed I could kill the entire herd, or as many as I chose.

After I had killed the number I wanted, I would mount my pony, ride to the nearest most prominent point, and signal my men to come on. Frequently, hearing the sound of my rifle, my team would drive as close as possible without scaring any game, and wait until I was done shooting. We would then proceed to take the hides and tallow, load our wagons, and return to camp.

The Indian method of hunting the buffalo was very different in those days. They hunted exclusively on horseback, and with bows and arrows. A bow and arrow is a much more destructive weapon and more effective in action than a muzzle-loading rifle. The Indians found no difficulty in killing hundreds and thousands of buffalo with a weapon which a white man would consider utterly useless. The objection to hunting on horseback was the danger of the horse falling and killing or injuring his rider, which not infrequently happens in riding over rough ground. The horses in the excitement and dust were liable to step into the holes of badger or prairie dog. Also the chasing of buffalo with horses would scare them out of the vicinity, making it necessary for the hunter to go to a longer distance from camp to find them. I once knew an Indian who was chasing a buffalo cow and just as he came near enough to shoot, his horse fell, throwing him violently to the ground in front of the cow, which turned on him and killed him before he could recover himself.

A young man—a friend of mine—was one day chasing an antelope with two young ones by her side, when his horse stumbled and fell, throwing him and breaking his collarbone. In this condition he picked up his rifle and killed the antelope before it got out of range, although running at full speed.

I never knew a buffalo to attack a person unless it was first wounded and then crowded upon. So long as a person lay down on the ground he could crawl around among wounded buffalo with perfect safety. I have had seven or eight wounded bulls lying down at one time, and have crawled right in among them to shoot at some further on, paying no attention to the wounded bulls. I found that I was perfectly safe as long as I lay on the ground, but if I stood up near one he would most likely charge at me, as I learned to my great inconvenience on several occasions.

One morning while in camp I saw a bunch of six cows and a bull feeding out in the bottom near the foot of a little hill. Taking my rifle, I crawled out to them, and shot the six cows, one after the other, killing each with a single shot. I did not want the bull, but as he declined to go away, I gave him a shot to get rid of him. He immediately lay down and, thinking he would die in a moment as the cows had, I walked up to the group. As the bull was not yet dead I laid down my rifle, took out my hunting knife, and walked up behind him with a view to seizing him by the hump and horn, throwing him on his side and cutting his throat, as I often did with wounded buffalo. Just as I was going to take hold of him I thought he looked a little too lively, but he did not pay any attention to me. I decided that I had better let him alone so I stepped back, took up my rifle, and walked round in front of him with my rifle ready. He then apparently observed me for the first time and instantly jumped to his feet and charged at me. While he was doing this I brought my rifle up, drew a bead on his forehead, and pulled the trigger. The gun missed fire.

In those days I was exceedingly active. My clothing usually consisted of a pair of light trousers and a shirt with a belt buckled tight around my waist. As the bull was coming for me with a rush, I let go of my rifle and "lit out." I could then run pretty near as well as a wild deer, and under the circumstances I made good time. Down the slope about fifty yards from where I started was a big buffalo cow lying dead—one that I had shot earlier—and I gave a few big jumps in that direction, landing on the other side of her. On looking back to see how close the bull was (I had not had time to look before) I found that he had run right up against the cow and stopped. He soon turned and walked slowly up the hill. I followed him back, got my rifle, put a fresh cap on it, and killed him for keeps that time.

It is a common opinion, and it has been published a thousand times, that a bullet will not penetrate a bull's head on account of his massive skull bone, and there being so much sand matted in the long hair that a bullet will not penetrate it. This is entirely a mistake. Among the thousands of buffalo heads which I have examined, I never saw one that had any sand matted in the hair. There is occasionally a little clay on the end of the hair where they have been horning a bank the same as domestic bulls do, but as soon as the clay becomes dry in the air it crumbles off, leaving the hair naturally clean. I have shot buffalo bulls a number of times in the forehead without killing them and then, after shooting them in a more vital spot, I have examined the head wound. Taking a ramrod, I found that I could insert it the whole length in the bullet hole in the forehead; the bullet having gone the length of the head and neck into the body of the animal without killing it.

This I have done repeatedly with a bullet weighing 500 grains and know that the bullet from an ordinary muzzle-loading rifle will go through a buffalo's skull as easily as it will go through an inch pine board. The reason it is supposed that buffalos cannot be killed by shooting them in the head, is the fact that the brain lies so far up between the horns that a hunter invariably shoots below it, and does not touch the brain. The head is so large and massive that the hunter is deceived as to where the vital spot is.

On several occasions I have killed a buffalo bull with a single shot with a round ball from a muzzle-loading rifle, happening to strike the vital spot high up in the forehead, causing them to drop dead in their tracks. After having long experience I found that standing behind a buffalo bull when he was walking a little quartering from me, and putting a ball right back of the base of the horns was certain and instantaneous death. I also found, after some experimenting, that I could readily kill a buffalo no matter in what position he might be standing. One of my favourite shots was to shoot them, when facing me, between the shoulder and breast bone, low down, reaching the heart and lungs. This was necessarily immediately fatal. Another sure shot was to cut the great artery which runs along under the back bone. A shot through the loins, penetrating the kidneys, would kill them in a few moments. Perhaps the most difficult shot of all was when a buffalo was walking quartering away, to shoot him low down in the flank so that the bullet passed below the paunch and ranged forward to strike the heart. After I learned to make this shot I could make it fatal almost every time.

Inexperienced hunters would frequently shoot buffalo broadside in the paunch or hump, and shoot a dozen or fifteen times before getting their buffalo. An experienced hunter would have little trouble in securing whatever number he chose to, and a miss was a rare occurrence. In fact I seldom shot unless I knew I was going to kill. The main cause of failure with inexperienced hunters was that they shot too high. The buffalo's heart lies low down close to his brisket, and the hump extends upward to such a great distance that they shoot entirely above any vital spot.

In my party was a young fellow—a youth about 18 years of age —without any experience in hunting, and pretty green generally. He took a notion into his head one day that he wanted to kill a buffalo. I asked him what gun he wanted and he picked out an old fashioned U.S. musket that someone had given me and proceeded to load it by putting in a handful of powder, then a musket ball, then a handful of buckshot, and a big wad of paper on top. He then went up the river to a big brush patch in which buffalo bulls were in the habit of wandering around and, getting behind a fallen tree he waited till a bull came along within two rods of him, broadside on, when he took a deliberate rest across the log and fired. The report was like a small cannon and the recoil of the musket knocked him backwards head over heels, bruising his face and nearly dislocating his shoulder. The musket fell back much further and the astonished bull "lit out" for the bluffs at the top of his speed, more scared than hurt. Whether or not he was hit, is to this day unknown. The young man returned to camp in a badly dilapidated condition and remarked that buffalo hunting was not as much fun as he had supposed.

That winter there was deep snow, and the starving buffalo travelled east in search of food. Several thousand passed by Salina and wintered in the valley of Gypsum Creek. The Kaw Indians reaped a rich harvest of robes and meat.

CHAPTER 5

Paradise Valley

TOWARD the end of my first winter on the plains the Kansas Indians, having completed their hunting, returned to their reservation, leaving us alone. For a while we felt rather lonesome, as there were no settlements near us and none between us and the Rocky Mountains. So we concluded that we would take a hunt in the unknown regions further west.

We first went up the Smoky Hill River about seventy-five miles, and found the country had been burned over and was entirely destitute of game. We then went north to the Saline River without finding anything, but while standing on the high plateau on the south bank of the river, in a quandary as to which way to go next, we looked north towards the divide between the Saline and Solomon Rivers and noticed that the tops of some hills in the distance appeared to be black. After watching them for awhile and noticing that they seemed to move, I became satisfied that the hill tops were covered with buffalo. There also appeared to be some timber in one of the canyons coming out of the divide, so I concluded that where there were buffalo there must necessarily be water and grass, and other game as well.

We crossed the Saline below some salt springs from which the river derives its saline properties, and traveled north. We soon found a large, dry, sandy creek coming from the hills in the dis-

James R. Mead

"I have been having my likeness taken by a sort of one horse artist. It is pretty dark. The day was cloudy. Folks say it does not look as well as I do. I have no particular fault to find with it. I have no doubt you will be glad to see what I look like after being in this heathen country so long, and after spending a winter among the Buffalo and Indians. . . . You must let me know just what folks and you think of my likeness." (JRM, Burlingame, Kansas, June 11, 1860.)

"I have been looking for a letter from you on receipt of my likeness, but have not heard from it yet." (JRM, Burlingame, Kansas, July 9, 1860).

Original letters and photograph in the Mead Collection, Wichita.

tance; following this up we came to beaver dams and water. The beaver held back all the water in the dry season.

Along towards evening we came to where I had seen the buffalo and found that there were large herds of them wintering there. Grass was abundant, there were groves of beautiful oak timber, and all the evidences of a magnificent hunting country of which we had been entirely ignorant up to that time.

I killed one of the buffalo for meat and then drove on until I came to the timber I had seen bordering a large creek of living water. We found groves of oak timber growing in the bottoms on each side, extending a great distance along the creek into the hills. It was one of the most beautiful valleys I ever saw, with canyons on the hill-sides filled with fine cedar timber.

There were numerous old Indian camps, though we found none of recent date, excepting that I discovered from the signs where one little marauding party of Indians had passed through on a raiding expedition against the Indians to the south. There were no signs of an axe or of white man's presence in any of it. I had found a stream unknown. As we drove into this beautiful spot I exclaimed, "Boys, we have got into paradise at last!" The contrast was so great from the burned and desolate country we had been in for the past week or two, that it really seemed like an Eden. The valley which I called Paradise and the creek which flows through it are called by that name today and it is a populous portion of Kansas. The town of Paradise is near the spot of our first camp. We had surely found a paradise of game: buffalo, elk, black-tailed deer in bunches of fifteen or twenty, turkeys in abundance, beaver, otter, and hungry wolves in gangs.

I got up at daylight and, taking my rifle, started out to see what I could find. Going down the creek I found a place to cross on a big log which had fallen across and lodged firmly. Midway on the log was a porcupine asleep. I walked out to him and nudged him with my rifle, but he was not disposed to move and struck the butt of my rifle with such force that he drove his quills into the stock of the gun. I pushed him off the log into the water and, passing along, peeked cautiously over the bank, having a view of the level open bottom beyond, which happened to be a prairie dog town. There, directly in front of me, was a large catamount,[1] which had come out

---

1. The puma or mountain lion, *Felis concolor*.

of the timber and was crawling up to catch a prairie dog for his breakfast. Seeing me, he ran back into the timber.

A little further out were two very large turkey gobblers fighting, the spring being their mating season. They were chasing each other alternately around the dog town, and finally they started running directly toward me. So straight did they come that I could see but one turkey and I thought I would try to kill both at one shot as they ran. I took aim and fired. The one in front dropped, while the one behind was untouched. The second one came up and walked around his dead enemy, evidently in great surprise, and tried to make him get up. He stood there until I rose up, and then he walked off. I hung the turkey in a tree out of reach.

About eighty rods ahead there was a bunch of buffalo feeding on a small knoll, and I shot three or four of them. Some distance beyond I found another small herd of buffalo and shot three cows. Noticing a great many wolves around, I dressed one of the cows and wrapped a part of the meat which I wanted in the hide to protect it, and then came back to the first ones I had killed. When I came in sight I found a great gang of wolves standing around them devouring the carcasses. They were so thick I could not see the buffalo. As I approached, the wolves were not disposed to go away, probably being very hungry or not apprehending any danger, not having seen hunters in that country before, perhaps. I discharged my rifle into the pack several times before they took alarm and ran away. On walking up to the buffalos I found them about eaten. Several wolves lay dead beside them. A ball had entered one wolf at the root of his tail and had come out at the end of his nose. He was very dead. Another the bullet had struck in the flank and ranged up through his heart and lungs. He was also dead.

About that time my wagon came in sight and we went back to the three cows I had killed. They were nearly devoured by the wolves, which had also eaten the meat I had wrapped up in the hide. But we secured enough for our immediate wants and got the hides and drove back to camp, where I enjoyed a good square breakfast after my morning walk.

I spent the balance of the day exploring the country, going up the creek to ascertain if Indians were about, and watching for Indian signs to see whether it would be safe for us to remain there. I found a large old Indian camp at the entrance to the hills, probably

ten years old. I also found a camp a few days old, where two Pawnees were returning from a successful horse-stealing expedition
from the Indians on the Arkansas, and had left a letter written in
hieroglyphics for the benefit of some of their comrades who were
behind. I added to it a short account of our hunt, our number,
where we were going, etc. in the same characters. Further up the
stream were cliffs of sandstone on which were recorded, in usual
Indian style, accounts of battles, and many other things, but no
white men's names.

While I found a great many old Indian camps, there was no other
evidence of Indians occupying the country at that time, and there
was no evidence of any white men ever having been there. There
was no tree cut, nor wagon trail anywhere to be found.

That evening we put bait round our buffalo carcasses for wolves.
In the meanwhile, on the afternoon of the first day, the two men
who were with me—inexperienced hunters—had found a number
of elk but failed to get any of them. The next day I was occupied
with looking about the country and did not go to look up my dead
wolves. But I put out more bait the second evening, and the next
morning we took our team and went to gather up our game. In the
course of the day we found eighty-two dead wolves; it was February and the weather being cold, the skins would remain good for
days. As wolf pelts were worth $2.50 apiece, we had no fault to find
with the wolves. The turkeys along the streams were abundant,
and almost as tame as the domestic birds.

While I was in the camp I noticed that the old buck elks went in
bands by themselves at that season, and that the old turkey gobblers were also in flocks by themselves, showing that in their native
condition—except in the breeding season—the males of wild birds
and animals go in droves by themselves. This fact I had frequent
opportunities of verifying in after years. While at this camp we
loaded our team in a very short time with the hides and skins of the
animals we killed, and returned safely home without any accident
or bad luck of any description.

This was Paradise Valley in its natural state, the Mecca of the
hunter's dream, and the Indian's delight. The beautiful valley, clear
cool water, plenty of wood for camp fires, abundance of game of the
grandest sort in the world! Well might we say, here roamed the
grand buffalo and stalked the noble elk, the timid deer, antelope,

lordly strutted the turkey gobbler and skulked the wolf, coyote, the lynx, the coon, possum, skunk, porcupine, beaver and other game in abundance. The ducks, geese, prairie chickens, and the quail here found their home, seldom disturbed by man, and now for the first time to hear the report of the white man's gun. What a pleasure it would give me to again find such a hunter's paradise where I could drink in the beauty I then beheld. If it could be found I would spend the balance of my allotted days there. It even now thrills me through to think of Paradise Valley as it was when I bestowed the name on it. No wonder the Red Man was loath to give up his hunting paradise to the Pale Face when he could be so happy in this home, as I have no doubt that he felt as happy among the game and wild grandeur as I did. I would that I could describe by word or pen my ecstatic feelings, but no one can and none but a true sportsman can have such thoughts or feelings. But, alas! the buffalo is gone, the elk, the turkey, grouse, etc. are only found as rare specimens.

During that summer I thought it would be a fine thing to have a little garden. So I ploughed and planted a small piece of ground near our camp on the bank of the river. I planted some potatoes, a patch of watermelons, also a little corn, which grew and flourished very satisfactorily. About the time the melons were getting ripe I discovered that some animals came at night and, making a hole in the side of the melon, would scoop out and eat the entire contents. On examining the tracks I found that it was raccoons. As this happened to be about the time of the full moon, I thought I would investigate a little in the night. So, taking my rifle and going along the bank of the river, I rose up opposite the melon patch with the full moon in front of me, giving a good view of the proceedings. There I discovered about two dozen raccoons busily engaged in scooping out the contents of my watermelons. I watched them for a while and then concluded that I would have some of the fun myself. Getting two coons in range, I fired and killed them both at one shot of my rifle, whereupon the rest of them made a break for the timber in the direction of which I was standing. After that night they seemed shy of my melon patch for some cause.

On visiting the point at which we had crossed the river the previous fall, I found some stalks of volunteer corn growing on the bank of the river. On one of them there were two well-matured ears of corn, indicating the future possibilities of the country should it ever

be settled. This was the first civilized corn grown on the banks of
the upper Saline. In the Smoky Hills in Saline country there were
no poisonous insects or reptiles, except a few rattlesnakes. But
in the Indian Territory and in southern Kansas they were quite
abundant.

On one occasion while hunting up the Smoky Hill River, we were
camped a short distance southwest of where the town of Wilson
now stands.[2] My partner—Abraham Boss—who was the best
hunter I was ever with on the plains, came into camp toward evening and said that from the racket he had heard up river he believed
there was a watering place up two miles, and he was going up to
see what it looked like. So he took his big muzzle-loading rifle and
traveled up the river. Not long afterwards I heard the distant boom
of his big gun, and these sounds continued at short intervals until
sometime after dark. Finally he came back to camp and I asked him
what he had found. He said that a creek from the south emptied
into the river at that point, and that there was a solid stream of
buffalo pouring down that creek to the river to get water. I asked
him how many buffalo he had killed. He said that he had taken
twenty-five balls along with him and had shot them all away, and he
guessed he had killed a buffalo about every time he shot, and that
was all he knew about it.

Bright and early next morning we hitched up our team and drove
up there. We found twenty-two buffalo lying round near the river
bank. Standing a little distance away I noticed a buffalo calf seemingly in a very stupid condition. On walking up to him I found his
head was swollen to about twice its natural size. His eyes were
swollen shut so that he could not see, and to get him out of his
misery I killed him with my knife. Shortly afterwards in going down
the bank of the river to get a drink, I saw a yellow diamond rattlesnake about four feet long and about as large as my arm, which I
also killed. This explained to me what was the matter with the calf.

In the course of the day, while skinning buffalo, I kept my rifle
within reach, and as any buffalo coming down the creek passed
near enough to shoot, I would use it. During that day our party,
which consisted of three men and a boy, skinned, took out the
tallow, and hauled to camp the proceeds of forty-four buffalo.

2. Near the northeast corner of Ellsworth County, Kansas.

At noon we went down to the sandbar in the river under the shade of the trees to eat our lunch, which was principally buffalo meat. While we were eating, buffalo cows would run down the steep river bank and go to drinking within a rod of us. I shot three or four while we ate dinner. In one instance I shot a cow through the back of the shoulders and she started running up the steep bank. Just as she got to the top she fell dead and rolled end over end down the steep path, making a dozen revolutions until she fell with a great splash into the water almost at our feet. The whole of the next day was necessarily spent in "pegging out" our hides on the ground, and in rendering out our tallow.

Two or three days after, while sleeping in our camp, we were awakened in the night by a horseman who proved to be a neighboring hunter named Joe Lemons. He told us that he was camped several miles up the river above us and in the evening after dark he thought he had heard drums up the river. Riding to the top of a neighboring hill he discovered that the valley was covered with the campfires of wild Indians. They had moved into the valley that afternoon or evening, and were engaged in their customary evening amusement—beating their drums, dancing, singing, and the various sports to which they were accustomed. He told us that his party was loaded up, that they were getting out of that country as rapidly as possible, and he advised us to do the same, as the Indians would undoubtedly discover us and our slaughter of their buffalo in the morning, and might take a notion to take our scalps. So we loaded up our wagons with all possible dispatch, but it was so late in the night and we had so much work to do in loading our hides, that it was daylight when we rolled out of camp. We travelled with all possible speed, considering our heavy loads, occasionally looking back to see if our unwelcome neighbors had discovered us. Fortunately, they were late sleepers that morning.

We travelled towards the East without stopping, keeping well back from the river and the gulches, until at noon we came to a little grove of cottonwood trees where a number of springs took their rise. The beavers had appropriated this by damming up the creek and forming quite a little lake of five or six feet in depth. My men imagined that they could catch the beavers by letting the water out and, against my earnest protests, proceeded to tear out the dam, letting the water out with a tremendous rush. Of course they did not get any of the beavers, as their holes extended quite a distance back under the bank, and we had neither the time nor the means to dig them out.

Now it happened that a party of explorers from the East with a team were camped beside the dry bed of the creek a couple of miles below us. There had not been a cloud in the sky nor had a drop of rain fallen for the past two months when, to their astonishment, the creek came down bank full of water. They could find no adequate explanation and on their return East they told the most remarkable stories about the wonderful phenomenon of the plains, which was too much for the credulity of their audience.

We saw nothing of the Indians, nor heard of them pursuing us. We went on to Salina, stored our skins and effects, and soon returned to our customary hunting grounds.

We were constantly on the alert, watching for Indians and trying to avoid them whenever it was possible to do so. The Indians in all cases were hostile to the hunter for his destruction of their buffalo, and occasionally a hunter never returned to camp. At some future time, perhaps, his bones would be found bleaching on the prairie. As an illustration of this, there was a well-known hunter named Tommy Thorn, who had a bachelor's hut at Salina known as "The Den." It had an earth floor covered with skins, a fireplace in the south end, and bunks on the side. It was very comfortable, being warm in winter and cool in summer. Fuel cost nothing, and at all times there was an abundance to eat and drink, free to all. Buffalo meat, flapjacks, and coffee gave men strength and courage. About twice a year Thorn would take a load of skins and hides to Leavenworth and bring back a load of provisions, consisting of flour, sugar, coffee, tobacco, and ammunition—not forgetting a ten-gallon keg of Kentucky whisky, of which he was very fond, but did not use to excess. On returning to "the den" he would unload his supplies, set his keg near the fireplace, put a faucet in it, hang a tin cup on a nail, and invite his brother hunters in to make themselves at home and help themselves to anything he had. Among other things, he had for a tobacco-box an Indian skull sawed in two. It was three-fourths of an inch thick, solid bone. Some congenial spirits would gather in, hang a few quarters of fat buffalo in a cool place, and for a week or ten days "the den" would be a place of joy, story, and song. It was not a disreputable resort, such as are found in cities, but a jolly hunters' club-house. [3]

Mr. Thorn was a man of many peculiarities, one of which was that he had no hair on his head, excepting a fringe of long hair below his hat. He made his last hunt alone out on Plum Creek, [4] where he made his camp. As he went down to the creek with a bucket to get water, leaving his gun in camp, a Cheyenne ran onto him and killed him. In order to get a scalp with a sufficient amount of hair, he had to take ears and all. Thorn's life and death were typical of many another man's who spent his life on the plains.

Most of the hunters on the plains met their death sooner or later by Indians or wild beasts, which were desperate when wounded, or by accident, which was liable to happen at any time from a variety of causes, such as the terrible extremes of weather to which they were frequently exposed. Those of us who escaped these vicissitudes are here to tell the story, while others—just as good men— left their bones on the prairie. So far as I am personally concerned, I was exceedingly fortunate, both in avoiding the Indians and accidents and in passing unharmed through a variety of dangers which proved fatal to many of our hunters. I attribute this immunity partly to skill and good judgment, and partly to what is commonly known as luck, which I had frequent occasion to think was but little less than the interposition of Divine Providence. I have been in positions where the chances seemed very largely against my being alive in the next few minutes. In my experience I find that the only fear of death is when you first see it coming, that when you are

3. On March 31, 1906, after reading the proofs of JRM's article "The Saline River Country in 1859," Alexander Spilman wrote to JRM from McPherson: "I received the proof-sheets of your article on the Upper Saline Country, which will appear in the next volume of the transactions of the Society. I have read and re-read that article with ever increasing interest. That country and those times had to me a fascination that will not wear off. I was especially pleased with your life-like sketch of old Tom Thorn and the 'den'. Tom was a typical frontier hunter, whose like we shall probably never see again. I am reminded that in those free and careless days I spent many idle hours enjoying his hospitality and good cheer. But few of us now remain who shared in the experiences of those days. . . . I have often regretted that I did not keep a diary of the important events then. But you and I have one advantage in any narration of the early days. There are now few who can dispute the accuracy of our recollections." Original letter in the Mead Collection, Wichita.

4. There are several Plum Creeks in Kansas, but the one in question may have been that which flows across southwest Ellsworth County into northwest Rice County.

brought face to face with it, you seem to become reconciled to the situation, and whatever fear there was at first—and I am free to confess that I have had my full share—is all gone before the critical moment. When you realize that probably in a few moments you will be killed, that your body will lie mutilated on the prairie to be devoured by wolves, that never again will you see your family and friends, that all your hopes, ambitions, and aspirations in life are about to come to a sudden end, all these thoughts rush through a man's mind when he first sees the danger coming. But when you are brought face to face with death, a feeling of resignation comes over a person which entirely takes the place of dread or fear, and I think that under these circumstances, a person can die without any mental suffering at all. I have several times been captured by war parties of Indians and expected to be killed shortly, but after I was in their power I had no feelings of fear of death.

In December 1861 I established a camp on Spillman Creek and, after collecting a quantity of furs, left one man in camp and went to hunt with my other man and team. It was winter, very cold, and the snow deep. In a day or two the man I had left came to my camp; said he had heard shooting all around, was scared, and had skipped in the night. I drove back, found the camp plundered and a big trail in the snow leading down the river. Directing my men to follow, I started after them on my pony. In a few miles I saw a party of Indians ahead on foot. Each one had a big wolf skin of mine hanging down his back, a slit in the neck going over his head. There were thirty-three in the party. I followed them, unseen, for some distance, and saw I could not possibly get around them, as my pony could hardly stand, her feet were so smooth; but I had to get to my ranch ahead of them for various reasons,[5] so I took a chance and rode into them, just after they crossed the creek, and was surrounded and captured.

I found they were a party of Sioux on a marauding expedition, some of them the most villainous-looking beings I ever saw. I gave them a good talk, let on I was glad to see them, proposed we all travel together, to which they agreed, had a jolly time for half a day, by which time I had so ingratiated myself with the chief, who was a fine fellow, that I was allowed to go on alone. Some of the Indians

5. "One of them being that I had just got married and my wife was there."—JRM.

loudly protested, but a chief's word is law. Our conversation was carried on in sign language, as not one of them could speak a word of English.

I had two men at the ranch, and my men with the team got in that night. The Indians came to my place the next morning and built a fortified camp in the timber back of the house. I treated them nicely, gave them tobacco, and got all of my furs back except an otter skin, which the chief had cut into strips, and wore a part of it braided in his head-dress and the other attached to his war club. I have some of their war arrows. Before leaving for the north-east they agreed not to molest any hunters they might meet, but they did go over to the Solomon and plundered and abused the few families they found there. What surprised me was that they traveled afoot in the winter long distances, with the thermometer at zero, and in deep snow, without the least inconvenience, seeming to like it.

And now I will give you a little unwritten history: In 1860 I took a load of goods to trade with the Kaw Indians at the "Big Bend" of the Smoky. I noticed some of them returned to camp full of booze. On inquiry I found they obtained it at a little shack hidden away in the almost inaccessible gulches of a creek coming into the Smoky from the South near by, now known as "Sharps Creek." A more secluded spot could not be found on the plains. No hunter knew of it. Its stock in trade was booze and tobacco. They said it was kept by a man with a "round foot" (club) from Council Grove. The proprietor has since been known as "Ex-Governor Sharp of Kansas" . . . and thus "Sharps Creek" obtained its name.[6]

6. The Sharp family, originally from Pennsylvania, are generally credited with being the first white settlers in McPherson County. They lived on what came to be called Sharp's Creek during the winter of 1859–60. Mrs. Sharp was the first white woman to reside in McPherson County. Her son Isaac Sharp moved to Council Grove, where he practiced law. In 1870 he ran for Governor of Kansas as a Democrat. McPherson County returned 198 votes, one of which was for Sharp. ANDREAS, 811.

CHAPTER 6

Smoky Hill Country

THE Smoky Hill River makes a bend in Saline County, swinging around to the south and then returning again a long distance to the north where it is joined by the Saline River, forming the "Big Bend." In this bend are several high, detached buttes, remnants of what was once a very high table-land composed of Dakota sandstone. In some early day of the earth—probably during the Champlain Era— there was an immense downpour of water which cut down most of this table-land of sandstone rock and, in the course of time, washed it away towards the sea. In certain places the rock was much harder than in others and consequently was not worn away, while between deep valleys were furrowed out, leaving standing in the air high pinnacles of rock which gradually, through the lapse of thousands of years, rounded down until they assumed the present form of what is known as the Smoky Hills or the Buttes of the Smoky Hill River. These buttes are prominent landmarks, resembling little mountains, and can be seen for a long distance in any direction. As during a large portion of the year the atmosphere is hazy, as if full of smoke, the Indians gave them the name of Smoky Hills and also to the river which sweeps around their southern base. I always understood that the Indians knew this river as the "Smoky Hill" and I suppose the whites adopted it.

The Saline River derived its name from its salty water, which

103

comes from numerous salt springs along its course until you have ascended the river for sixty miles, above which point the water was perfectly sweet. The Saline and big bend of the Smoky Hill were favorite hunting-grounds of the Kaw Indians in the fall and winters of 1859, 1860, and 1861. A majority of the tribe were there.

In June, 1861, the Otoe Indians, whose reservation was up in the eastern part of Nebraska, and who were kinsfolk and friends to the Omahas, came south to the branches of the Saline River on the plains north of Spillman Creek, about forty miles west of my place, on a buffalo hunt. With them came two or three white men who were employed at their agency, sent along by their agent to prevent their getting into trouble with frontier settlers or hunters. While they were camped on Spillman's Creek with their families and all their belongings, engaged in killing buffalo and curing the meat, they were discovered by the Cheyennes and Arapahoes, who claimed that country and were very jealous of other Indians hunting on their territory, especially semi-civilized or reservation Indians. The Cheyennes and Arapahoes armed 300 or 400 warriors, intending to wipe out the Otoes, who were a feeble band comparatively, and they got into the vicinity of the Otoes before their presence was discovered. But the Cheyennes were afraid to charge the camp, as the Otoes had guns. The first intimation that the Otoes had of danger was when two of them, who had gone quite a distance from camp, were shot from ambush. The other Cheyennes immediately showed themselves, and the Otoes gathered into their camp and sent their warriors out on the prairie to do battle. A skirmishing fight ensued all over the prairie.

They fought over that prairie for two or three days while the chiefs of the Cheyennes watched from the summit of high buttes to the north. Both sides fought on horseback with bows and arrows. The Indians never charged in a body, but each Indian would pick out an adversary and they would fight on horseback while riding at full speed. In one instance an Otoe and a Cheyenne, after exhausting their arrows, rode together at full speed, each grasping the other with his left hand, and stabbing with their knives until both fell dead from their horses, still grasping one another.

The Otoes gradually fell back along the creek into positions that were easily defended and where their warriors, who were better armed with guns than the wild Indians, were able to stand them off from their camp. At the end of three days, seeing that it was impossible for them to do any more hunting, the Otoes retreated down the river and came to my ranch. They had succeeded in killing and securing the bodies of several of the Cheyennes, and had with them, tied to poles, the fingers, toes, ears, and scalps of some of their enemies.

Shortly after, I rode over the prairie where the battle had occurred[1] and saw dead horses lying around over the prairie and found arrows in every direction, showing much wild shooting. This may account for the fact that in certain localities in the U.S. large numbers of arrow points are found scattered over quite an extent of country, indicating a favourite hunting resort, or a battle fought in which large quantities of arrows had been expended and lost, or in the vicinity of a permanent camp.

On several occasions while I was living at my ranch on the Saline, small war parties of Cheyennes, who were scattered over the country hunting for their hereditary enemies the Pawnees, came to my place and, in one instance, camped there for a couple of days. Although they rode down to the ranch at full speed and with every indication of hostility, they were friendly. I had a pasture fence around my ranch and a short distance from the house was a set of bars where we came in. On one occasion a war party of Cheyennes charged down the road at full speed as though they were going to exterminate us in a minute, but when they came to the bars and found them closed, they halted and shouted for me to come and let down the bars so that they could get in. I did so and they rode in and we all had a jolly good time.

I noticed that the chief of the party—a jovial, good-natured fellow with a big Roman nose—had lost his forefinger. I asked him how he lost it, expecting that he would tell of some fight he had been in. He told me that a pony had bit it off when he was a boy, which occasioned a hearty laugh. I gave them the use of a building which I had vacated for the purpose and in which they found some clothing belonging to the wife of one of my men. The Indians took the woman's skirts and, putting them over their heads, let them

1. "The fight occurred in the northern part of Lincoln County, over a large piece of ground within a circle between Denmark and the west branch of Salt Creek on Brown Trail and Little Timber Creeks, branches of Spillman's Creek."—JRM.

hang down from their shoulders. They then marched round in that costume, performing a war dance which seemed to afford them great amusement.

On one occasion I took my wife and another lady with her infant child out into the hills for recreation and a little buffalo hunt. We drove through timber for a short distance and out into the hills, and I shot several buffalo. One buffalo bull—mortally wounded— walked over a little ridge out of sight. When I had killed the others I told my wife to walk up on the ridge and see what had become of the other bull, which she did. She came back with the word that he was "standing on his head," which I thought a very extraordinary circumstance, so I immediately went over to investigate. I found the bull, in a last effort to remain on his feet, had put his head on the ground nearly between his front feet to steady himself. His hind parts were up the hill and, in reality, he was nearly standing on his head. He died in a few moments.

When we had taken what meat, tongues, etc. we could use, I drove back to the ranch where we found half a dozen armed Cheyenne warriors. The only person I had left in camp was a colored man who had taken a notion to come out on the ranch with me. He had formerly been the servant of an officer at Ft. Riley. He was nearly scared to death. He had never seen a wild Indian before, and some of the Indians apparently had never before seen a negro. So they had a mutual admiration society all to themselves. The Indians had had much fun with the colored man during my absence, but he was too badly scared to enjoy it.

In conversation with the Indians they told me that they had been lying in ambush within a few feet of us as we drove through the timber going out on our hunt. They described minutely everything we had with us and what we were doing, and how we were sitting in the wagon. Evidently they were telling the truth. We had not had the slightest idea that there was an Indian in the vicinity.

The buffalo I hunted ranged from the British line South to the Gulf of Mexico, coming North in the Spring and most of them returning in the Autumn to fresh pasture and a milder climate. Over the entire extent of this range Nature had provided that the streams ran toward the East, affording the buffalo abundant water on their annual migrations. Through this entire range salt springs came through the surface at short intervals, affording them all the salt they required without any effort on their part to obtain it.

One of the peculiarities of the buffalo is that they shed their heavy coat of fur every Spring, excepting the long heavy hair on their heads and shoulders. Their heavy coat of fur becomes loose in the Spring and seems to be very annoying and unpleasant to the buffalo. So to get rid of it they lie down on a smooth spot in the prairie and, kicking vigorously with their hind feet and digging the ground up with their horns, spin round and round on the ground and stir up a considerable amount of loose soil in a circle, at the same time removing a portion of their surplus winter fur.

The violent winds at this time of the year will blow away the dust they have loosened. Presently along comes another buffalo and he will lie down in the same place and go through the same performance. When he gets up, the wind immediately blows out the dust he has loosened up. This process is continued indefinitely until, in the course of time, there is a circular depression in the shape of a shallow bowl that finally becomes 12 or 18 inches deep. It permanently remains in that shape and, so long as it is dry, is used by the buffalo, its hollow oval shape fitting their bulky round bodies. These innumerable depressions on the prairies and in the valleys are known as "buffalo wallows." In times of heavy rains they become filled with water, and where the sub-soil is of a clayey, tenacious nature, they will hold water for a considerable length of time and are then used by the buffalo for drinking purposes. But in all my experience I never saw a buffalo lie down in one of these "wallows" when it contained water or was muddy, contrary to the common opinion that buffaloes wallow in the mud. On the contrary, buffaloes seem to avoid mud as much as possible. I have been told, however, that in the British possessions of the North where mosquitoes and flies are exceedingly numerous and troublesome, the buffalo may lie down in mud and water to protect themselves from these insect pests. But on the great central plains there were no mosquitoes or flies to annoy them.

A buffalo is built after a fashion all his own. A bull has an immense heavy head and his shoulders reach up higher in proportion than any other known animal. His hind parts are comparatively light and compactly built, but at the same time very muscular and strong.

This arrangement throws nearly all the weight on the front legs and enables the bull to balance himself on his front feet and keep his head directed in any position he may choose. This peculiarity is noticeable in the fierce battles which are constantly occurring between the bulls during the rutting season, which commences on the first of July simultaneously all over the plains.

During this season the bulls—which are more numerous than the cows—are constantly engaged in fighting. The wonderful agility and skill they display in protecting themselves from the horns of their adversaries is astonishing, considering the great weight and bulk of the huge animals. Two bulls will rush together something after the fashion of two rams, always meeting head on. The effort of each then seems to be to push the other back until he can get a chance at his adversary's ribs with his horns.

I have seen two bulls, evenly matched, lock horns and strain every nerve, their hoofs sunk deep into the sod, revolving about a common center until utterly exhausted. Their tongues hang out of their mouths and their bloodshot eyes nearly bulge out of their heads without either gaining any apparent advantage or being able to harm the other in the slightest. When—as it sometimes happened—one bull found that his strength was failing him and that the other was too much for him, he would jump backwards and get out of the way before his opponent could touch him with his horns. I have seen bulls thus engaged in fighting spin around, balancing on their forefeet with all the agility of a cat.

In many fights I have witnessed—and I have frequently sat within fifty yards of two bulls fighting, and enjoyed the combat to the end—I never saw a bull injured by his opponent. While engaged in fighting they paid no attention to me, although I may have been within a few yards and in plain sight. No more exciting scene could be imagined than two of these immense brutes with their shaggy heads and bodies engaged in desperate combat; their great weight of fifteen or sixteen hundred pounds adding tremendous force to their charge as they rushed at each other with all the ferocity imaginable, tearing up the turf with their hooves and covering the grass with foam from their mouths.

Buffalo do not bellow like domestic cattle, as is frequently erroneously stated. They have a peculiar deep, rumbling grunt which, in the still night, can be heard for a long distance. It is constantly heard when they are travelling, especially at night, and seems to be a signal from one band to another which is well understood. There are various modulations of this grunt which the buffalo fully understand, and thus communicate with one another their movements.

All birds and beasts have a language of their own by which they can communicate to one another all that nature considered it necessary for them to know. It is as intelligible to them as our language is to us and from long experience I learned to understand it as well as the animals themselves, so that, like Audubon, I could tell their species and sex by their voice.

Speaking of the language of animals, the most thrilling as well as—to me—the most soul-stirring music I ever heard was the clear deep bass voice of a big gray wolf on a clear cold winter night rolling out over the ice-covered prairie. It would commence on a high note and then run down the scale to the bottom, soon to be answered by his companions from every hill and canyon for miles around. From the intonations of their voice, I understood whether it was a call to assemble or come to a carcass, or to take up their line of travel for some other locality.

There are certain instincts and faculties possessed by buffalo and other animals which are equal, if not superior, to the intelligence of mankind. For instance, a string of buffalo may be travelling along a well-used trail. Should they be disturbed, they will turn off from the trail in some other direction. Soon another band of buffalo will come travelling leisurely along the same trail, apparently half asleep and paying no attention to anything. But the instant the leaders come to where the advance buffalo had scattered, they would immediately stop with every indication of alarm and, all alert, would survey the country in search of possible danger. Yet the entire prairie was so completely covered with tracks crossing and recrossing in every direction that there was nothing to indicate to my observation that any disturbance had occurred. How they were able to instantly detect that some disturbance had occurred at that point, I could not discover. Every buffalo appeared to know where the herds were grazing and which way they were travelling, though they might be miles distant and entirely out of sight. When the time came for them to move to another locality, they would all start simultaneously over a large area of country, and apparently with as good a general understanding as though they had previously communicated with one another. Yet they had no messengers to convey intelligence over the different portions of their range.

I was forcibly reminded of this fact on one occasion. I had driven down to the Smoky Hill River at the big bend late in the evening, and found the whole country covered with buffalo quietly grazing or lying down in perfect contentment and peace. We did not disturb them, and so far as I knew, our presence was unknown a hundred yards from our camp. Yet by some common impulse for which, as far as we could see, there was no cause whatever, they took a notion that they wanted to travel South. We could hear their grunts, which were apparently signals to one another, all through the night. In the morning not a buffalo was to be found in that whole scope of country. Word had evidently been passed through that whole Smoky Hill Valley to move South and they all went without a dissenting voice.

Perhaps some atmospheric phenomenon influenced them, for the next morning there set in a drizzling rain. I covered myself and horse with a big rubber blanket and started to ride up a ravine along a well-travelled trail. Soon I noticed a big buck antelope walking down the trail towards me. He evidently thought I was a lone buffalo bull going the wrong way, and paid no attention. He walked along until he met me and then simply turned out so close that I could have put my hand on his neck. Then he happened to smell the horse or myself and he lit out in evident surprise and astonishment, running to the top of the nearest ridge, where he stopped and satisfied his curiosity by an extended look.

CHAPTER 7

Civil War Raiders

In the summer of 1862 I was up the Smoky Hill River in the buffalo range on a hunt. With me were my usual two teams and two men. Having nearly secured our loads of hides we concluded to drive North to the Saline and finish our hunt. It happened that we came to a very precipitous branch known as Hell Creek, where we decided to camp.[1] The bluffs on either side were so precipitous that we had considerable difficulty in finding a place where we could get our teams and wagon down. While we were on the high land looking round, we saw some horsemen about a mile up the river, chasing buffalo furiously. We supposed they were wild Indians, not having a field glass to bring them closer, so we started down the bluff with our teams to get into the timber on the creek to escape their observation if possible.

While making our way down, one load of hides slipped forward onto the horses, causing them to run and tipping one of the wagons over so that both axles were broken off short. This left us in a very unpleasant predicament with no tools to mend our wagon and with an enemy close at hand. But we had no intention of abandoning our possessions at that time.

After considerable labor we got our broken wagon and load down to the creek where there was an immense spring coming out from

1. Now known as Elkhorn Creek.

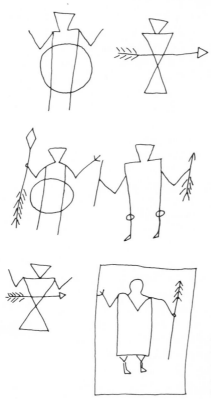

Petroglyphs copied by James R. Mead from a sandstone cliff along the Smoky Hill River. From a notebook in the Mead Collection, Wichita.

under a sharp over-hanging sandstone cliff, completely surrounded by timber. The spring formed a large, deep pool of the purest water I ever saw, flowing out over a rim of pure white sand. This cliff, I noticed, was covered with Indian hieroglyphics depicting events of war and the chase and horse-stealing expeditions in which the various parties of Indians who camped there at various times had participated, inscribing their adventures for the benefit of other parties who might come that way.

We went to work with no tools but an ax and an inch auger, splicing the broken axles of our wagon, and making liberal use of buffalo hides cut into long ropes to lash the splices firmly together. And on the second day, with our heavily loaded wagons, we drove home to Salina. Our wagon-mending proved to be such a good job that I

then drove that same heavily loaded wagon through to Leavenworth—a distance of 230 miles—without any further repairs.

One morning just at daybreak, two or three days after we arrived in the little town of Salina, a band of about thirty-five heavily
armed horsemen rode into town.[2] They surrounded the building
used as a hotel and proceeded to place every man under guard that
they could find. At that time Salina contained no more than thirty or
forty families all told and most of the men were either absent on the
plains hunting, or down at the Missouri River after supplies. The
horsemen were unshaven and dirty, dressed in buck-skin, and were
a true picture of outlaws.

My wife and I were living in the home of Congressman Col.
Wm. A. Phillips, who was then in Washington. He had invited us to
occupy part of his residence as company and protection for his family while he was absent. I saw at once that it would be utterly
useless for the few of us who were there to make any resistance.
So I told the ladies not to be anxious, as I didn't think there was any
special danger. I then went alone to meet the Captain of the party
and three of his men who were marching in our direction. Each man
was armed with two double-barrelled shot guns, two big revolvers,
and a huge knife in a belt around his waist.

On meeting the party I halted them and asked what they wanted.
They said they were going round gathering up what horses and
arms they could find, and if we didn't make any resistance they
were not going to hurt any of us, but if we made them any trouble
they were going to burn our little town for us. I asked them what
they were going to do that for, telling them that we never had
wronged anyone, and asking why they wanted to rob us. The Captain replied that they were good Confederates and were going
down to join their brethren in the South. They knew about our little
town and thought they would take it as they came down from the
mountains, and fit themselves out with some things they wanted.

The Captain of the party then told one of his men to take me
over to the hotel where they had the others under guard. He then
went on to the door of the house. My wife, who had been watching
the proceedings from the door, asked him what he wanted and
what he was going to do with me. The Captain took off his fur cap,
made a very polite bow, and said, "Madam, don't be alarmed. We

2. The date was September 19, 1862.

Agnes Barcome

"I have half a notion of getting married, but I suppose you will laugh at the idea." (JRM, Burlingame, Kansas, August 26, 1860.)

"I have come across a young lady out here whom I think a good deal of, and who thinks considerable of me. I think considerable [more] of her than of any one I ever met before." (JRM, Burlingame, Kansas, September 2, 1860.)

"I am going to get married this fall, I expect, to a poor girl, and not very good looking, but she likes me and I like her and I guess we could make a living." (JRM, Leavenworth, Kansas, May 1, 1861.)

"If I had my farm under good improvement I should get married this spring, but as times are, we will wait awhile. What do you think of that? Maybe you think I have been jokeing along back." (JRM, Burlingame, Kansas, May 15, 1861.)

Original letters and photograph in the Mead Collection, Wichita.

are not going to hurt anybody. But if you have got any guns in the house we would like to have them."

It happened that I had an old muzzle-loading musket that some-one had given me, and an Indian rifle with the barrel full of sand that I had found lying out on the prairie. These guns were standing by the door, while my own good hunting rifles were back in the kitchen. My wife handed him out the two guns and the Captain made a polite bow, took them, and walked off, molesting them no further.

In the meanwhile, other members of the party were scouting round the town, gathering up all the arms and horses they could find. They brought all the guns over to the hotel and threw them in a heap on the ground. They also went into the little stores and helped themselves to all the guns, knives, revolvers, etc. that they could find, and all the ammunition and tobacco they wanted. Where a man needed a pair of boots or a hat or a shirt, they took it. Other-wise they took nothing. They didn't want to load themselves up with useless plunder. Among other things, they got seven or eight big stage mules out of the stage barn.

A number of young men had claims in sight of the town in dif-ferent directions, where they had built little cabins to hold their claims. They would go out there to spend nights, riding their ponies back and forth. On this particular morning, on getting up early and seeing an unusual commotion in town, they jumped on their ponies and came galloping in to see what occasioned the un-usual stir in town. On riding up to the crowd at the hotel, some of the guards would step out and, putting a revolver under their noses, invite them to dismount. It was amusing to see the look of utter blank astonishment on their faces, and at first they could not understand the situation.

Adjoining the town on the North was the claim of a man named William Bean, who had two large American horses. It chanced that one of these horses was picketed on the prairie near the trail by which the guerrillas entered the town. And as they came in, one of the party cut the rope with his knife and turned the animal into their herd. Mr. Bean was standing in the door of his cabin and he ran out and shouted to them to let the mare alone. They of course paid no attention to him. So he ran into his stable, put a blind bridle on the other mare and came galloping in at the top of his speed, wanting to know what they were doing with his mare, and ordered them to turn her loose. When he rode up to where the party had halted, one of them stepped out and, holding a revolver in his face, invited him to get off the other mare, as they wanted her too. He was about as astonished a man as there was in the party. Mr. Bean was shortly after killed in a railroad accident while returning home East with his bride of twenty-four hours.

It so happened that I had a very fine rifle down at the gun-smith's, having broken the loading rod. The guerrillas captured the shop, scaring the proprietor, Charley Cresson, pretty badly, and appropriated my fine rifle. They also took a number of others and secured a large stock of pistols, cutlery, and ammunition. This capture seemed to please them very much. They threw all the guns into a pile on the ground, and each man picked out such as he wanted.

I noticed my rifle among the others, and saw the man who got it. He was one of the finest-looking men I ever saw, over six feet in height, not over twenty-five years of age, with a face as rosy as a young girl's, and flowing raven hair. About the time they were ready to go, I went to the Captain of the raiders and told him that one of his men had my gun, that I was a hunter and depended upon that gun for support, and that I really could not get on very well without it. After talking with me a moment, he said he would get my gun if I could find it. I pointed out to him this man who had saddled and mounted a big stage mule.

The Captain went up to him and said, "Lieutenant, what are you doing on that darned big mule? You can't ride him. He will buck and throw you off. Better get on a horse. And you have got this man's gun. He seems to be a clever sort of man and you had better let him have his gun."

The man, however, who proved to be the Lieutenant of the company, said he wanted that gun himself. Besides, it was too good a gun to leave behind. So, after parleying a moment, the Captain turned to me.

"I would like to get your gun for you," he said, "but you see it won't do to raise a fuss with one of my own men about it, and I guess I will have to let it go."

I then began talking to the Lieutenant about the gun, and in the meantime got hold of it and was pulling it away from him when he jerked it back.

"You wouldn't take a man's gun right away from him, would you?" he asked.

So I had to let it go.

When they had all mounted and started to leave, the Captain lingered a moment and made us a little speech. From his dialect I should judge he was raised somewhere in the backwoods of Missouri or Arkansas.

"We aint got nothing against you folks, and I suppose we have used some mighty fine men pretty damned rough. But we have been done that way ourselves and we had to do this to get even. The best thing you can do is to go and get even on somebody else. You folks have treated us like gentlemen, and we aint got nothing against you, and wish you good luck. If you happen around where we are, come and see us and we will treat you white."

And, bidding us good day, he rode off in a gallop.

The party followed the old military road running from Ft. Riley to Larned, and robbed two or three ranches along the road. Finally they met the stage coming in from Larned, with its four mules and some extra animals tied behind. Among other passengers was William Greiffenstein,[3] known on the plains as "Dutch Bill," who had a little trading establishment on the Walnut Creek. The party stopped the coach and surrounded it. Covering the driver and passengers with their guns, they made them dismount and stand out beside the road while they unharnessed the mules. They took every hoof of stock they had, leaving them afoot and alone on the prairie.

It seems that this party were Southerners who had been mining in the mountains. On deciding to go back to Texas and join the Confederacy, they had followed down the Smoky Hill River and stopped out on the range fifty or sixty miles West until they had sent spies

3. William Greiffenstein was born in Germany in 1829. He arrived in the United States in 1848 and became an Indian trader running freight wagons to and from Leavenworth. One of his drivers was William F. Cody, who later borrowed the nickname Buffalo Bill from William Mathewson and became famous as a showman. Greiffenstein went to Sedgwick County, Kansas, in 1865 and settled on Cowskin Creek. He was later mayor of Wichita for six and a half years between 1877 and 1888. See SOWERS in BENTLEY, vol. 1.

JRM wrote the following of Greiffenstein: "I can write a lot of interesting stories of 'Dutch Bill' Greiffenstein; smart, shrewd, unscrupulous. . . . He was the man who supplied the wild Indians (Cheyennes, Comanches, etc.) with ammunition in 1866–7" (JRM to George Martin, February 11, 1908, KSHC, Topeka). Later the same year he added:

down and found out our defenceless condition and what we had, and then made the raid.[4] They were the party I had seen chasing buffalo in the distance while I was on Hell Creek. After gathering up all the horses and mules there were in the settlement—which occupied possibly an hour—they left on a gallop, riding sixty miles before they stopped to rest their animals on the head of Cow Creek at some springs.[5] From there they struck South across the plains and, as I afterwards learned, arrived safely in Texas and joined their brethren in the war.[6]

"Wm. F. Cody, in his new book, speaks of 500 lbs of powder and 1000 lbs of lead found in the Sheyenne [*sic*] Camp at the Battle of the Washita. Greiffenstein furnished that ammunition before the battle. I personally know of his furnishing Black Kettles Camp with 250 lbs of powder and 500 lbs of lead on one trip. Some things of that kind I do not like to write for publication. Mr. G. said, in explanation, that Black Kettle and his band were 'good Indians' and never on the warpath, and I always understood Black Kettle to be a peaceable, friendly Indian" (JRM to George Martin, October 13, 1908, KSHC, Topeka).

4. "The guerrillas from the mountains who captured Salina, camped a couple of days at my ranch, after I had abandoned it, before striking Salina."—JRM.

5. The party stopped near present-day Beaver, Kansas, in Barton County. On the way they also visited the hunting camp of Henry and Irwin Farris. This was on the Fort-Riley-to-Pawnee Road at the Elm Creek (now Clear Creek) crossing, about four miles east of the Page and Lemon (Lehman?) Ranch. The Farris brothers lost their horses and rifles to the raiders. See Note 7 in MEAD [14].

6. On that same day, September 19, 1862, JRM wrote the following brief account of the raid in a letter home: "'Verily we know not what a day may bring forth,' especially in this country. This morning about sunrise a band of mounted men gallopped into town, took the men prisoners before they could get together for defence and, after placeing them under guard, collected all the horses, the best guns, and whatever they wanted out of our two little stores, and cleared out the Gun Shop and left after bidding us good morning.

"They have gone south west towards [the] Arkansas [river]. There will be a hundred troops after them in the morning, but I have no hope of their being over taken. I lost three head of horses and a very valuable rifle, which happened to be at the Gun Shop.

"As soon as they had left we dispatched runners to Fort Riley, and then went to our work as usual. I done a job of surveying in the afternoon.

"I have been thinking I had better bring Agnes back to Davenport till the war is over and matters are settled, as Kansas is in a very critical position. We are very much exposed here in case of an Indian war. . . . [I] want to get my wife in a place of safety untill peace returns to our unfortunate country."

JRM mentions that "runners" were sent to Ft. Riley, but according to BLACKMAR 2:637, the raiders overlooked one horse, which Robert Bishop rode to Ft. Riley to give the alarm. Despite JRM's pessimism about the recovery of any stolen property, he was able to write home only 9 days later to say, "I got two of my ponies back which the Robbers took a short time since, so I am only out one mare, $60, and one rifle, $5.00, and ten days time" (letter from Salina, Kansas, September 28, 1862, in the Mead Collection, Wichita).

CHAPTER 8

A Winter's Hunt

DURING the early winter of 1862 I went East on a visit to my father's and I did not return until nearly the first of January to my ranch on the Saline. There I rigged out two teams and, taking with me two men—one an old hunter[1] and the other a green hand—started out for a winter's hunt.

We followed up the North side of the Saline for two or three days, camping one evening at a large spring on a creek which was dry above. There were a large number of trails leading down to this spring where the game came for water. While making camp, I saw three bull elk with immense heads of antlers following in Indian file down one of the trails towards the spring. They were about a quarter of a mile away when I first saw them. I took my rifle and ran up the creek, got behind a sand hill, and as they came marching down the trail about a hundred yards from me, I shot at the leader. They all stopped in their tracks, looking towards me, and in a moment the leader tumbled over dead. I loaded my rifle and shot at the second one, and he tumbled over dead. The third one had not moved, but stood looking steadily at me. I shot at him, and after standing a moment or two he commenced staggering and tumbled over as the others had done. I then started towards them, loading

1. Abraham Boss.

my rifle with powder and ball as I walked. I had just finished loading as I got to the elk when, to my surprise, one of them sprang to his feet, his hair all turned toward his head (which is a habit of theirs when they are in a fighting mood) and his eyes green with rage. He was not more than five yards distant from me, with his head lowered for a charge, when my bullet killed him.

At that time, not appreciating the beauty and the value of large elk horns, I left them lying on the prairie, taking only the hides, which were worth about five dollars apiece. Fifteen dollars, I thought, was a very good half hour's work.

The next morning on walking up the same trail I saw a coyote trotting down towards me. He came along entirely unconcerned, paying no attention to me, and as we met he simply turned out of the path to pass. When he got my scent he suddenly had business in another direction, looking over his shoulder as he ran. He had probably never seen a human being before.

From there we travelled on up the river until we came to Paradise Creek, which we followed to its head. On looking for our evening's camp on the creek we found it was entirely dry, and the ground frozen hard. But I found a place where wolves had been scratching in the sandy creek, and with an ax I sharpened a hard wood stake and drove it down into the ground through the frozen crust, breaking it out in big chunks. Directly I found an abundance of pure living water not more than a foot below the surface.

From this place we passed north to the first branch of the Solomon River. Here we found numerous elk, antelope, and a few buffalo. That night we made an immense fire, thinking that if there were any Indians or hunters in the country we would attract their attention. But we failed to find any.

We continued North to the middle fork of the Solomon, now known as Bow Creek, and from there North to the main branch, where we found an abundance of buffalo, as well as great numbers of black- and white-tailed deer, and some elk. We were in a country that was new to us, and in which no hunters had been apparently. We camped on the river for a couple of weeks, killing large numbers of buffalo and deer, and especially gray wolves, which were the main object of our hunt, as their skins were quite valuable and easily packed in bales and carried long distances.

About that time there came a heavy fall of snow some two feet in depth, and as we were afoot we found it a very laborious business wading through the deep snow after game. During this time of deep snow I found out why buffalo were able to subsist while domestic cattle would starve. The buffalo would go on the hills and jam their noses down through the snow to the ground and, using their nose and head as a broom, would sweep the snow away from a space of ground. They would then eat the short buffalo grass they found under the snow. That method enabled them to keep in good condition while domestic cattle would starve to death under the same conditions.

In a customary day we got our breakfast early in the morning, eating a hearty meal of buffalo meat and coffee, with a few flapjacks, as we called them, made of flour. Then my partner, Abraham Boss, would take his rifle and go in one direction and I would take mine and go in another direction, leaving our man in camp. He was to take care of what skins we had got the day before, chop down elm trees for our cattle to browse on, and attend to camp duties generally. We would be gone all day, and evening would bring us back to camp with our loads of wolf skins that we had collected during the day, and such other skins as we might be able to bring with us. Sometimes, however, it would be necessary to take a team and go after them.

While the snow was still on the ground I took a notion to move camp up the river about four miles on to the head of a small timbered creek. Instead of following up the valley of the river as was customary in such cases, I drove off South from the river on to the divide, which I followed up to the head of the creek, then down the creek to a suitable camping place in a big grove of timber. The next day I followed the creek down about a mile to the river, when I found from tracks in the snow, that a large band of Indians had passed down the river the evening before. On following their trail back down to our old camp, I found they had been there and had followed our trail out until they saw it going into the divide. Then, supposing that we had left the country, they did not see fit to follow it any farther, but went on down the river to the next grove of timber and camped. There they made a fortification by setting up a large amount of fallen timber around a small tree in the form of an Indian lodge. They made a crooked entrance to their lodge which, in case of attack, made it impossible to shoot inside.

As I afterwards learned, this band of Indians went on down about sixty miles to the forks of the Solomon, where they found a small party of hunters whom they robbed of their teams, guns, provisions and, in fact, everything they had. And the hunters claimed that they would have been killed had they not slipped away from them in the night. We would probably have shared the same fate, or worse, but for the seemingly guiding providence which prompted me to move camp in the peculiar manner in which I did, and at that special time.

There was a similar occurrence once down on the Saline when I left a young man to attend to camp and kill wolves, while I, with the team and another man, went west ten miles to Wolf Creek to hunt. It was in winter. In a few days I returned afoot, carrying my rifle, revolver, and a red blanket which, for a joke, I wrapped around myself as I came near my camp through the timber. To my surprise I found the camp in confusion. A lot of wolf skins I had left out to dry in the sun were gone, and my young man was gone. I threw off my blanket to investigate. Pretty soon he came out of the brush, nearly naked, and so badly scared that his teeth chattered. He said that two Pawnees going north with five horses had come to camp, saw he was scared, and compelled him to cook all they could eat; then stripped him of his clothes, took what provisions and skins they wanted, leisurely packed their ponies and went their way. And there were two loaded guns in the skin-covered camp, under some hides. Some people were so uncharitable as to suggest that if the writer had been present there would have been other game than wolves to skin.

On one of my daily hunts from camp I had wandered about five miles away when, looking across a broad valley, I saw in the distance two sharp ridges of land extending out into the valley, very steep and precipitous. On the sharp backbone of one of them, near the end, were three large animals lying down. After some little time, I made them out to be elk. At that time there were two big buck deer standing within shooting distance looking at me, but as I was more interested in the elk, I let them go. I saw that the elk were in such a position that it would be impossible to approach them except from behind, as the wind was blowing directly down the ridge and they had an unobstructed view of all the country around. So I made a wide detour and approached them from behind the parallel ridge and, climbing up the steep side until I got to the top, I peeped over and saw the three elk lying there two hundred yards distant, with a gulch probably three hundred feet deep between us.

I lay there with my rifle until I had made a calculation just where to place the ball in order to kill one and then, taking very deliberate aim, I fired. They all sprang to their feet and stood looking in my direction. In a moment the one I had shot at commenced getting weak in his hind legs, and directly he fell backwards with a great crash, raising considerable dust, stone dead. He was shot through the heart. The other two paid no attention, but stood still looking in my direction. I loaded up my rifle and shot again, when the second one commenced staggering on his feet and presently he fell over on his back dead. I began to get excited and thought I was doing them up in great shape, and so when I shot again I was a little careless. The third elk humped himself up at the crack of the rifle, moved a few steps, and stood still, looking pretty sick. I loaded as rapidly as possible and shot again. He humped himself up some more and stood there. Then I began to think it was time to stop such foolishness, and I got down to business. Taking a very deliberate aim, I fired again. In a moment he commenced staggering backwards toward the opposite side of the ridge and, his hind legs giving away under him, he turned a summersault backwards out of sight. From the noise and dust, and rattling stones, I judged that he had turned end over end down the opposite bank for a couple of hundred feet. This I found to be a fact after I had made the journey down the steep canyon and up its opposite side. I found that my three balls had struck him at exactly the same height, but the first one went too far back to reach his vital part, going into the paunch; the second one had gone through his neck, just in front of the shoulder, while the third one went through the heart.

As their skins were valuable and I was afraid that the wolves would tear them up that night, I skinned off one side of each of them so the wolves could get what meat they wanted. I then made a lot of strychnine baits which I put around for the benefit of whatever wolves might come, as well as for my own benefit. By that time it had become dark and I was about six miles from camp. The country was particularly rugged and I was pretty well tired out from my long day's tramp so it was nine o'clock at night before I reached camp. My two companions, in discussing the situation, had come to the conclusion that the Indians had my scalp, and if they were lucky enough to get away, they would have to go home without me.

The next morning I made a bob-sled out of the fork of an elm tree, and hitching a yoke of cattle to it, started out after my game. On the way I gathered up seven wolf skins that I had taken off the day before, and on arriving at my elk found seventeen dead wolves lying around them. So we returned to camp with our three elk hides and twenty-four wolf skins for that morning's trip.

We continued our hunt along the river at different places with very considerable success, killing all kinds of game common in that country. We also discovered several immense Indian camps which had been made the previous summer by some Indians unknown to us.

After getting what hides we could haul, we broke camp along in the middle of March and started back home. On arriving in the valley near Salina we found that the grass was a foot high. We had been gone on the expedition for three months and had not seen a single human being. We were given up by the people of Salina as dead. There was a general rejoicing when we drove into town, fat and hearty and rugged, and without any accident. We brought back a thousand dollars worth of fur, besides having had one of the most enjoyable hunts of my experience.

The magnificent heads of elk antlers which I left lying on the prairie on that trip would be worth a little fortune if I had them now.

CHAPTER 9

The Valley of the Arkansas

To begin at the beginning, I will tell you how I first heard of the Walnut and the Whitewater Rivers. From 1859 to the Spring of 1863 I was engaged in the fur trade and hunting on the Solomon, Saline, and Smoky Hill Rivers. In the Autumn of '62 I took my teams and some men from Salina and went to the South side of the big bend of the Smoky to get some buffalo meat, hides, and furs. On arriving there in the evening, I found the country covered with buffalo quiet and almost as tame as domestic cattle, and very fat. So we made our camp, anticipating some great sport and success on the morrow.

During the night we heard the buffalo moving, and their peculiar grunt could be heard in every direction. Evidently the word was passed round that the grass was eaten up; Autumn had come and it was time to travel South. When the sun rose in the morning not a buffalo was to be seen in the country. I asked my men where they supposed the buffalo had gone.

"I guess they are down on the Whitewater by this time," one of them replied.

That was the first intimation I had that such a stream existed in Kansas and, little thinking that it would be my home for several succeeding years, I asked the man what kind of a country that Whitewater was. He said there were but a few people there, and about half of them were horse thieves from Arkansas—not a very flattering or true description.

In the Spring of 1863, having spent most of the time on the Solomon, far beyond where any of our hunters had gone before, and having several loads of furs, I took the trail for Leavenworth and sold everything to W. C. Lobenstein, realizing about $1,000. While unloading, I saw leaning against the side of the building a long-haired man clothed in a suit of well-worn buckskin, a revolver and knife hanging from his belt. He wore a broad-brimmed slouch hat and nothing about him seemed acquainted with soap.

Recognizing him as a plainsman in typical garb, I approached and asked him who he was and where he was from. He replied that he lived on the Walnut and that his name was Bill Bemis.[1] (How came it that so large a number of plainsmen of more or less notoriety were named Bill?) I had a long conversation with Bemis. He gave me a very flattering account of the beauties of the Walnut and Whitewater country, of the abundance of game there, and the countless herds of buffalo nearby on the Arkansas, and of the Osage Indians, who four times a year passed through on their semi-annual hunts. He said that tanned buffalo robes could be bought for six bits apiece in trade and that nobody knew a buffalo hide was worth anything. There were no traders there except Stein and Dunlap, whose entire stock of goods could be hauled about in a one-horse wagon.[2] The few people there knew nothing about hunting, except for securing supplies of buffalo meat.

I thought surely this must be a hunter's and a trader's paradise, and in justice to Mr. Bemis I must say his description was not overdrawn. I had contemplated changing my location, as the Indians in the north were treacherous and hostile, frequently killing or robbing hunters when they caught them away from the settlements and could do so without danger to themselves. They were threatening to wipe out the border settlements, which they afterward attempted. I had had my sufficient share of that kind of experience,

1. William Bemis and H. Bemis were among the first settlers to arrive on the site of El Dorado, Kansas. This was in July, 1857, and they built houses and cleared land along the Walnut River near the townsite. Bemis Creek, which flows into El Dorado from the northeast, is named after them. MOONEY, V.P., 68–69.

2. Stein and Dunlap were originally Stone and Dunlap. Daniel Stein bought out their trading establishment at the old El Dorado site two miles below the present city. Daniel Stein later lived in Augusta, though he continued to serve as postmaster of El Dorado. STRATFORD, 32, and MOONEY, V.P., 66.

as well as having my wife and son[3] to think about, and did not care to have our scalps adorn the shield of some enterprising Cheyenne, Pawnee, or Sioux, with all of whom I had had some adventures not suggestive of health or pleasure. So I determined at once to visit this country of beauty, simplicity, and peace.

After purchasing necessary supplies of provisions and ammunition and employing two young men,[4] we rolled out of Leavenworth. Our trail passed through Lawrence and Burlingame to an ambitious young town called Emporia,[5] passing by Superior, J. M. Winchell's offspring,[6] Waterloo and Mickel's Hotel, a now forgotten town.[7] Thence by Jacob's Creek and mound across to the South Fork of the Cottonwood,[8] past Bazaar. We followed the Cottonwood up to its source, stopping at "Mitchell's" on the way. Crossing the high prairie divide, we soon came to the head of the "raging Walnut" at Sycamore Springs, where a fine spring boiled out of the limestone rock under the roots of tall sycamores. Here, camped in the timber, we found Dave Ballou, a Cherokee, with his three wives,[9] also Dick Pratt and Don Carlos,[10] who seemed quite inquisitive as to our destination and business. Their "wild and woolly" garb did not impress me favorably, but I afterwards had considerable dealings with them and had no occasion to regret their acquaintance.

Following the trail down the Walnut we soon came in sight of

3. Agnes Barcome Mead had given birth to a son on January 13, 1863, at the Mead farm at Rockingham, Iowa. They named the boy James Lucas Mead, but to friends and family he was known throughout his life as Bunnie.

4. JRM later mentions that "a young man named Mounts" had come out with him from Leavenworth, presumably one of the two young men he mentions here.

5. Emporia, Kansas, was founded in February, 1857, by P. B. Plumb, Gen. G. W. Deitzler, G. W. Brown, Lyman Allen, and Columbus Hornsby. ANDREAS 2:847.

6. Superior was a short distance almost due south of Burlingame. J. M. Winchell set up Superior as a rival to Council City, as Burlingame was first called. Before Osage County was organized Superior looked so promising that it was proposed as the state capital, and Topeka won by only two votes. GREEN [1].

7. Some early maps of Kansas show Waterloo on Elm Creek, approximately midway between Burlingame and Emporia and not far south of present-day Miller, Kansas, in northeast Lyon County.

8. An early notice of the Cottonwood River is that given by Zebulon Pike, who camped on the South Fork of the Cottonwood on September 11, 1806. BARRY, 54.

9. Two years later, in 1865, Davis Ballou was employed by JRM and supplied with goods to trade with the Indians at Cowskin Grove west of the junction of the Big and Little Arkansas rivers. BENTLEY 1:120.

10. "Don Carlos and his Indian wife were later among the first settlers on the Wichita site. His place was close to the Alamo Addition, between the rivers, and up the river on the east side a quarter of a mile at a fine crossing. There he built a cabin and sold goods in a small way."—JRM.

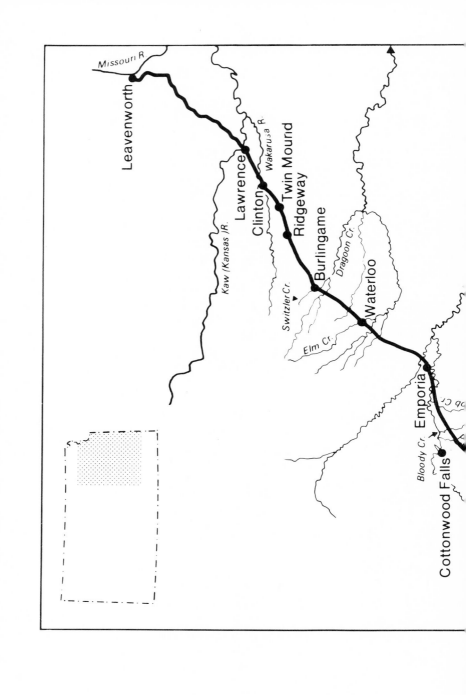

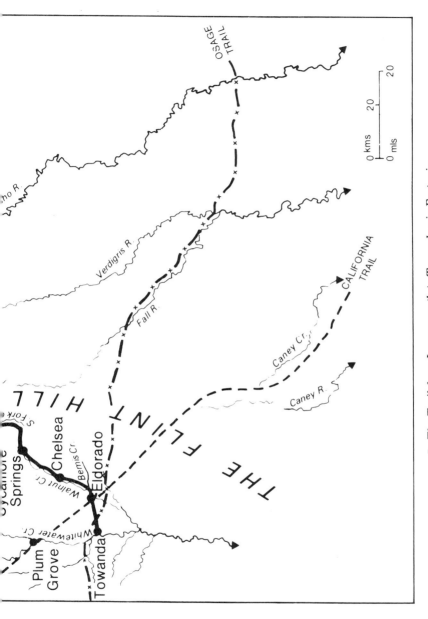

5. *The Trail from Leavenworth to Towanda via Emporia*

Chelsea,[11] and a valley as beautiful as my eyes had ever beheld. This was the first of May, 1863. The prairies were covered with a lovely coat of fresh grass and flowers. The converging belts of timber along the streams in the full glory of spring foliage furnished a background to this picture of nature in her holiday attire. Nearby were the neat and cozy homes of J. C. Lambdin,[12] George T. Donaldson,[13] and others whom I found to be, with their families, intelligent, cultured people of whom any community might be proud. With my family, I enjoyed their society and hospitality on many occasions in succeeding years.

These gentlemen tried to induce me to locate with them, and Mart Vaught[14] offered me 160 acres of bottom land, well timbered and watered, with a field fenced and in cultivation, with a log house hewn and put up, ready to roof in, for $200. Amazing bargain! But I had been living where earth, timber, water, and sky for unnumbered leagues, covered with the "cattle on a thousand hills" were all my own, so far as I had any use for them. What did I want with a little "patch" of ground half a mile square? I had no use for land in severalty. I seemed to have the happy-go-lucky Indian idea that the earth was the Lord's and the "fullness thereof" and no man should say, "*This* piece of land is mine," except as he occupied it at his convenience.

The next morning, leaving our kind friends of Chelsea, we proceeded on down the Walnut, then in a state of nature almost untouched by the hand of man. Occasionally there was a log house with a few acres in cultivation, enclosed by a rail fence. Doctor

11. Chelsea was established in 1858 by Martin Vaught, "Prince" G. D. Morton of Boston, and others. STRATFORD, 22.

12. J. C. Lambdin first arrived in Butler County in 1857. In 1859 he was elected probate judge and elected to the Upper House of the Territorial Council. He was a member of the Constitutional Convention in 1860. Under that constitution Kansas was admitted as a state on January 29, 1861. Together with his two sons, Judge Lambdin served the Union Army during the Civil War. STRATFORD, 22–23,33.

13. Donaldson, together with J. C. Lambdin and Martin Vaught, reached Emporia in August, 1857, and then travelled down to the Walnut River, where he settled to farm 800 acres. He became Chelsea's first postmaster, was elected county commissioner in 1859, then was killed ten years later, on November 4, 1869, while hauling logs, when one of them rolled off his wagon, crushing him against a wheel. M. Vaught, "Chelsea Township," in STRATFORD, 22 and 24.

14. Martin Vaught was a pioneer settler of Butler County, arriving there in August, 1857. See note 13 above.

Lewellen[15] was living on the West side of Walnut near Chelsea. Several miles below were families named Caskins—colored refugees from the Nation then in the toils and turmoils of internecine war. On a hill lived the Bemis family,[16] and not far beyond we crossed the Walnut at a rock bottom ford, with the clear, sparkling water, shaded on either side by tall walnut, hackberry, sycamore, and oak, in marked contrast to the sandy, cottonwood-lined streams common to the plains.

Near the ford lived Henry Martin,[17] trying to make a home and farm. He held the office of county treasurer and, to the best of his ability, kept his books on scraps of paper at home, as did the other county officers, if there were any. Butler County was at that time organized, but there seemed to be no regular organization records, county seat, nor process of law. Happy country! Happy people! Many of the settlers had enlisted in the Union Army at the outbreak of the war. Others had moved away on account of a year of drought (1860), or the dangers to be expected in their defenceless situation from the roving bands of the Indian Territory to the south, and the wild Indians of the plains whose country joined theirs on the west. Those who remained were mostly ready to roll out or "hide out" at an hour's notice, and the country was in a demoralized condition.

From Martin's to the old townsite of El Dorado, we noticed a number of settlers. The original El Dorado was two miles below the present city, at the point where the old California Trail from Arkansas to the mountains crossed the Walnut. This trail entered Kansas near the southwest corner of Chautauqua County, thence northwest between the Caney Rivers across the corner of Elk, entering Butler near its southeast corner, reaching the Walnut at the Osage

15. One of the first white settlers on the Walnut, Doctor Lewellen was not an M.D. or Ph.D.; "Doctor" was his first name. In 1859 he was elected sheriff of Butler County. He was later among the early settlers on the Wichita site and ran a store there before returning to Butler County. STRATFORD, 12–13.

16. It was from William Bemis, met by chance in Leavenworth, that JRM first learned of the Walnut country.

17. Henry Martin, who was from England, was among the third group of settlers in Butler County, arriving with W. and H. Bemis over the Osage Trail on July 9, 1857, when he was 28 years old. He built the first store in El Dorado, served as probate judge and justice of the peace, and was county treasurer for four years. He froze to death while on a buffalo hunt near Medicine Lodge in 1870. STRATFORD, 33.

crossing near El Dorado, then northwest to the Whitewater crossing below Plum Grove, and pursuing a course to the Old Santa Fe
Trail at Turkey Creek, in McPherson County. This trail bore evidence of heavy wagon travel in former times. When I passed over
it in 1863 it was then abandoned, and in places grown over with
grass.

The great Osage Trail, worn deep by the Indians in many generations of travel to and from their hunting grounds to the west,
also crossed at this point. This trail extended from the Neosho
(Dacotak: *ne*, "water"; *osho*, "clear") River to the Little Arkansas
buffalo range, crossing the Verdigris River just above the junction
of Fall River, at Chief Little Bear's (*Mint sho shinka*) town; following up Fall River on the north side to the Flint Hills, then west to
the Walnut River, which it crossed at the old townsite of Eldorado,
as mentioned. This great Osage Trail reached the Whitewater at
the junction of the west branch, near Towanda—a favorite camping
place for the Osages, as it is just a day's march from the Arkansas
and furnished abundant fuel and shelter. The trail reached the
Little Arkansas six miles above its mouth. This Osage Trail was
much used by the early traders, hunters, and settlers, and occasionally by parties passing from the east on up the Arkansas to the
mountains. It bore evidence of age and much use, from the deep
gullies worn in the river banks and slopes of the hills by rains and
horses' hooves. For several succeeding years the Little Osages,
with their chiefs Mint-sho-shinka and No-po-walla,[18] passed through
from the Neosho to the Arkansas on their summer and winter
hunts. They camped along the Little Arkansas in the timber and
made their lodges of rows of green poles set in the ground about
eight feet apart, bent over and tied together, forming an arch about
six feet high; other poles would be lashed to the sides with willow
withes, and all covered with dry buffalo skins, forming very comfortable houses ten, twenty or more feet in length.

On the west bank of the Walnut Eldorado, "the Land of Gold,"
was founded and named. Its location was excellent, commanding
the traffic over the trails and the trade of the Walnut and Whitewater settlements, yet when I first saw it on that bright May day of
1863, it was practically abandoned. A family lived at the crossing;

---

18. Research has not revealed further information about these two Osage leaders.

Stein and Dunlap kept a little store. Several frame buildings which had been erected were partly torn down for the lumber they contained.

At this point we camped for several days, getting acquainted with the people and the country. The inhabitants were particularly easy to get acquainted with; most of the men seemed to have nothing to do and well pleased that they didn't, while the women were always busy at something. Yet somewhere within the broad boundaries of Butler County there then resided as brave men and as fair women as can be found within her limits today. At a social gathering I met a number of ladies and gentlemen of intelligence, refinement, and grace. I can now only recall the names of Lieutenant Cowley[19] and his wife and Jerry Connor.[20]

My object being to engage in the fur trade and also to do some hunting occasionally, and wishing to get as near to the game country as possible, I took the old Osage Indian Trail west to the Whitewater, and camped at Mr. C. L. Chandler's.[21] There I found a magnificent spring pouring a volume of clear, pure water from one of the limestone caverns which underlie the rocky prairie between the Whitewater and the Walnut. A little hackberry tree grew from the bank just over the spring, while about a hundred yards back on the hill was a very rough log building called a school house. Near the spring in the valley was a small log building, and a little further away was Mr. Chandler's story-and-a-half hewed log house and a cultivated field. A post office was kept here, supplied once a week

19. Matthew Cowley enlisted in the Union Army along with 26 other men from Butler County, and together they made up Company L of the Ninth Kansas Cavalry. Lieutenant Cowley died of malaria at Little Rock, Arkansas, and is buried in the military cemetery there. STRATFORD, 26, and MOONEY, V.P.

20. Jerry D. Connor was born in County Kerr, Ireland, on June 20, 1837. He arrived in the U.S. at the age of 9 and lived in Portsmouth, New Hampshire, where he attended school and became a printer. In 1857 he travelled west, and in the spring of 1858 he followed the California Trail to Butler County. In staking his claim on the Walnut, he became the first settler to make a land entry in the county. In 1862 he enlisted in the Ninth Kansas Cavalry and served until the end of the Civil War, having gone up through the ranks from private to lieutenant. He was a member of the Kansas Legislature in 1866 and 1867 and was Butler County treasurer for four years. STRATFORD, 12.

21. C. L. Chandler was from Ohio. He took part in the 1849 gold rush. In 1858, on his return east over the Santa Fe Trail, he met some travellers who praised the waters, timber, and grazing to be found along the Whitewater. In September, 1858, having followed the river down from its head, Chandler reached the big spring. There he built a cabin. He lived in Towanda until 1863, when he sold his property to JRM. STARR, 3–4.

James Kelly, who was employed by James R. Mead at Towanda, Kansas,
from 1863 to 1868. Mead Collection, Wichita.

from Cottonwood Falls by horseback service. Nothing else was in
sight but prairie, timber along the Whitewater River, and sky.

This was Towanda, at that time the extreme western settlement
and the eastern edge of the buffalo range.[22] Occasionally buffalo

22. JRM called the settlement Towanda or Towando from the start, as is shown by
his letters home. The letter in which he speaks of Quantrill's destruction of Lawrence,

came into Towanda to graze. Here by the big spring I concluded to locate. There were then two families living south on the river: William Vann[23] and Sam Huller. Dan Cupp lived at the junction of the west branch of the Whitewater with the main stream where the Osage Trail crossed, and where he lives today.[24] The widow Kelly had a cabin nearby, and James and Abe Kelly—the latter as plucky a boy as I ever saw—were stopping somewhere about. Dave Meser and Morris Harrah were on the river, old man Gillian lived five miles above, while Joseph Adams and his excellent family lived at Plum Grove.[25]

Up the west branch, adjoining the claim of Anthony Davis, who was then in the army, was a colored family named Buckner, from the Cherokee Nation. Buckner was quite an enterprising man. He owned a bunch of cattle, kept hogs, and made excellent bacon. He was also quite a hunter and caught and attempted to raise a bunch of buffalo calves, but on one of the family's periodic stampedes from imaginary Indians, he left his calves shut up in their pen and upon his return found them starved to death. All of these people, and others whose names I do not now recall, assisted me in every way in their power.

For a trifle I bought a set of hewn house logs across the river, hauled them over, and with the assistance of Dan Cupp and young George Adams, soon had a house close by the big spring.[26] I

Kansas, on August 21, 1863, is dated "Towanda, Irvin County, Kansas, Wednesday, September 2nd, 1863," and yet throughout the remainder of the 1860s the place was widely known in Kansas as Mead's Ranch (*KSHC* 12: 483). One account of the origin of the name Towanda is that given by Mrs. Dan Cupp (see n. 24 below). She stated that it is an Osage word meaning "many waters" or "rushing waters," in reference to the big spring (STARR, 16–17).

23. William Vann and his wife and seven children were from Missouri. They were among the first settlers in Towanda Township, having built a house in the area as early as 1859. MOONEY, V.P. (p. 72) says that they arrived in July, 1868, but JRM clearly remembers that they were already there when he arrived in 1863.

24. Daniel Cupp arrived in Towanda in 1860, driving a covered wagon in which, among other things, were his wife and a Seth Thomas clock. It was said that Dan Cupp's clock was the only one between the Whitewater and Santa Fe, New Mexico. Cupp was a hunter and trader until the Civil War began. He enlisted in Jim Lane's cavalry regiment and served the Union throughout the war. After returning home, he took up farming at Towanda. It is said that he killed the last buffalo seen in El Dorado township. He died at his Towanda home on January 12, 1930. STRATFORD, 12–13.

25. Joseph Adams was from Dwight County, Illinois. In 1863 he built a house in Plum Grove Township and took up farming. He is credited with being the first permanent settler in that township. He had a son named George. STRATFORD, 44.

26. JRM purchased the Chandler claim for $3 an acre. STARR, 6.

bought sufficient lumber for doors, floors, etc. from one of the old buildings at El Dorado. Lime, sand, and stone for a big fireplace were obtained nearby. In a few days I was at home and had a place to store my belongings while I went on a hunt, the particulars of which I will attempt to give.

After deciding to locate at Towanda, it was necessary to make a trip across the country to Salina to bring down a team and other things I had there. Taking with me a young man named Mounts who had come out with me from Leavenworth, I got ready a team, riding pony, blankets—in those days we always took our bedding along with us—and a camp kit, which consisted of a bake oven, fry pan, bread pan, camp kettle, coffee pot, tin cups and spoons, bucket, an ax, lariats, and stakes with which to picket our animals. Each man, of course, carried in his belt a knife used for all purposes.

Our usual supply of provisions consisted of flour, coffee, sugar (three essentials), a piece of bacon, if we had it, and a little salt. My tried and trusty rifle furnished meat, the choicest and the best, and our main dependence for food. The rich, juicy steak of buffalo, elk, deer, or antelope fried in their own fat or roasted before the fire, or joints boiled in a camp kettle, gave us health, strength, and vigor. Together with a little bread in the form of "flap jacks" and coffee, this furnished a perfectly satisfactory ration.

On one occasion after several months camping in the hunting range of the Solomon and the Saline, on reaching the first settlements I purchased for a supper for five of us, a bucket of milk and five dozen eggs. We dispatched all of this, with the usual accompaniments of bread and coffee, at a single meal! And then one man was growling because he thought he had not quite got his share of the eggs. There was some heavy snoring and sleeping that night, but no other ill results.

Our route was up the Whitewater to the California Trail, which crossed the stream just below Joseph Adams' place. We followed this trail to the northwest until it left the county near its northwest corner, thence continued in the same direction across the corner of what is now Harvey County, just touching the corner of Marion County, into McPherson County, where it joined the great Santa Fe Trail at Turkey Creek ranch. This was the only habitation between Adams' and Salina. All else was a wild, uninhabited plain, roamed over occasionally by buffalo and Indians.

Mead's Ranch at Towanda, Kansas, which included his trading post, a post office, an Indian agency, over-night accommodations for travellers, and the Mead home. From a contemporary drawing by James E. Taylor in the Mead Collection, Wichita.

From this point we turned north across the divide of the Arkansas and Smoky Rivers to the head of Gypsum Creek. We saw no buffalo, but quite a number of antelope. My companion, a novice on the plains and ambitious of killing something, expended considerable time and ammunition, but invariably came back to the wagon empty-handed. That evening as we went into camp in a bend of Gypsum Creek, a fine buck came bounding up the valley, stopping opposite us about a hundred yards off, to take a look. His curiosity furnished us with meat, for a shot from my rifle dropped him dead in his tracks.

On returning to Towanda from Salina with the things I had gone after, the time seemed propitious for a hunt and I wished to see the famous hunting grounds of the Arkansas. Buckner was ready to go at the same time, and proposed to go along. As he knew the country well, there were no objections. My outfit consisted of myself and two inexperienced men, a large freight wagon drawn by three yoke of cattle, a horse team and wagon, and a riding pony. Buckner had one team and a wagon into which he piled his entire family, consisting of a heavy-weight wife and six or seven children and, in addition, about all the bedding and cooking traps he had.

The road from the Whitewater to the Arkansas followed the old Osage Trail, worn in places into deep gullies. The uplands were covered with buffalo grass common to the plains. The other grasses did not grow until the buffalo had left the country. In all central Kansas the buffalo grass died soon after the buffalo ceased to tramp it, and "blue-joint" and other grasses took its place. The prairie dogs disappeared or perished at the same time and apparently from the same cause.

There was nothing of interest to be seen along the trail, the buffalo ranging at that time farther west, until we reached the bluffs overlooking the Arkansas River.[27] Here a vision of beauty and interest greeted our eyes, such perhaps as no other spot on the plains could furnish. A level valley spread out before us as far as the eye could reach. The fresh green grass, cropped close by the buffalo and bordered by belts of timber resembled a well-kept park. Through this valley wound the great and little Arkansas Rivers,

27. JRM's first view of the Arkansas Valley may have been from a point near the present site of Wichita State University.

their banks fringed with stately trees. Scattered about over this landscape were groups of buffalo, fat and sleek, their bodies covered with a new coat of fur, black as Jet. Some were grazing and others were lying down in the warm sun, or standing motionless as if asleep. This was their country and their home, and in all the broad valley there was no human being to disturb them. So long as earth endures man will labor with hand and brain, but with all his labor, wealth, and art, he can never restore the beauty and life of that valley as I saw it on that bright June day of 1863.

Man is the most destructive and cruel of all the creatures upon the earth. What other animal will destroy life beyond its need or for greed of gain, or slaughter its own kind? We were of the race of man and descended into that peaceful valley to slay its inhabitants. Soon we came near a group of bulls lying down. The men with me were anxious to see me kill a buffalo, so with my rifle I crawled along the grass in plain sight to within seventy-five yards, raised my hand and motioned to the men to get up, which they did. Selecting a fine bull, I shot just in the edge of the shoulder, low down. He jumped forward, stood a moment, and fell dead. The ball had pierced his heart. The others stood looking, not knowing what to make of the strange actions of their companion. I loaded my rifle—a muzzle-loader—as I lay on the ground, and shot again. In a moment another bull tumbled to the earth. So I might have continued till the last one was dead, but these two were enough to show how it was done. I arose to my feet, when the buffaloes immediately "lit out." Taking the tongues and some of the humps, we drove on to the crossing of the Little Arkansas at a gravelly riffle.

Here on the east bank, in the fall of 1859, Moxley[28] and Mosley[29] built a cabin (called a ranch, of course) at the Osage crossing to trade with the Indians. It was the first ranch in that country. They had come out from Coffey County in 1857 to hunt and trade.

28. Ewing Moxley was among the first group of white settlers in Sedgwick County, Kansas, having arrived in 1857 with C. C. Arnold, Ed S. Mosley, Robert DeRacken, and others. In 1858, Moxley was in Walnut Country, in the Chelsea area. Martin Vaught described him as "a thorough frontiersman, born in the wilds, an unerring marksman, fearless, honest, and simple and tender as a child. He had been a Government scout and guide on the plains." STRATFORD, 23, and ANDREAS, 1384.

29. Ed S. Mosley came into Sedgwick County in 1857 after leaving a claim in Wilson County. Sometime later he moved to Humboldt, Kansas, in Allen County. JRM has more to say about Ed Mosley in Chapter 17. ANDREAS, 1384.

Moxley left the ranch at the beginning of the war and went as a sort of a side show to the army, picking rebels off their horses and taking the plunder for his pay. He was drowned at Lawrence, Kansas, while taking some contraband stock across the river. Mosley returned to Humboldt and their trading house was burned. This was in 1862 or 1865. I received this information from Daniel Stein, now of Augusta, whom I have always found to be a reliable man. C. C. Arnold,[30] Jake Carey, Bob DeRacken, and others went up the big river a few miles and built a cabin and, it is said, broke up some ground on the same site where the Jewett farm[31] and, later, old Park City were to be located.[32] But Arnold and his associates left for Butler County, and soon no trace of their occupation remained.

In that summer of 1863 I noticed on the bluffs along the Walnut and Whitewater rivers and their tributaries in Butler County frequent low mounds from six inches to two feet in height and from fifteen to twenty-five feet in diameter. They were usually overgrown with the same coat of short buffalo grass which at that time covered the highlands and were as compact and solid as the surrounding land; originally they may have been higher. They evidently were made long before historic times, as the Osages and other Indians, who at times occupied the county since Kansas was known, did not bury their dead in mounds.

Some of these mounds have since been explored and proven to be burial places. Several bodies were sometimes found in one mound, and with them were placed various articles of their belongings; heavy stone axes of granite or other stone not found in the vicinity, occasionally flint spades, and always flint arrow and spear points, knives, etc.; sometimes bones of animals and shells. The writer opened one of these mounds, situated on a rocky point of bluff overlooking Four Mile creek, in the summer of 1902. The

30. C. C. Arnold is sometimes mentioned as the first white settler in Sedgwick County, having reached the Arkansas Valley in 1857 with a party of hunters from Coffey County, Kansas, including Ed S. Mosley, Ewing Moxley, Thomas Crawford, Robert Dunlap, Robert DeRacken, and Joseph Carey. ANDREAS, 1384.

31. William T. Jewett had a farm three miles west of present-day Valley Center, Kansas, on the Big Arkansas. ANDREAS, 1384.

32. In 1870 the two small hamlets of Wichita and Park City were keen rivals, competing with each other for settlers and business. Wichita won, as JRM recounts in Chapter 17 below, and Park City died. Park City was west of Valley Center on the Arkansas River and is unrelated, except by name, to the recently established Park City which lies north of Wichita between Broadway and Kechi.

earth and stone had been excavated to a depth of two feet. There were found portions of the hard, dry bones of three persons, two adults and a child, with them a buffalo bone, and a few *Unio*; the excellent drainage aiding in preserving them. Some arrow and spear points were found, of dark bluish chert, of fairly good workmanship, and covered with a hard lime deposit.

It must be remembered that very few of the articles which are originally buried in a mound remain after the lapse of ages—usually nothing but stone, bone, or pottery. Such articles as buckskin clothing, furs, buffalo-robes in which the dead were wrapped, head-dress, the ornamented shafts of lances, bows, and arrows, all disappear in time; so that what we find is but a small remainder of the original burial, almost nothing remaining by which to judge of the dress, food, or customs of the people. Then, burrowing animals nearly always have invaded the mounds, and small articles, such as ornaments or beads of stone, bone, or shell, are scattered, mixed with the earth, or thrown out, and difficult to find. In these mounds everything had disappeared save some of the larger bones and whatever implements of stone or pottery may have been placed in them.

Stone implements similar to those found in the mounds have been picked up over the country, some of them fine specimens of hammers, axes, grinding-stones, pipes, spear-points, etc. Probably a wagon-load has been gathered, and several fine collections shipped out of the state.

The junction of Whitewater and Walnut Rivers seems to have been the center of a considerable population of these ancient and unknown people. On the high bluff coming abruptly to the Walnut on the east are numerous low mounds and camp sites; under the rocky bluff is a big spring, and in the vicinity are sink-holes. On the high prairie, in a cavity in the rocky sides of one of these mounds, were found four Indian pipes, peculiar, unique, skilfully carved, and drilled from red quartzite, only found in Kansas along the southern limit of the Glacial ice-sheet.

A fine example of the pink and red quartzite can be seen in a field of boulders just west of the Wakarusa, in Douglas County, near Clinton. Other pipes, duplicates of these, have been found in the same county. These pipes were exceedingly hard; it would seem that nothing but a diamond would cut them.

The washing down of the side of a clay bank disclosed some large pottery vessels of excellent make, and there were found also a cache of spear and arrow points.

In the narrow strip of valley between the two rivers where they join many implements were found on the surface by the first settlers of the country. About 1870 Daniel Stein took it as a claim. He plowed up many more implements, and later sold to another party who, with a strong plow and four big horses, turned up the ground much deeper than before, and brought to view a third lot of stone implements. Among these were well-shaped hammers, weighing five or six pounds, with a groove around the center, cut from the same red quartzite. This black gumbo land has not increased perceptibly by surface deposit in the forty years I have known it.

These mounds extend down the Walnut to near its mouth. I think it probable that this valley long ago was the home of a numerous people antedating the roving tribes found in Kansas when first explored. The abundant streams and springs of pure water, rich soil, abounding in game of all kinds—buffalo, elk, deer, antelope, otter, and wild turkeys—and bearing abundant timber, combined to make a primitive man's ideal home.

From the Little River (the Little Arkansas) we followed the trail a couple of miles to the Arkansas and camped in a cabin built by William Ross. In the spring of 1860, William Ross, a farmer, moved from Wilson County, Kansas, and settled on the east bank of the Arkansas River on what is now the southeast quarter of section four, township twenty-six, range one west. His family consisted of his wife and two small children. He brought with him teams, some farming implements, and household effects. He chose a beautiful spot for his home, a bend of the river adjoining a grove of timber about three miles beyond the Osage crossing on a high bank of the Big River. He built a house of logs, 14 × 20, the roof formed of poles split and covered with earth. A fireplace occupied the west end of the building, and near his house he built a log stable for his horses. As soon as this was done he commenced ploughing and planting corn and such garden seeds as pioneers usually carry with them. To assist him, he had a hired man, and his faithful wife, who was happy in their new home. For neighbors they had encountered thousands of buffalo, antelope, and wolves, and occasionally elk and deer. In the month of June the Osage Indians, with their chief Mint-sho-Shinka, or Little Bear, came on their annual summer hunt, to the Arkansas, which had been their chosen and allotted hunting ground from time immemorial. Following the Indians for the purposes of trade, Ewing Moxley built a cabin at the crossing of the Little River, and the DeRacken brothers also built a cabin on the Big River, in a grove several miles above. Rumor said Indians traded ponies for fire-water at this place and that sundry horses missing from the settlements were traced in that direction.[33]

The Osages were friendly and did not disturb Mr. Ross. Little Bear, their Chief, was a portly, good-natured, well-disposed Indian, fonder of his ease and the good things of life than of the war path, and while their flour and coffee lasted, was a frequent visitor at the Ross cabin. Ross was killed, probably by Indians, that same fall while hunting near the Cowskin a few miles from here. Part of his remains were found by a searching party from the Walnut and were buried on the bank of the river near his cabin. A mound of stone was placed over his grave. His hired man, who was with him, and the team were never found, but the wagon was discovered in the weeds on the river that winter by the Osages.[34] His family returned east and the two Arkansas Rivers reverted to their original solitude. Ross was the first actual settler with a family in what is now called Sedgwick County.

At the time of which I write, this country was virtually a part of Butler County and the hunting ground of her people. And here a number of them met their death from arrows, bullets, blizzards, or exposure. When we arrived and camped in the Ross cabin there

33. Mrs. DeRacken was among the earliest settlers at Chelsea on the Walnut, arriving in August, 1857. She had three sons: Robert, John, and Reuben. They took a claim on what came to be known as DeRacken Creek, shown on some maps as Durachen Creek, and on the U.S. Department of the Interior Geological Survey Map of Kansas (1963 ed.) as Durechen. Regarding the "sundry missing horses" mentioned by JRM, Martin Vaught wrote: ". . . let me say that horses had mysteriously disappeared, were traced close to DeRacken's, and Bob was suspected. A Vigilance Committee called on him, but he was discreetly absent. His younger brother was ordered to tell where Bob was. He refused. A rope was brought and he was hung by the neck repeatedly, but he was steadfast, said they might take his life, but they couldn't make him tell, and they didn't. The DeRackens, however, did make themselves scarce." STRATFORD, 22–23.

34. H. Craig Miner suggests that the hired man may have murdered Ross. See H. C. Miner, *Wichita: The Early Years, 1865–80*, p. 6.

was not another human being in what is now Sedgwick County, nor another vestige of human habitation, as we learned by driving all over it. But of animal life there was plenty.

Passing on up the river, we proceeded to the business of hunting. I found Buckner entirely impractical and useless to me. His way of hunting was to get on a horse and run the buffalo until he had killed one or two, which would very soon scare them all out of the country. I loaded him up as soon as possible and he started home. As soon as he was well underway, I rode down the river a short distance and saw a fine buck elk crossing the river. I shot him, but as he kept on, I shot again as he went up the opposite bank, and he fell. I rode across, tied my pony nearby, and knife in hand, went to skin him. Then he sprang to his feet, but with one stroke of my knife I hamstrung him, which settled his fate. I carried his hide and some meat across the river, leaving the head of horns with the carcass, as at that time they had no special value.

By the time I had my pony unpacked at camp, a herd of buffalo which Buckner had disturbed, came travelling toward the river. I lay in wait for them and shot seventeen bulls in a very short time, all of them lying in the space of a hundred yards. They were very fat and we saved a large amount of tallow. The hides we pegged out on the ground until they were perfectly dry.

Thus we worked from day to day, killing all the buffalo we could handle. On the last day's shooting, I rode four miles from camp before I saw a herd, and there I killed thirty-five in the course of two hours or less, all lying on about two acres of ground. I ran out of bullets, and the last five or six I killed with bullets cut out of dead buffalo. These bullets I whittled with my knife until I could load them. A buffalo usually dies lying on the side at which the ball has entered. The bullet, battered and flattened by striking bones, would frequently lodge under the skin on the opposite side, pressing it out into a prominence that was easily noticed. Thus the bullet could be recovered and used again, if needed. Once I had several hundred balls, each of which had killed a buffalo.

This lot of buffalo, nearly all cows and young animals, became so tame before I was done shooting that the last were shot at a distance of not more than thirty feet, and I had to get up and wave my hat to scare the last of them away. I remember skinning, cutting up, and taking the tallow of eleven myself that afternoon, my two men finishing the most of the balance. We had to leave some of them until morning. This occurred on the Cowskin about ten miles northwest of where Wichita now is.

We got back safely to Towanda after an absence of three weeks with our load of 3,500 pounds of tallow and a large number of hides, having killed 330 buffalo and secured various other game.

CHAPTER 10

Home on the Whitewater

AFTER getting safely back to Towanda with our heavily laden teams, you may inquire what we did with our loads or how we got to market with our harvest of the plains. In this case, after a rest of a few days, we rolled out for Leavenworth, 200 miles distant, the nearest market. There were at that time, 1863, no railroads in Kansas. We used oxen for heavy freighting as they were less liable to be stolen than mules or horses, cost much less, were easily kept, and as time was no particular object, we got along nicely. Twenty miles was a usual day's drive with good roads. On one occasion I found it necessary to drive a heavily loaded ox train thirty-five miles in one day from one watering place to another. Starting at four o'clock in the morning we drove until nine o'clock at night, with a short stop at noon. Some of the Cherokee cattle were almost as good travellers as horses. I owned one pair of these cattle of remarkable size, weighing over 4,000 pounds. They could move anything except a county seat! There were very few fences along the route and grazing was free, as was fuel on all the timbered streams. In those days freighters had certain well-understood rights which were the laws of the road. One was the right to graze their animals on any unoccupied land—which comprised about all of it. Another was to camp in any of the timber and use as much fallen timber as needed and take along sufficient wood to reach the next camp.

Water, grass, and fuel were free, and as we took along our own provisions and bedding, we were as independent as a ship on the ocean. There were settlers at the crossing of most of the streams, and they would come down the river to our camp evenings to hear news and get acquainted. Many were the pleasant evenings spent round our campfire. Acquaintances thus formed grew into friendships which continued in after years.

"Mitchell's" on the South Fork of the Cottonwood was a favorite stopping place. Mr. and Mrs. James Mitchell were elderly people, had a good farm with comfortable buildings and plenty to eat for man and beast. For a trifle they entertained all who chose to stop with them, which included about every person travelling the road. They had no children and seemed to enjoy the company of travellers and thus learned all the news. In fact, Mitchell's in its way was a general intelligence station. I believe they knew nearly all about every man, woman, and child in Butler County, and what they were doing or intended to do. Newspapers were scarce in those times. *The Emporia News* was the only paper published in what used to be called Southwestern Kansas—at that time including all the country South and West of Emporia.[1] Butler County was generally known as the "Walnut Country" and the news from there was obtained by word of mouth.

Norton's on "Bloody Creek" and Old Man Dietrich's on Jacob's Creek were also stopping places. Mickel's Hotel at Waterloo,[2] a day's drive beyond Emporia, was a very popular camping place. Burlingame was the next town beyond Emporia; the next was Ridgeway;[3] and then Clinton[4] on the Wakarusa near Lawrence.

1. *The Emporia News*, first published in August, 1857, was run by Jacob Stotler, Alexander Butts, and Frank McLennan. Regular publication continued until October, 1889. CONNELLEY [4], 31.

2. "The first Waterloo in Kansas was north of Emporia. The name now remains on a township in Lyons County."—RYDJORD, 128–29.

3. The "ridgeway" was an upland stretch 30 to 40 miles in length lying between the Wakarusa River on the north and the Osage River on the south. It was a natural roadway and was used as such beginning in the 1820s by overland travellers on the Santa Fe Trail. The town of Ridgeway attracted few settlers because of its exposed location on the open prairies. GREEN 3:7.

4. Clinton, Kansas, is located between Rock Creek and the Wakarusa about nine miles southwest of Lawrence in Douglas County. It was founded by John A. Beam, N. Alguire, and M. Albin in June, 1854. On August 1, 1858, a post office was opened at Clinton with J. A. Beam as postmaster. ANDREAS 1:359.

Some of these towns are now forgotten. In the winter we were often glad to avail ourselves of the comfort and shelter afforded at these places in severe cold or stormy weather.

It was our intention to get in most of our freight during the beautiful weather which always prevailed in Kansas in the fall season, but there was always some teaming to be done in the Winter. After the first year or two I used mules and horses exclusively, as they became plentiful and cheap. In fall weather we slept on the grass in our blankets.

"Where shall we spread our bunks down?" became a common inquiry soon after a hearty supper had been dispatched. If a storm came up in the night we would crawl into the covered wagons. Before daylight we would be up, build a bright fire, feed our animals or turn them loose to graze, and soon have breakfast under way. We baked our bread in a Dutch oven or made pancakes, while strong coffee and plenty of it seemed a necessity to active outdoor life. It was usually drunk from a pint tin cup twice or more filled for one person. I have often wondered why coffee drunk from a bright tin cup in camp seemed so much better than the coffee of more civilized life.

Breakfast finished, the dishes would be washed and put in the mess box, the bedding tied up, each man would hitch up his team, and in a few minutes we would be on our way. At noon we usually stopped, made a pot of coffee, and spread our blankets in the sun while our animals were feeding. We had regular drives on the way to Leavenworth, and knew each day just where we would make camp at night, usually on some creek where wood and water were abundant. There were no bridges, so of necessity we forded all streams. In a season of heavy rains we were sometimes compelled to wait several days for the waters to subside. At Lawrence there was a rope ferry across the Kaw. Sometimes we forded that stream before the bridge was built. On one occasion I passed through Lawrence just after the "Quantrill raid," when her business houses were smoking ruins and her sidewalks red with the blood of her best citizens. And yet some call Indians savages.[5]

5. Lawrence was burned by W. C. Quantrill and his gang on August 21, 1863, and 150 of the town's citizens were murdered, an act that blackened Quantrill's name forever in Kansas history.

From Lawrence to Leavenworth the road was through the Delaware Indian country, mostly timber land. Here I saw flocks of Carolina parakeet, a bird now almost extinct in the United States.[6] Arriving in Leavenworth, we camped in a wagon yard until our loads were sold and goods purchased for the return trip. On this, my first trip to market from Butler County, the proceeds of my three weeks' hunt were $400. The goods we purchased were to supply our own and the wants of the settlers in the county, and were almost exclusively staple and necessary articles such as flour, coffee, sugar, salt, pepper, soda, bacon, tobacco, powder, lead and caps, knives, axes, rope, nails, camping utensils, wagon covers, blankets, shoes, boots, clothing, calico, muslin, woollens, and such other goods as women and children wear, not forgetting ribbons to deck the hair of the fair maidens, whose cheeks were as rosy and smiles as sweet as they are today.

Flour was usually bought at Soden's Water Mill at Emporia,[7] and later at Cottonwood Falls.[8] I have paid Soden $8.60 per hundred by the wagon load for flour, and he at that time paying $3.00 per bushel for wheat. Those were war times and war prices. We managed to get along without pine lumber or much furniture, as the cost of transportation was too great. We built houses from the forest with our axes and made most of our own furniture, rude though it was.

On our return journey I was joined at Burlingame by my wife and infant son (the latter known to some who will read this by his pet name of "Bunnie"). They had been visiting with relatives at Burlingame while I was preparing a home on the border of the wilderness. In due time we arrived safely in Towanda, healthy, hearty, happy, and contented, and found the sparse settlement increased

6. By 1900, Carolina parakeets were said to be "exceedingly rare." The last recorded sighting was in the Florida Everglades in the early 1920s. AUSTIN, 147.

7. W. T. Soden was born in Ireland on November 22, 1835. In 1836 his family moved to America and lived in Clinton County, New York. They later moved to Iowa before settling in Kansas. In 1857, W. T. Soden purchased a sawmill seven miles west of Emporia, which he converted into a flour mill in August, 1858. It was the only flour mill south or west of Burlingame. In the spring of 1860, Soden sold the mill, moved into Emporia, and built the Emporia Water Mills. ANDREAS 1: 860.

8. Cottonwood Falls in Chase County, Kansas, was established in 1860. ANDREAS 2: 1357.

by the arrival of several settlers, among others that most excellent citizen and neighbor, Samuel Fulton and his family;[9] also Mrs. Lawton and her son Jack; and Sam Carter.

Along in October the Osage Indians came out on their annual fall hunt, following their great trail from the vicinity of Neodesha. This trail passed near my ranch on to the Little Arkansas five or six miles above its mouth and had been travelled for generations.[10] That same fall came the affiliated bands comprising the Wichita Indians. They were refugees from the south; had wintered along the border in eastern Kansas and nearly starved to death, and most of their horses had perished.

The Indians comprised in the general term of Wichitas were remnants of tribes affiliated together when first known to history, more than a century ago. They were the Wichitas, Wacos, Towakonis, and Kechis, who speak the Wichita language, and the Caddos, Ionis, and Nadarkos, who spoke the Caddo language. The Nadarkos are practically extinct.[11]

Each of these bands lived in separate villages and preserved their tribal identity. They had built their villages of grass houses on the Brazos River in Texas, and on the Washita River and its tributaries and other streams in the Indian Territory, and ranged in former times from Arkansas to the Wichita Mountains and from the Cimarron River to central Texas.

At the outbreak of the Civil War the Indians of the Wichita agency were living quietly and peaceably on the Washita River and other streams near old Fort Cobb, Indian Territory. The Indians of the plains and the civilized tribes of the territory were their friends. They were an agricultural people, had fields and gardens, an abundance of horses, and lived in a paradise of game—buffalo, elk,

9. Samuel Fulton arrived in Towanda in the spring of 1863 and built a log cabin one-half mile north of the present town. Mrs. Fulton organized and ran a subscription school. The Fultons stayed in Towanda for JRM, in a letter dated April 4, 1892, mentions meeting "Sam Fulton and his two daughters" when he went to Towanda to survey tornado damage in the spring of that year.

10. For a description of the Osage and other trails in Kansas see MEAD 1893a.

11. According to James Mooney, the Kechis, although affiliated to the Wichitas, spoke a cognate but different language. The Wichitas themselves are of Caddoan stock, closely related linguistically to the Pawnees. The Tawakonis and Wacos are Wichita sub-tribes. The Ionis or Nai'nais are mentioned as one of the 12 divisions of the Caddos along with the Anadarko (Nädäko). See MOONEY [1] and HODGE.

deer, antelope, and wild turkeys constituting their bill of fare, with corn, beans, melons, pumpkins, and wild fruits as side-dishes. Each year at the time of roasting ears, watermelons, and garden-truck, the Comanches came in from the plains and spent a season feasting, visiting, and having a good time generally—an agreeable change from their usual fare, which was buffalo meat straight.

When the Civil War came the Wichitas were loyal to the Union. To the east were the powerful civilized tribes, who were slaveholders; on the south, Texas. The Wichitas were driven out, together with many Shawnees, Delawares, Kickapoos, and other loyal Indians, leaving all behind except such articles as could be gathered for hasty flight. With their wives and little ones, they fled north across the pathless wilderness to Kansas and safety. They were pursued, and some of them killed, on the Salt Fork. A few had wagons, which were mostly broken or abandoned on the way. There were no roads or trails to follow. After many hardships the scattered bands collected in southern Kansas, on the border, destitute, hungry, among strangers. The Government afforded them scant relief. The first winter all of their horses starved to death, and many of their people died from want and sickness. In their distress they sought aid from the Osage Indians, who at that time owned nearly all of southern Kansas, including millions of buffalo, and secured their permission to move to the mouth of the Little Arkansas and subsist on the buffalo. So in the summer of 1863 they set out for their new home, afoot, hungry, almost naked, and established their temporary camp in the dense timber at the mouth of the Little River, just across from the present Murdock Avenue bridge, Wichita.

They managed without horses or guns to kill enough buffalo to eat and lay up a scant supply for winter. Some of the men went south to their old homes and gathered up what horses they could find. Others visited the Comanches, who gave them presents of many horses, a custom among the Indians to their less fortunate brothers. By spring the Wichitas were mostly mounted and able to take care of themselves. They could make their saddles and equipment, weapons and clothing, while the women were industriously at work planting gardens, which in time yielded abundantly. They were the first to demonstrate that the Arkansas Valley was the garden spot of the state.

The Wichita Indian grass lodge built on Mead Island in Wichita in June, 1927. In front are Mrs. Fern Mead and Suck-a, a Wichita woman who helped build the lodge. Mead Collection, Wichita.

All took a hand in building their very comfortable and peculiar grass houses. These were usually made of forked posts about five feet high, set in the ground at intervals in a circle which was twenty or twenty-five feet in diameter. Horizontal poles were then securely fastened to the top of the posts; then smooth poles, twenty or more feet long, were set upright in the ground outside the posts, converging, cone-shape, to a common center at the top; very small poles bound with withes crosswise, holding the whole structure securely together. The squaws weave the long, tough, reddish bunch-grass in and out in such an ingenious manner that each bunch of grass overlaps the bunch immediately below. When complete, it is a substantial structure, does not leak, and is warm. A low door opens to east and west; it is made of grass or skin.

Arranged round the inside are raised bunks for sleeping, and underneath there is storage room. In the center a fire, with an opening at the top for smoke. The inside and floor are sometimes plastered with gypsum, and for fifty feet on the outside the ground is kept smooth, hard, and clean. These houses are unique, comfortable, and unlike any others in America. I have seen those built twenty years and still in good condition.[12]

Not far from these houses were their gardens, surrounded by fences made of small poles set upright in the ground. There the Wichitas grew an abundance of native corn, pumpkins, melons, and Mexican beans. These grass houses were built in groups along the Little Arkansas River for a mile, on the east bank. The water of the river was sweet, clear, and pure; it was full of fish. There was plenty of timber and game was abundant.

When I first saw the Wichitas in 1863, many of the older women were artistically tattooed in pink and blue zigzag circles and lines according to ancient custom. Their village was known all over the plains as "the Wichita town." There were also considerable numbers of Shawnees and Delawares and Kickapoos camped down the Whitewater and Walnut Rivers, so that I had about me nearly two thousand Indians who came to my place to trade.

Occasionally I would load a wagon with goods and go to their camps on the Arkansas or other streams within a day's drive, frequently alone. When I arrived at an Indian camp, I would go to the chief and make some presents of tobacco, and "have a talk." He would then direct me to some lodge in the village, usually the best and occupied by some Indian and his family who would assist me in trading.

It was the custom of all traders in coming into an Indian camp to make some presents to the chief and his principal men, and also to supply the lodge in which he stopped with flour, sugar, and coffee for the family. They would furnish the meat and do the cooking. The Indians would carry the goods into one end of the lodge, which

12. Seventeen years after JRM's death his widow, Fern Mead Jordan arranged for a group of Wichita Indians to come up from Anadarko to build a grass lodge on Mead Island in the Little Arkansas River as a gift to the city of Wichita. The lodge stood intact for nearly a quarter of a century until destroyed by fire.

would be vacated and swept clean for that purpose. After the goods were all properly arranged and the price of the various articles agreed upon, either with the chief or someone he designated to stay with me and see that there was exact justice done by both Indians and trader, and to settle any possible differences that might arise, we would commence business. If it happened that the Indians had on hand a quantity of robes and furs, the trading would proceed very briskly, after satisfactory prices had been established for the goods I might have, and also for the robes and furs which they brought in to trade. From the price first agreed upon between us, there would be no deviation so long as that stock of goods lasted, which might be one or two days or a week.

Our staple articles of trade were flour, coffee, sugar, tobacco, Mackinac blankets (two and three point), bolts of imported save list strouding[13] and broadcloth costing from $2.50 to $5 a yard wholesale, calico, Chinese vermilion, knives, small axes, hair pipe (a bead two to six inches long and pearly white, made from the lip of a conch shell on the Atlantic coast),[14] Iroquois and abalone shells from the Pacific ocean, beads from Germany, and many minor articles of use, adornment or fancy.

After the trader was once in the Indian camp and established there by the consent of the chief, he and his property were absolutely safe, while a party coming in and attempting to trade without first making satisfactory arrangements with the chief would have a sorry experience. While I was in their camp the Indians would take my horses out on the range with their own ponies and herd them on the grass, and I would not see them again until ready to go home. During all my trading experience neither myself nor my property was ever molested while in an Indian camp. Sometimes I left a quantity of goods in an Indian's charge for him to trade on while I was gone after further supplies, and they were all accounted for on my return.

13. Strouding was woollen cloth green on one side and red on the other. It was manufactured for barter or sale in the North American Indian trade. It was probably named after the town of Stroud in Gloucestershire, England.

14. By the 1850s many traders were supplying the Plains Indians with dentalia ("Iroquois beads") and the long tubular shell beads, later made of bone, that were manufactured in New Jersey and known among traders as "hair pipe." EWERS.

On one occasion I rode down to a small camp of Kickapoo Indians near the forks of the Whitewater and Walnut. They had just returned from a hunt in the Indian Territory and showed me 400 deer skins they had taken on that hunt. Those Kickapoos were the most independent Indians I ever met. They were successful hunters, dead shots with the rifle, never wanted something for nothing, and invariably bought and paid for such things as they required.

Not all Indians knew the value of money. During the Civil War the Cheyennes captured a paymaster's train on the Platte, and in the plunder they found a chest of greenbacks, something new to them. As they were pretty, they took them along for the children to play with at home, and for cigarette papers. Before they were used up, Colonel Bent, a famous trader, happened in their camp, and gathered in the remainder for about the price of waste paper. This was the story told to "Dutch Bill" Greiffenstein, who unfortunately arrived in their camp too late to get his share. Our people along the Little river knew the value of a dollar in paper or gold.

Along later in my experience I sent wagon train loads of goods to the wild Indians on the prairies. They had no fixed place of abode, but roamed from place to place according to the season of the year, following the migrations of the buffalo to some extent. They usually wintered in the western part of the Indian Territory on the upper waters of the North Canadian, the Washita, and other streams of that country. There they were within reach of the buffalo on their winter range.

Once, while in a large Comanche camp, a war party returned from a raid into Texas. They gave us a graphic account of their fights with the Texans, the number of men they had lost, the number of Texans they had killed, and the amount of stock they had captured and brought back. To us they were perfectly friendly and believed that we belonged to another nation. We who lived in the north were called by them "cold white men," while the Texans were known as the "warm white men." They were constantly fighting the Texans, claiming that they had been driven out of Texas, which was their own country, by violence, and had received no compensation for their lands and had never made a treaty with the Texans, and were going to fight them as long as they had a man left.

Among other things, they told us that a small party of them were pursued on the prairie by a much superior force of Texas Rangers. Finding it impossible for them to reach the timber, one of the young men, willing to save his party at the expense of his life, called out to his companions to make their escape and tell his people what had become of him. He then turned and fought the Texans alone until he was shot to pieces. This occasioned such a delay that his companions made their escape. A white man who would perform such a deed would be immortalized for his bravery and fidelity to his comrades.

We frequently trusted some of the wild Indians that we became acquainted with for considerable amounts. They would tell us that the next spring, or the next fall, as the case might be, they would be at a certain place on some river, perhaps a hundred miles from where we were at the time, and that when we met them on our next trading expedition they would pay us, which they invariably did.

As an illustration of the honor among Indians, just at the close of the war a party of seven Indians and one white man came across the plains from the southern part of the Indian Territory to my ranch on the Whitewater. Their ponies were loaded with furs and skins to trade. During the war they had had no source of supplies and were therefore destitute of everything but bread and meat, which their country provided in abundance. I bought all they had with them, paying them in goods, which seemed so satisfactory to them that they proposed I should return with them, taking a stock of goods into their country.

I had never seen anything of them before and knew nothing of their country. During the war they had been fighting our people of the North and were considered our enemies. I therefore declined to make the trip with them. They then asked me to credit them with goods to the extent of three hundred dollars apiece, stating that they would return in the fall (this was in the spring of the year) and pay me, which I did. I saw or heard nothing from them during the summer, but one evening along about the first of November, they rode up to my ranch with their ponies loaded to pay their debts. One of their number had died in the meanwhile, and his friends had sent up three hundred dollars worth of stuff in payment. Those Indians had no object in making that long trip of two hundred and fifty miles, except to make good their pledge to me that they would come back and pay for the goods.

Chief Ten Bear of the Comanches. Courtesy Kansas State Historical Society, Topeka.

Once while in a Comanche camp about where Ft. Supply has since been built, having with me a number of teams and men, the Cheyenne tribe went on the war path owing to some difficulty up north on the old Santa Fe Trail. One band of Cheyennes was camped nearby. They sent a messenger over to the Comanche camp where we were, saying that they were going to take the scalps of the white men who were trading there. This was reported to our friend Chief Ten Bear, who was reclining on some robes in his lodge. He jumped up and ran out, calling his warriors to arms. In fifteen minutes two hundred warriors rode out to the ridge between the camps, drew up in line of battle in view of the Cheyenne camp, and sent a messenger down to tell them that if they wanted to take those white men's scalps, now was a good time to come and get them; that they had come out there to see about it.

The Cheyennes sent back word that they were only joking, that they just wanted to see if they could scare those white men. Shortly after that we started for home, and Ten Bear sent a guard of thirty warriors with us. They slept round our camp every night on their blankets with their weapons in their hands, holding the lariats of their horses, until we were past any danger. They did not ask any compensation, showing that when an Indian is a man's friend, he is a friend under all circumstances and, if necessary, will fight for him.

On another occasion, while hunting on the plains with two men and teams, we saw a party of Indians charging down on us at the top of their speed as though they intended to wipe us out in a moment. My men were greatly alarmed and thought their last hour had come. I told them to keep quiet as possibly I knew the Indians. They rode up to us at full speed with their weapons in their hands, but the instant he saw me, the leader of the party jumped off his horse, rushed up and threw his arms about me, hugging me as though I had been a long-lost brother.

When he turned and explained to the other Indians who I was, they all dismounted and crowded around, shaking hands and all talking at once, saying how glad they were to see me. The leader of the party was my old friend *Notta-tunka* or Big Mule.[15] From being

15. *Notta tunka* means "big ears," which means "mule." The name of the tribe is not recorded, however. MURDOCK.

half scared to death one moment, the next my men were perfectly at ease. Such incidents as these were the spice of life to those of us who ranged upon the plains and almost every day furnished some adventure of interest. After we had gotten out of one scrape we would laugh over it and wonder what would happen next. Sometimes these happenings did not end so pleasantly, but I was fortunate, and passed through them all unharmed, while some of my acquaintences never returned to tell their story.

The love I had of hunting and trading and wild life took me onto the plains and, incidentally, I found it a very profitable business, along with all our fun. We could make money rapidly and easily and at the same time have all the sport and adventure we wanted, which appeared to be our main object in life. Hunting of itself was very profitable. I thought nothing of getting $50 worth of skins in one night, and as my business grew I found it necessary to employ a considerable number of men to assist me about the ranch and in my expeditions on the plains, and in driving my teams back and forth to the Missouri River, which was at that time our only base of supplies.

Occasionally we took a trip to Philadelphia or New York to purchase goods in quantity. A frontier trader who had proven himself capable and reliable could command almost unlimited money or credit in any of the great cities. I once drove one wagon loaded with furs and robes from the White Water to Leavenworth, which sold for a sum equal to thirteen carloads of wheat, estimating the average price and capacity of cars for the past ten years. I have on numbers of occasions sold as much as $3,000 worth of goods in one day, and yet when I came on the plains I had nothing but a fine riding horse, a team, two rifles as good as could be made, plenty of good clothes, and provisions for six months, with a little money in my pocket. Within three years I made a visit back to my childhood home on the farm near Davenport, Iowa, and I had a nice wife and baby boy, $7,000 in the bank, $1,500 in my pocket, and did not owe a dollar in the world. I had made it all with my rifle and by trafficking on the plains. At the same time I had made many friends, established unlimited credit in commercial circles, and acquired an acquaintance with the Indians which was not only very pleasant, but was an important factor in connection with trade and in the protection of the frontier settlements of Kansas in our vicinity from the hostility of the wild tribes who ranged along the border.

Many of the friendships formed in those days, both with Indians and with whites, have continued down to the present time, but most of my associates have long since gone to the happy hunting ground of the unknown hereafter. Especially is this true of the Indians. I know of but one living Indian with whom I was associated in my early life on the plains some thirty years ago. That Indian was then a bright, active, intelligent young man. He is now Chief of the Caddos and weighs 250 pounds. His name is Tawakoni Jim and a more reliable or companionable associate I never met.[16]

On one occasion he and I, with a white man and an Indian boy, were returning with our teams from a trading expedition on the plains. On arriving at the Arkansas River we found it covered with a sheet of rotten ice from bank to bank, about one thousand feet in width. Although the ice was six or eight inches thick, it would not bear our teams. The country behind us was burned off clean, and we were out of provisions and compelled to cross or starve. So at daylight the next morning we took our axes, and taking off our boots, we worked all day in the ice and water, cutting a road through the ice and shoving the cakes under. When our feet and limbs got so cold working in the ice water that we could stand it no longer, we would stand on the ice and our bare feet would apparently get warm in a few minutes. We could see our feet bleeding where they were cut by the ice, but they had no more feeling than if they were sticks. My Indian friend Jim worked all that day in the water and ice, cheerful, always laughing and joking, and never made a complaint.

Just at evening we had made an open way across the river, through which we drove our teams. Ten minutes after we had passed, the ice moved down and closed up our passage. At that time the only human habitation on the east side of the river was a lone cabin occupied by a half breed Indian family. We drove over there and turned our animals loose and lay down in front of a big fire. The Indian woman soon brought us some dry clothing and fur-

16. The Tawakonis and Wacos speak a dialect of the Wichita language and are Caddoan tribes of the Wichita group. Tawakoni Jim was probably chief of the Tawakonis, a subdivision of the Caddo confederacy. BOLTON, 701.

nished me with a pair of trousers which would fit a man thrice my size. I was a slender youth, weighing about 130 pounds. She also made us a big pot of coffee with some bread and meat, and we soon made ourselves warm and comfortable. The next morning, feeling no worse for the excessive hardships of the previous day, we hitched up our teams and rolled out for home on the Whitewater.

CHAPTER 11

The Country of the Wild Horse

IN the Autumn of 1863, I outfitted from my trading post at Towanda a number of Butler County citizens and sent them out on hunting expeditions. I furnished them with arms, provisions, ammunition, and whatever else they lacked—which was nearly everything— and they paid me on their return out of furs and skins they secured on the trip. I also supplied their families during their absence with any provisions which they might need. The parties I equipped for wolf hunting mostly came back empty.

The buffalo did not winter on the unprotected treeless plains which extended further than our knowledge. Their trails led to the Southwest to some country unknown to us, and with the advent of Winter, they departed after the fashion of wild geese. The wolves, of course, went with them. As our hunters did not feel safe in venturing more than fifty miles West of the Arkansas into the apparently limitless, blizzard-swept, Indian haunted, inhospitable plains, they found nothing. I was impatient at their lack of success. My curiosity as to where the buffalo went was aroused and I began to have the hunting fever which usually came on after I had been home a month or two. I had unlimited confidence in my ability to find game and put to shame the fellows I had sent out.

My neighbor, Samuel Fulton, who still resides on his farm South of Towanda, was also anxious for a trip and proposed to furnish his excellent team of big horses, wagon, etc., if I would go and direct the hunt. So we employed Sam Carter, a very faithful, willing young man, and Fulton and I went as partners. We took feed for the horses, a gun apiece, I taking my inseparable companion—a heavy steel-barrelled rifle.[1] Fulton took bread and butter enough to last us a week or more, something I never did as I preferred warm bread and the oily fat from the back of buffalo, spread with marrow from the large bones, which is better than butter to my taste. And of course we took flour, coffee, sugar, and salt as part of our outfit.

We started out in January, 1864, following the Osage Trail to the Arkansas. Our first day's drive thence followed a hunter's trail to the Cowskin, where we turned Southwest across the smooth rolling treeless plains and made our second camp on the "Ne-ne-skaw" (good spring water)[2] below the fork. Continuing the same course over the same character of country, we camped at the Willow Grove on the Chikaskia River, where all knowledge of the country beyond ceased.

We started early next morning, still following the buffalo trails to the Southwest with some anxiety as to what this terra incognita might have in store for us. Prairie dogs, the only game we had seen so far, stood upon their mounds and gazed at us in evident surprise. The soil was red, and in spots bare of the usual buffalo grass, hinting at a possible "Great American Desert" somewhere beyond.

In the course of a day we reached the divide and in the far distance could see timber. Joyful sight! For where there was timber there was also shelter, fuel, and game, and food for man and beast—and possibly Indians, which we were anxious to avoid. That night we camped on a sandy creek with groves of timber in sight all along the horizon in front of us. In the morning we drove joyfully toward the largest body of timber across a wide alluvial valley, eaten off closely by buffalo, and soon we came near isolated groves of large trees like islands in an ocean, growing in groups of shifting sand hills which in some instances had buried tall trees to their topmost limbs.

While crossing this enchanted valley, a bunch of 15 or 20 ante-

1. This is probably a reference to JRM's single-shot breech-loading 45-90 Sharps, now owned by Mr. Mead's daughter, Ignace Mead Jones.

2. The North Fork and the South Fork of the Ninnescah meet a few miles northwest of Clearwater. In 1865, JRM built a trading post near present-day Clearwater.

lope came feeding along, passing directly in front of us. As they were within a couple of hundred yards I stepped in front of the team, took a rest on my knee, held to the top of their backs, and shot at the bunch. At the crack of my rifle two of them dropped, one shot through the shoulder, the other through the hips. The ball had passed through both animals and went singing on its way beyond. One could get upon its hind feet, the other upon its forefeet. They spun round in vain efforts to get away, but my knife soon ended their struggles, and we loaded our first game seen so far on the trip.

Soon we crossed two large dry sand creeks with a few immense dead cottonwood trees still standing or lying prostrate, rotten and half buried in the sand. In every standing tree was an eagle's nest, but not a living tree or bush grew along these creeks. What calamity had overtaken those large trees we could not discover.

On arriving at the large body of timber, we found that we were at the junction of two considerable rivers.[3] The first one apparently rising in some broken mountainous country to the Northwest, while a heavily timbered creek between the rivers emptied at their junction. A few buffalo could be seen scattered about over the country, evidently wintering there.

We halted on a high bank while I rode across into the timber to select a suitable camping ground. Dismounting with the bridle on my arm, I had gone but a few steps in the brush when I saw a dozen fine deer looking at me not a hundred feet distant. I raised my rifle, fully expecting to kill two or three of them, as they were so close together. Just as I pulled the trigger, my pony jerked my arm and the bullet flew wide of the mark. We had hardly driven across the river and unhitched when four big gray wolves came out on the high bank about a hundred yards distant and leisurely inspected camp, curious to know what this strange intrusion into their country meant, and they found out in a day or two. We did not wish to disturb them.

Building a big fire, we soon had our antelope roasting, broiling, and frying, and to which we did ample justice, not forgetting the usual quart of coffee apiece. In those days Fulton had a very healthy appetite and Carter and I considered ourselves full hands at

3. "I now know that point to be at the junction of the Medicine Lodge and the Salt Fork in Indian Territory."—JRM.

the "grub pile," at least. Dinner finished, the next thing in order was to explore our surroundings to see if any Indians were in the country and to look for signs of game. While Fulton and Carter arranged camp, I rode up the timbered Creek and in the big grass and brush soon saw where large bands of horses had sought shelter and feed during storms. I naturally supposed we were near some Indian camp, but on looking for Indian signs I found that not a bush or twig had been cut nor a campfire made on the creek within two years. I then realized that we were in the country of the wild horse.

Birds new to us were seen, among others the scissors-bird with two such absurdly long tail feathers that they could hardly fly in a moderate wind. Eagles sat in the trees carefully watching us, while in the marshy regions of the river were black and white plover. Red birds hopped about in the thickets. Geese were feeding in a marsh close by, and droves of glossy bronze turkeys stretched their necks and looked at me curiously as I rode by. Raccoons travelled about in the day time, while out on the prairie the buffalo were feeding.

I returned to camp satisfied that we had found the winter home of the game we were in search of—a country unknown to white hunters and seldom occupied by Indians. Riding a short distance below camp to the junction of the rivers, I shot two big buffalo bulls and, splitting them open to attract the wolves, left them as they lay, taking only that choicest bit of all, the tongues. I scattered about a few baits for the benefit of the coyotes that are always on hand when an animal has been killed.

That night we sat round our camp fire well-pleased with the prospect: plenty of game, no Indians, no hunters to bother us, and a new and unknown country to explore. Even the rivers we had discovered had no place on the map. None of us smoked—the fire did enough of that—nor drank, except coffee. We were happy and content. Fulton and Carter were then in the prime of life, full of energy and fire, and as pleasant, genial companions as could be wished.

In the morning after breakfast I rode down to see how my two bulls were getting along and to my astonishment found them gone. Where they had been were two bunches of chewed grass about the size of a bushel basket. On looking around I saw a head some distance off, but all else—legs, hide, bones—and all, were gone. A short distance away were sand hills and on these were gangs of gray wolves lying down enjoying the warm morning sun. My two bulls were inside them; they had good appetites as well as we. The half dozen coyotes my bait had killed were torn to pieces and eaten by eagles and ravens. On riding toward the gray wolves, they lazily trotted off South on the prairie. I counted forty in one string. That was an interesting sight under any circumstances, but especially so as I knew their pelts would all be in our possession within two or three days.

I immediately returned to camp and we soon arranged our plan of action. Fulton went up the creek a couple of miles and killed three bulls. Carter went up the river and killed two, while I went down the river two or three miles and out on the bare prairie South of the river shot five buffalo. Returning to camp we prepared our "medicine," using eight dram bottles of strychnine, which should make 240 baits. A bait for wolves, such as we used, is a small piece of meat—two or three ounces—on which is rubbed one thirtieth of a dram of strychnine. At dusk each man went to his carcasses. The ravens would pick them up if put out before they had gone to roost, and the coyotes that came first would get them all if too easily found. So we hid them about in various places, some in and some under the dead buffalo in order that the big grays might have a show when they came round later.

That night we went to bed with great anticipations which were fully realized on the morrow. By daylight each man was on the way to his carcasses, leaving the camp to take care of itself. On reaching my baits, I saw dead wolves scattered over the prairie in all directions. Tying my pony to a buffalo head, I rapidly stripped off the hides. While at work, the coyotes, with their usual curiosity, came trotting up close. I shot five of them as I worked, scarcely delaying me five minutes. Towards noon I packed on my pony all the skins he could carry and led him to camp. No sign of Fulton or Carter, which was good evidence that they too were busy. I ate a hasty dinner and went back to "wolfing," finishing with another pony load.

I hunted up, skinned, and packed to camp that day 34 wolves, while Fulton and Carter came in with enough to make our number 72 for one day's killing. Next in order was to dry our skins, which was done by pegging them out on the ground, stretching them as tight as a drum. As each skin required 24 pegs there were from this day's work 1,728 pegs to be made and driven through an equal number of holes in the edge of the skins. We put our baits out and killed 20 or 30 more that night.

A short distance down the river on the South side was a plain five or six miles across, covered with salt and looking like a lake of frozen ice or snow. I ignorantly supposed that this came from the hills to the South, washed down by some creek. So the next day I determined to explore it and find where the salt came from. My rifle was so heavy for a long day's ride that I foolishly left it at the camp. I was not hunting for game that day, but for a hill of rock salt.

I rode South towards a creek that was coming out of the hills six or eight miles distant, when out of a ravine sprang a dozen wild horses that gazed at me a few moments before galloping off to the divide. They continued running until out of sight. Finding no salt coming from that direction, I turned East and rode rapidly along over a smooth prairie South of the salt plain. A violent wind was blowing and filling the air with dust.

Suddenly I reined in my pony, for lying stretched out eight or ten feet long, the bushy end of his tail moving to and fro, lay an enormous mountain lion. His tawny hide was almost the exact color of the dry buffalo grass. He was within a hundred feet and refused to move. I asked him what he was doing there and why he did not go on about his business, but he seemed sulky and refused to talk. So I rode round him, just out of reach of his possible spring. His round eyes and huge head followed me intently and watched every movement. Alas, my rifle was at camp, and I rode on, leaving him to his meditations and to further feasts on wild horses, buffalo, calves, and deer.[4]

Getting round to the East side of the plain and finding no salt stream running into it, I concluded to ride directly across towards camp. The salt was blowing like a snowstorm, filling my eyes and mouth. When partly across I saw what appeared to be three Indians riding at a tremendous pace directly across my course to intercept me. As we were trespassers in an unknown Indian country and I had noticed a lodge pole trail that morning, I felt quite uncomfortable. As the supposed horsemen passed close in front of me, I

---

4. "In 1865, I saw a mountain lion on the White Water in Butler County where Towanda now stands. It came out of the tall grass, close to where my children were playing in the road, and leisurely bounded along to the bluff in the east."—JRM (MEAD 1898c).

saw they were three ravens flying low with the wind. Seen through the storm of blowing salt, the mirage magnified them into phantom horsemen.

The next day I rode ten miles down the river to some timbered hills on the North side. On the South side of the river was a high bluff rising nearly perpendicular several hundred feet above the river, and on the almost inaccessible front of the bluff were some little grassy benches on which were several buffalo bulls feeding like flies on the side of a wall. How it was possible for them to get there, I could not see. On the high narrow top of the hill, commanding a view for miles in every direction, was a herd of elk lying asleep in the warm sun. I did not care for them, but rode on into the big timber where I saw droves of big glossy turkeys as tame as though raised in a barn-yard. I did not disturb them, and rode back to the foot of the salt plain, where I shot two bulls on a sand bar in the river for wolf bait. I did not care to destroy animal life wantonly for the sake of killing. While I was away from camp, nearly all the time hunting and exploring, my companions were equally as busy and as usefully employed at camp attending to the skins we had taken.

The next day we moved camp down to the mouth of the big sand creek near two bulls I had killed. At dusk Fulton and I went to put out baits, wading through the loose sand. On approaching the bulls there was such a gang of gray wolves at work that we could not see the carcasses until the wolves had trotted off. One big fellow, that was all inside except his tail, was too busy to notice us. As I stepped close to him he backed out, pulling at some choice bit he had hold of, and backed almost against me. With one stroke of my hunting knife I split him nearly in two lengthwise. He whirled, snapped at his assailant, ran a short distance and fell dead. We put out our baits and in the morning found fifty gray wolves lying about, some of them nearly buried by the drifting sand.

At the end of ten days' hunting we found that the grain for our horses was about gone. Big American horses could not live on the range like Texas or Indian horses and oxen. We did not care to tempt fortune further. We had 302 wolves, some buffalo, and other skins—all our team could conveniently haul—so we started for Towanda, taking a bee-line across the country, not following the somewhat circuitous route by which we had come. Driving one day in a furious snowstorm, keeping our course only by that instinct acquired by Indians and plainsmen, we struck the Arkansas just below the junction of the Big and Little Arkansas where the city of Wichita now stands. We reached home the next day, safe and sound. Our furs reached market at a time of exceptionally high prices, and we realized $70 for each day spent on the hunting ground.

I have related principally my own experiences while on this hunt. Those of my companions were equally as interesting. In a short time Fulton made up a party and returned to the hunting ground, and came to grief.

CHAPTER 12

Indians, Frontiersmen, and the Treaty of the Little Arkansas

THINKING to duplicate our hunt on their own hook, Samuel Fulton and Sam Carter outfitted and started back to the happy hunting ground as soon as possible. In due time they reached it and camped in the same place, expecting to repeat the wonderful success we had made a short time previous. As a precaution they took most of their provisions and part of their ammunition and hid it under some brush not far from their camp.

Early next morning a large party of Comanche Indians made their appearance and ordered them to cook breakfast. Under the circumstances they could not refuse. They kept on cooking, and the Indians continued to eat, and more Indians came, until they had eaten all there was in the camp. When Fulton and Carter told the Indians they had nothing more to cook, the Indians replied that they had better go and bring in the stuff which they had hidden in the brush pile last night. The two men tried to convince the Indians that they had nothing more, that they had cooked up everything. But some of the Indians told them to come along with them and they could show them that some provisions were hidden in the brush.

So the Indians brought the remainder of their grub back to camp and kept Fulton and Carter cooking until they had eaten what they could. Then, loading the remainder on their ponies and bidding them good morning—mentioning that they would be glad to see them again whenever they had plenty of provisions—the Indians went on their way. The two hunters were so thoroughly scared that they hitched their teams up and made a bee-line for home without securing a single pelt. They concluded that they were not born under a lucky star and would wait until I had time to go along to keep them out of trouble.

In the summer of 1865 there came to my ranch on the White-water two Indians, one of them Satanta, the noted Chief of the Kiowa tribe, at that time the most dreaded warrior on the plains.[1] Among other things at the ranch I had the Indian Agency. Major Milo Gookins, an old-fashioned gentleman from Indiana, was in charge of this, sent out by the Government in 1864 to look after the numerous Indians in this part of the country. He knew nothing about Indians and had at first nothing to aid them, and the Indians nearly worried him to death. I helped him out considerably, as I had abundant supplies and much-needed experience.

Satanta had a record of forty white men he had killed. One of them was George Peacock, whom Satanta killed at Allison's Ranch, along with Peacock's clerk and Mexican herder, on September 9, 1860. The "ranch," or Trading Station, had been built by Allison of Independence, Missouri, in 1857. It was situated on the Santa Fe Trail about 100 yards from the crossing of Walnut Creek, on the east side, and on the north side of the road. Allison had died suddenly of heart failure at Independence, and Peacock rented the ranch. Peacock was killed for personal reasons only. Among other things, Satanta came to Peacock and asked for a letter of introduction stating that he was a Chief of importance, in order that he might be treated civilly and entertained when he came to the camps of freighters, or others travelling the trail, as was customary on the plains.

Peacock wrote a letter as follows: "The bearer of this, Satanta, is

1. Set-t'ain'te, or White Bear, was born about 1830 and rose to occupy the second-highest place among Kiowa leaders. Sometimes known as "The Orator of the Plains," he had unquestioned courage and ability. His boldness and skill, while admired by many whites, often got him in trouble as the U.S. Government extended its military power, and as settlers and broken promises swallowed up more and more of the free range-lands. On October 11, 1878, he committed suicide in the prison at Huntsville, Texas. After years of petitioning by relatives, Satanta's remains were taken to Oklahoma in 1963, and he was reburied at Fort Sill. MAYHALL.

Satanta (White Bear), war chief of the Kiowas. From an original photo-graph by Will Soule in the Mead Collection, Wichita.

the dirtiest, laziest, louseyest vagabond on the plains; if he comes to your camp, kick him out." The next train that came along Satanta presented his letter of introduction, and to his surprise he met with derision, contempt, and abuse. It occurred to Satanta, who was a very civil, decent, and proud-spirited Indian (at least I always found him so), that there was something wrong with his credentials. So he went to Mathewson's ranch on Cow Creek to see William Mathewson, the original "Buffalo Bill." Mathewson read the letter to Satanta, who swore vengeance. Mathewson sent word to Peacock as to what he might expect, but he laughed at it.

The killing was adroitly planned. Peacock had a tall lookout built on top of his trading house. Satanta, with some of his men, came to the store and told Peacock that there was a lot of soldiers coming. Peacock climbed to the top of his lookout to see, and Satanta shot him. If Peacock had treated the Indians decently, probably he would not have been disturbed.[2]

Satanta was a perfect specimen of manhood, both mentally and physically. His brawny breast was covered with scars, mementos of many a battle and adventure. With him came "Heap of Bears," a noted Chief and medicine man of the Arapahoes. Each of these men were leaders of their tribe, then at war with the whites. They came to my ranch alone from their distant camps on the plains, perfectly unconcerned as to their own safety, to hold council with the Government Agent and signify their desire to make a treaty of peace.

I called these chiefs' attention to the fact that there was a squad of soldiers stationed about an hour's ride distant and that they were on the watch for wild Indians. I intimated that the soldiers might get after them. Satanta laughed and said he was not afraid of soldiers; that he had had plenty of fights with them on the plains.

The two chiefs remained several days and, as they did not appreciate white man's food, I killed a beef for their entertainment. They found this a very satisfactory change, and cooked it after their own fashion, roasting it before a fire. One peculiar custom I noticed was in their method of smoking. It seemed to be a religious observance, as they first took off their moccasins, went out of the house, and the first whiff of smoke they blew towards the sky as an offering to the Great Spirit.

This battle-scarred warrior, Satanta, would take my little baby boy, Bunnie, on his knee and talk and play with him as I presume he

2. After Peacock's death this trading post was operated by Charley Rath. Rath had been a teamster at Fort Riley in 1858. Later he hauled wood for Theodore Weichselbaum at Fort Dodge. Weichselbaum described Rath as "a very nice fellow [who] went later to New Mexico and freighted down about Las Vegas." WEICHSELBAUM, 570.

Heap of Bears, chief and medicine man of the Arapahoes. Courtesy Kansas State Historical Society, Topeka.

did with his own little children at his distant prairie home, showing that at least he had one tender spot in his heart that was not calloused by a long life of war, rapine, and murder on the plains.

Their trip resulted in the Treaties of the Little Arkansas and Medicine Lodge, by which peace was restored to the plains for the time being.[3] I was present at the Treaty of the Little Arkansas and, as the agent was sick, I represented the Wichita Indians on that occasion. The treaty was signed on the east bank of the Little Arkansas, about six miles above its mouth, in the middle of October, 1865.[4] The Commissioners on the part of the United States were William S. Harney,[5] Kit Carson,[6] John B. Sanborn,[7] William W. Bent,[8] Jesse H. Leavenworth,[9] Thomas Murphy,[10] and James Steel.[11] In addition to

3. Jesse Leavenworth was the moving force behind the treaty of the Little Arkansas, of which one purpose was to work out a means of keeping the Indians and white settlers apart. MINER, 20.

4. Treaties were made with the Cheyennes and Arapahoes on October 14; with the Apaches, Cheyennes, and Arapahoes, on October 17; and with the Kiowas and Comanches on October 18. See "Indian Treaties and Councils Affecting Kansas," *KSHC* 16 (1923–25): 746–69, and KAPPLER, 887–90.

5. William Selby Harney (1800–1889) was born in Tennessee and spent his life in the U.S. Army. He saw active service in the Mexican War, served in Kansas in 1857 and 1858, commanded the Department of Oregon from the autumn of 1858 to 1860, and was then given command of the Department of the West. It is said that his temperament was revealed in a large vocabulary of expletives upon which he drew liberally at the slightest provocation. *KSHC* 12:306.

6. Christopher ("Kit") Carson's first notice in the press appeared in the *Missouri Intelligencer* of Franklin, Missouri, on October 6, 1826. At the age of "about sixteen" he had run away from a saddler to whom he had been apprenticed, and the notice was designed to secure his return. But Carson had joined a wagon train and made his way to Santa Fe, New Mexico. For some years he was employed by William Bent. Between 1842 and 1848, Carson was a guide for J. C. Frémont. In 1848 he entered service with the Indian Department. During the Civil War he rose to the rank of brigadier general, by which time many of his earlier exploits had entered the mythology of the West. He died on May 23, 1868, at Fort Lyon, Colorado. GRINNELL [1], 28–91.

7. John B. Sanborn was a brevet major general commanding the Upper Arkansas District.

8. See n. 25, Chap. 1.

9. Jesse H. Leavenworth was the son of Gen. Henry H. Leavenworth, the man who in the spring of 1827 established Fort Leavenworth. Jesse graduated from West Point in 1830. He served in the Second and Fourth Infantries until 1836, at which time he took up civil engineering. In 1862 he was in command of a cavalry regiment known as the Rocky Mountain Rangers at Fort Lyon, Colorado. Later he was appointed agent for the Kiowas and Comanches in Indian Territory. Convinced that peace could be established and maintained between whites and Indians, he was active in arranging the Treaty of the Little Arkansas. MAYHALL, 222, 237, and 243.

10. Thomas Murphy was superintendent of Indian affairs.

11. Commissioner Steel is not to be confused with the James Steele who was later part of Wichita's early history.

Satanta and Heap of Bears, the Indians were represented by Moke-ta-ve-to (Black Kettle),[12] Oh-to-ah-ne-so-to-wheo (Seven Bulls),[13] Oh-has-tee (Little Raven),[14] Oh-hah-mah-hah (Storm), and other chiefs and head men on the part of the Indians.

There were present at that treaty about three thousand Indians camped along the river on either side, as did the one or two companies of soldiers who were present. The Wichita, Waco, Caddo, Ioni, Tawakoni, Kechi, and other Indians, some 1500 in number, were living here at the time and were scattered along down the river to the junction where Wichita now stands. They had cultivated extensive gardens and had scaffolds covered with sliced pumpkins, beans, and corn drying for winter use, with plenty of melons in their gardens, which were a feast to visiting brethren.

Kit Carson came down the Arkansas River from New Mexico with an officer's ambulance and army wagons, with teamsters, cook, and an escort of six soldiers, and was well-equipped with tents, provisions, etc. Colonel Bent, the noted Cheyenne trader, came down from his fort on the big river up towards the mountains. General Harney and Kit Carson were the most noted persons present. The former, a noted Indian figher and athlete, was six feet four in his moccasins, his luxuriant hair as white as snow. He was a famous story-teller. Kit Carson was his opposite in everything but fighting qualities. I found him to be quite a different man from what he is depicted in dime novels. He was short-legged, standing I should think about five feet five or six, stoutly built, with short arms, a round body, ruddy face, and red eyes with rays running from the pupils like the spokes in a wheel. His silky, flaxen hair reached almost to his shoulders. He was a man of fierce, determined countenance. With a kind, reticent, and unassuming disposition, he combined the courage and tenacity of a bulldog. He had nothing to say about himself, though occasionally he might be

12. Black Kettle, Cheyenne chief and famous warrior, brother of Gentle Horse, was killed three years later on November 27, 1868, when Custer, acting on Sheridan's orders, attacked Black Kettle's village on the Washita. MOONEY [2].
13. Seven Bulls was a Cheyenne chief.
14. Little Raven was an Arapaho chief who felt that the best chance for his people lay in peaceful relations with the U.S. Government. He represented his people at the signing of several treaties and consistently urged them to adhere to the terms of those treaties. He died at Cantonment, Indian Territory, in the winter of 1889. HODGE 1:770–71.

drawn out by some question. He was bluff, but very gentlemanly in his conversation and manner, with nothing of the border bravado about him. His prominent characteristics seemed to be utter fearlessness, infallible judgement, and instant decision and action.

Carson and Bent were much together. Colonel Bent had a fort on the upper Arkansas which the Government afterwards bought and converted into Fort Lyon. Bent was quite a noted man with a wonderful history acquired during a lifetime spent as a trader with the Indians, among whom he married and raised a family which he educated in St. Louis. He was almost as dark as an Indian, with piercing black eyes and a very prominent Roman nose. He personally knew nearly every Indian from the Rocky Mountains to the settlements of Kansas. He and Kit Carson had more influence with the Indians than any other two men of their time. Largely through their efforts and influence the treaty terminated to the satisfaction of both the government and the Indians.

All kinds of rumors were floating about during the progress of the treaty and there was considerable uncertainty and anxiety as to its success. The Indians were friendly, but very independent and indifferent, and reluctant to relinquish their rights to all of their country north of the Arkansas, and much of that to the southwest. They justified their depredations and cruelties by the wanton slaughter of their women and children by white men at Sand Creek a year before.[15]

While the treaty was in progress a rumor came that a party of Indians coming down from the north to attend the treaty had been attacked by soldiers on the Santa Fe Trail, and thirteen of them killed. At once the camp was in an uproar. A runner came into the tent where I was sitting with Carson and Charley Rath, and told of the rumor. Carson instantly said, emphatically, "I don't believe a word of it. Those Indians could not possibly have been there at that

15. The Sand Creek Massacre occurred in the autumn of 1864 when the Colorado Volunteers, led by Col. J. M. Chivington, attacked Black Kettle's village of Cheyennes near Fort Lyon, Colorado. Black Kettle had made peace with the government, and his people had kept it. As a symbol of this peace, Black Kettle flew the American flag over his village. Chivington and his volunteers launched a surprise attack and killed 69 Indians, many of them women and children, some of whom were scalped and otherwise mutilated by the whites (MAYHALL, 229–30). According to H. C. Miner, Chivington and his militia killed 450 men, women, and children on this occasion (MINER, 20).

time." Turning to me he said, "But if the rumor is true, the treaty is gone to hell. I had six soldiers coming down, and would need a hundred going back."

Carson and I slept in the same bunk and occasionally took a nip from the same bottle, though neither of us drank habitually. He seemed to be awake at all times of the night; if a horse got loose or anything occurred during the night he seemed to know all about it as though he had been standing guard. I found him one of the most intelligent and pleasant companions I had ever met on the plains.

I asked him about some of his adventures of former years, of which I had read in the papers. He replied, "Some of these newspaper fellows know a damn sight more about my affairs than I do." The origin of one story he told as follows: "When I was a young man I was going out to Santa Fe with a pack-train of mules. We camped at Pawnee Rock and were all asleep in our blankets in the grass when a party of Indians rode over us in the dark, yelling to stampede our stock. I jumped up and fired my rifle in the direction they had gone and shot one of my best mules through the heart."

About rattlesnake bites on man or animals, he said: "I cut the bite open and flash powder in it three times, and it is all right. One of my men was once bitten on the hand by a big rattler. I cut it open, flashed powder in it three times, and that afternoon he killed and scalped two Injuns."

Among other noted hunters and frontiersmen whom I knew was William Mathewson, known on the plains as Buffalo Bill. He had a ranch on Walnut Creek, on the old Santa Fe Trail, and also at the crossing of Cow Creek. He was a noted hunter and Indian trader, a man of great influence among the Indians of the plains, and was also a Government scout during part of his career. His ranch was the headquarters for army officers and all the noted characters who passed back and forth on the Santa Fe Trail. Among others, Generals Sherman and Hancock were his frequent guests, as was Henry Stanley who later acquired fame in Africa. He was sent onto the plains by the *New York Herald* as their correspondent. Stanley was then an unknown young man. He spent a month or two at Mathewson's ranch, and the interesting letters which he wrote back were largely based on information given him by Mrs. Mathewson, a most noble and energetic lady, who was as well versed in the affairs of the plains as was her distinguished husband.

William Mathewson, the original Buffalo Bill. Mead Collection, Wichita.

Elizabeth ("Lizzie") Inman Mathewson. Mead Collection, Wichita.

Mathewson was the hero of many a hard-fought battle and hand-to-hand encounter with hostile Indians, in which they suffered heavy losses, while he escaped unharmed. They finally came to regard him with superstitious dread, and at last the chiefs made a personal treaty with him by which, in consideration of his never fighting them or leading soldiers against them, he might travel at all times over the plains and to any of their camps in time of war or peace in perfect safety.[16]

The first years of my life on the plains were spent in a country almost unknown excepting to Indians and buffalo, and distant from any line of travel. It was seldom that I was brought into much contact with white men, and Indians were avoided as much as possible. The opportunities for notoriety and fame and renown which sometimes accompany life on the plains were entirely wanting, while other men, engaged in the same business, located for instance on the great Santa Fe Trail, were in constant association with the military department of the Government, as well as the great commerce of the plains, and also with the wild Indians. In the business in which I was engaged it would have been foolishness to have attempted to fight the Indians where it was possible to avoid it. Consequently, I have not had as many adventures with Indians nor as many scalps hanging from my lodge pole as Mathewson and some other frontiersmen have.

16. William Mathewson was the original Buffalo Bill. The nickname was bestowed on him by Kansas settlers during the severe winter of 1860–61 when he supplied all who came to him with fresh buffalo meat. He married Elizabeth Inman of Yorkshire in 1864. The Mathewsons and the Meads were close friends, and when JRM's wife, Agnes, died, Elizabeth Mathewson took care of the three Mead children, "Bunnie," Elizabeth Agnes, and Mary Elenora. Of William Mathewson, V. P. Mooney wrote that he was "a man of splendid physique, with a heart of like proportion, a good comrade; quiet, modest, unobtrusive, but the master of all he undertook, all under him obeying his nod, wave of hand, or quiet command without a murmur; beloved by all with whom he came in contact. A typical man of a typical country, he passed away in the city of Wichita in March, 1916" (MOONEY, V. P., 97).

CHAPTER 13

With the Indians on the Plains

My acquaintance and experience with the Pawnee Indians extended from 1859 to 1867, and that acquaintance was confined to one phase of their tribal character—that of relieving distant tribes and peoples of their surplus horses. They were expert horsemen and had long been noted as inveterate marauders, especially given to horse-stealing.

Next to their semi-annual buffalo hunts, on which, together with some agriculture, they relied to obtain their supply of food, clothing, and camp equipage, the quest for horses was their chief and most important industry. It was possible for a young man with nothing to secure horses enough on one expedition to set up housekeeping and become a man of consequence. The successful return of a raiding party was the occasion of feasting, dancing, and joy in the camp of the returning party, similar to the return of a victorious war party. In fact, the danger and honor were about as great in one as in the other. Then again, there might be occasions for mourning when the remnants of a party after weeks or months of absence, returned afoot, hungry, almost naked, to tell a tale of surprise, slaughter, and woe.

These raiding parties of Pawnees were the special objects of hatred of all the tribes of the plains, both north and south, who fought and, if possible, killed them, wherever found, and faithfully aided each other in their crusade of extermination against the Pawnees, whom they called "prowling cowards." But they often found to their sorrow that there were no more skillful or brave warriors on the plains than the hated Pawnees.

The Pawnees invariably went on these expeditions afoot, in parties, as I observed them, of two to thirty-five, composed mostly of young men. With a large party there would be an experienced middle-aged chief in command, whose orders were implicitly obeyed. They went lightly armed, each with a very serviceable bow and quiver of arrows and a knife. A few carried a light rifle. Each Indian carried, tucked under his belt, from four to six extra pairs of new moccasins, and one or more lariats. Each man also had a pack weighing twenty pounds or more, containing dried meat, both fat and lean, some pieces and straps of tanned skins to repair their moccasins and clothing, and also useful for bridles. A strip of tanned hide looped around the lower jaw of a horse was bridle enough on the plains. The above-mentioned articles, with a pipe and tobacco, an occasional light squaw axe, and a few trifles, comprised all that was necessary for a thousand mile journey.

Wolf and Spillman Creeks were on the road of war used by the Pawnees from the Platte River region. They knew the country perfectly, as they formerly occupied it and still claimed it, so they told me. These Pawnees had a regular route of travel, coming into the state near the north-east corner of Jewell County, south across Mitchell and Lincoln counties, across the northwest corner of Ellsworth County, into Barton County and the big bend of the Arkansas, and from there wherever Indian camps could be found, travelling by night when near other Indians.

These excursions combined the pleasure of a picnic with the excitement and joy of a hunting or war party. The country traversed, from the Solomon to the Smoky Hill inclusive, was the most beautiful and interesting of all the plains with its rolling hills, timbered streams, pure water, sandstone cliffs, and all the country covered with a coat of soft buffalo grass, over which ranged unnumbered buffalo, elk, antelope, and deer, while turkeys and all small game were everywhere in evidence, so that it was an easy matter through all of Kansas and the territory south to kill an abundance of game for each day's needs, be the party large or small; and a fire to cook it could be easily made from the friction of two cedar sticks by those

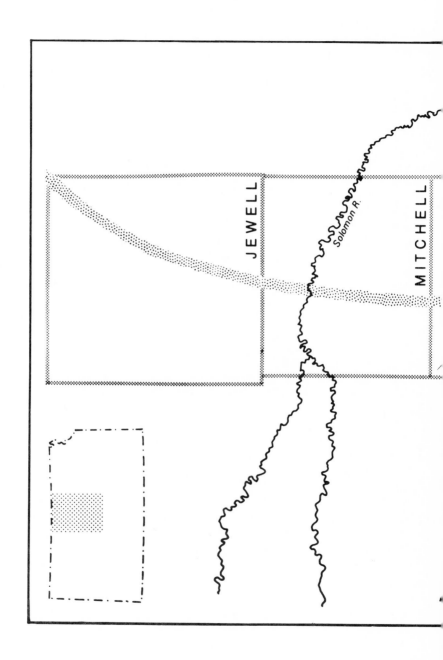

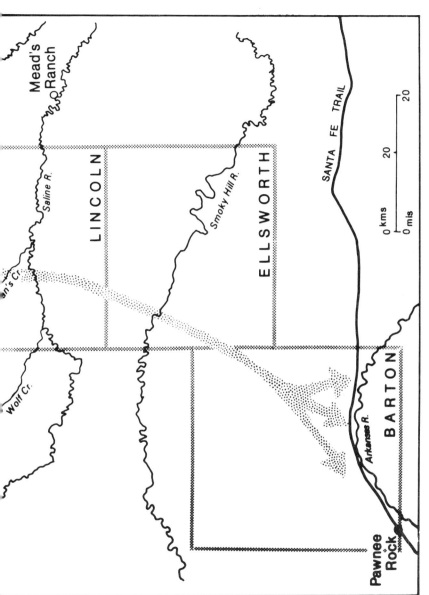

6. *The Pawnee Trail from Nebraska to the Arkansas River*

who knew how. The air was so clear and pure that at night the planet Venus cast a distinct shadow.[1] This country was indeed the paradise terrestrial for the roving Indian and the hunter and adventurer such as I.

During my experience on the Saline from 1859 to 1863, Spillman's Creek was one of my principal camping and hunting grounds on account of the great abundance of game and its convenient location. We soon discovered that we were directly on the route of the Pawnee and other Indians, as well of their pursuing enemies. Frequently the writer and his men, who had gone on the plains for the love of sport, adventure, and danger, found considerably more of each than was agreeable from contact with the Pawnee, Cheyenne, and Sioux, as well as wild animals.

One of our favorite camping places was on the east branch of Spillman's Creek upon, as we supposed, a very secluded spot. Here we were twice visited by raiding parties of Pawnees on their way home. The place can be easily located, as a petrified log two feet in diameter and fifteen feet long was exposed on the side of a bank within 100 yards of camp.

The first party came straggling in on foot. They were gaunt, lean, and almost naked. For a party of a dozen they had no weapons but two bows. They were a very dejected looking party. They had found a camp of Comanches somewhere south and were about to make a round-up of horses when they were discovered, pursued, and some of them killed. They had thrown away weapons, blankets, everything to escape. Whenever the Cheyennes or Comanches discovered that a bunch of their horses were stolen, they would start in hot pursuit, like a swarm of angry hornets.

The Pawnees then scattered and later met at a pre-arranged place. One of them was shot through the thigh with an arrow, but he hobbled along with the rest. We had the quarters of several buffalo lying on the grass at camp, which we gave to the Indians. They cut the meat from the bones, cut it into little squares, and borrowing some large kettles from us, they first filled them with meat, then with water, and set them on the fire. When the kettles came to a boil, foamed, and ran over, their contents were consid-

---

1. I am grateful to the astronomer Patrick Moore for confirming in a personal communication that during a near approach to Earth the planet Venus will indeed cast a shadow.

ered done and they were emptied out on the buffalo grass, the Indians sitting around in a circle until all was devoured, when the process was repeated. When they could not possibly eat any more, they lay down on the grass and slept for a couple of hours, then resumed their journey to the north-east.

The second visit was in May 1861. We were sitting quietly in camp one morning when we were surprised to see some mounted Indians who had almost got into our camp before we discovered them, or they us. They immediately bunched up their horses and prepared for defence, not knowing what they had run into. Then, seeing it was only the camp of some white hunters, they sent a couple of their party to us, asking if they could also camp there, to which we consented. They were a jolly, good-natured crowd.

Two or three buffalo cows which I had killed the day before were lying on the side of the hill and, as the weather was very warm, they were swollen up as tight as drums, for we had not skinned them. The Pawnees asked for these buffalo to eat. They went and cut them open, got what meat they wanted, which was badly tainted, removed some of the small intestines, and brought everything into camp and proceeded to feast. They put the meat into kettles which they borrowed from us and boiled everything up. After eating they said it was "heap good." The small intestines they braided into mats and roasted before the fire and ate them, including their contents. These also they pronounced "heap good." They invited us to join them, but I excused myself on the ground that I had just eaten heartily and was full.

These Pawnees told me that they had left their reservation directly after receiving their payment the previous fall, when the leaves were yet on the trees, and had been absent seven or eight months. Observing that a number of their horses and mules had Mexican brands on them, I suggested that they had been to Mexico. The chief said, "Yes, Mexico," but very likely he lied. These Indians had gone south and stolen the animals, some ` thirty or forty, somewhere—possibly on the frontier of Texas. As I was well-acquainted with the country and the rivers for a long distance south, I got one Indian to make a map on the ground of the different rivers they had crossed to get an idea of where they had been. He marked out quite accurately all the rivers so far as my knowledge extended and, in addition, marked out seven or eight rivers of which I had no knowledge. So I gave up the idea of trying to find out where they had been. They claimed the country as theirs. Taking a handful of earth, a piece of wood, and a bunch of grass, and with a circular sweep of the arm, one exclaimed, "All Pawnee." They pointed out the North Star, gave their names for various others, and seemed well-versed in the movements and direction of the heavenly bodies.

They had two or three ponies loaded with blocks of salt, two chunks of salt making a load for a pony. They had drawn a green buffalo calf skin over each block of salt, and then suspended two of these blocks across a saddle on the pony, making a comfortable load. They gave us several chunks of salt, which was the first evidence I had of the existence of rock salt to the south, though I had frequently heard of it from the Indians. They also showed me an old axe, very badly dented, which they used in chopping out blocks of salt. "This," they said, "made the axe stick." The rock salt was evidently obtained from the salt plains of the Cimarron—a district that was visited by the Indians for the purpose of obtaining salt for their own use and as an article of trade. It was a place well known by all the Indians from the British line to the Gulf. This was the only locality on the plains where rock salt could be found on the surface.

These Pawnees had been away from home since the previous fall and were feeling very anxious to get home. While sitting around the fire that night it was plain to see their condition. They stayed with us all night, filled their stomachs to the utmost capacity with tainted buffalo meat, and got a good night's sleep. They also mended their clothing and saddles, all of which seemed to be of their own manufacture, and made a number of drums by stretching a piece of green hide over a hoop for the purpose of making a grand entry into their home camp, about a week's travel distant, which to them was almost home. They took their departure the next morning in fine spirits and without molesting us beyond attempting to steal some small articles. It is as natural for Pawnee Indians to steal as it is for them to eat.

It was the greatest ambition of an Indian to be the owner of a band of horses. His chance of success was nil without them; his wealth and social standing were determined by the number he possessed. So the bold Pawnee hiked off to the Arkansas and its tributaries to the south where the wild Indians often congregated with their numerous herds, and where the great Santa Fe Trail also gave them opportunities. They carefully refrained from molesting Government mules or wagon trains, as they depended on the Government to protect them on their reservation.

Travelling on foot, the Pawnees extended their forays to great distances. Dakota, Wyoming, Colorado, New Mexico, and northern Texas acknowledged their presence and work. Tradition states that they penetrated as far as the frontiers of Old Mexico. It was the usual custom of these parties to return home mounted, and frequently with quite a bunch of loose horses besides.

The usual objective of the Pawnee raiding parties south from their villages in Nebraska was first to the Big Bend of the Arkansas, and from there on to wherever opportunities seemed most favorable. Their route passed through the center of what is now Lincoln County, crossing Spillman's Creek about five or six miles above its mouth. They had no defined path to follow, but kept to a general course about 15 degrees west of south and east of north, within a strip of country a mile or more in width.

On one occasion I was out with two green, inexperienced young men—one of them was Joseph Thompson of Auburn, Kansas,— hunting buffalo for hides and tallow. I had been on foot two or three hundred yards in advance of the team after buffalo, leaving the men sitting in the wagon, when to my surprise and dismay, I saw that it was surrounded by thirty or forty Pawnee Indians.

I hastened up to the team and found that the Indians had already taken all the arms and other things the young men had, under the pretext of wanting to look at them. My young fellows were so badly scared that they could hardly stand up, and were incapable of doing anything. I used some rather expressive language in giving them my opinion of their folly in allowing the Indians to get possession of their guns, though in their condition of mind they would have been utterly unable to have made any use of them.

Some lively things happened in the next few minutes. With more energy than judgement, I immediately commenced getting the things away from the Indians which they had taken from my men. But some of them refused to give them up and I got into a row with one young fellow about a knife which he had taken. I undertook to get it from him by force, when he slung down his pack and the other Indians did the same. They took out their arrows, strung their bows, and formed a semi-circle in front of me. I cocked my double-barrelled rifle and moved back a few steps, holding it in position for instant use if an Indian made a motion to draw his bow on me. At the same time I began talking to them as rapidly as possible to divert their attention.

Just then the old chief of the party, who up to that time had not said a word, and who had refused to shake hands with me, which showed a very bad spirit, seeing that dangerous proceedings were about to commence, began talking in a loud voice to his Indian braves.

"What are you fellows trying to get into a row with that young white man for? Some of you will be killed in about a minute if you don't stop, and you don't know which one of you it will be, either. We didn't come down here to get into a fight with somebody and get killed. We are Pawnees and we are on our way to steal horses and get home safely if we can. Now you had better give that young man his knife and go on about your business. You give it back to him. If you don't, you are likely to have a bullet through you very soon and never have a chnce to steal any more."

At this the young fellow came forward and, with every indication of anger, handed me the knife and, at the same time, hit me over the head with his bow. If he had been the only Indian present, I would have made a good Indian out of him, but as there were thirty-five, and I was the only white man prepared for the defense, I concluded I had better let him go with the best grace I could.

The Pawnees then went on their way, while I secured the buffalo I had killed, fully resolved that we would get out of that country as speedily as possible, and that they would never catch us there again. But when we reached camp and had made a pot of hot coffee and fried a lot of buffalo meat, we soon forgot our Indian scares and troubles.

On another occasion, while camped at the springs near the head of Cow Creek, [2] a band of thirty-five thieving Pawnees came along from the north on one of their frequent horse-stealing expeditions. They were skulking around in the brush near our camp, watching

2. This site is due north of Cheyenne Bottoms near present-day Beaver, Kansas, in Barton County.

for a chance to steal our horses and possibly to get away with us if an opportunity presented itself. Knowing their intentions, as soon as it was dark we dispatched a messenger over to a Cheyenne camp about twenty miles distant. At daylight the next morning the Cheyenne warriors surrounded the Pawnees and sent twelve of them to the happy hunting ground. The rest of them scattered out over the country and made their way back home on foot.[3]

In 1864 I built a trading post between the Great and Little Arkansas Rivers, two miles above their junction, in a walnut grove where converging bends of the rivers bring them near together, affording a beautiful and commanding location.[4] Here hundreds of Indians camped, came and went, and built houses of logs or poles. On one occasion Jesse Chisholm, going south to Washita, bought of me $3,000 worth of goods saying he would pay me on his return, whenever that might be. The next spring he returned, camped by my place with his train. I took supper with him and he said, "I am owing you. I have no money, but have buffalo robes, wolf skins, beaver, buckskins, and you can take your pay from any of them." I chose coyote skins, which were legal tender for a dollar, and he counted out three thousand. We also sent wagon trains of goods to the camps of wild Indians 200 miles southwest.

On another occasion Mr. Chisholm returned from the south with some Indian families and Mexicans whom he had bought from the Comanches when children and trained to be expert teamsters, herders, and campmen. He camped at the "Walnut Grove," a beautiful and favorite camping place between the rivers. Here he was met by two traders, Charley Rath and Louie Booth, who bought all

3. On March 10, 1868, while JRM was away from Towanda, a raiding party of Pawnee Indians arrived at Mead's Ranch and, despite the efforts of those present, took "one sorrel horse, 5 years old, valued at $75.; one bay Texas mule, 9 years old, valued at $50.; one black mule, 8 years old, valued at $100.; one bay horse, 7 years old, valued at $90.; one black riding pony, valued at $50. Total $365." Both JRM and his assistant Timothy Peet made depositions to this effect in court in Shawnee County, Kansas, concluding with statements "that said party of Indians were armed and on a raid through the settlement, that every effort was made to prevent the said property from being taken, and that all diligence possible was used in order to recover said property, but without avail, and that said property or any part thereof was never recovered." Such statements were made in the presence of frontier officials for the purpose of claiming government compensation. Original documents in the Mead Collection, Wichita.

4. The historian O. H. Bentley has described this as "the first stationary place of business set up on what was to become Wichita." BENTLEY 1: 115.

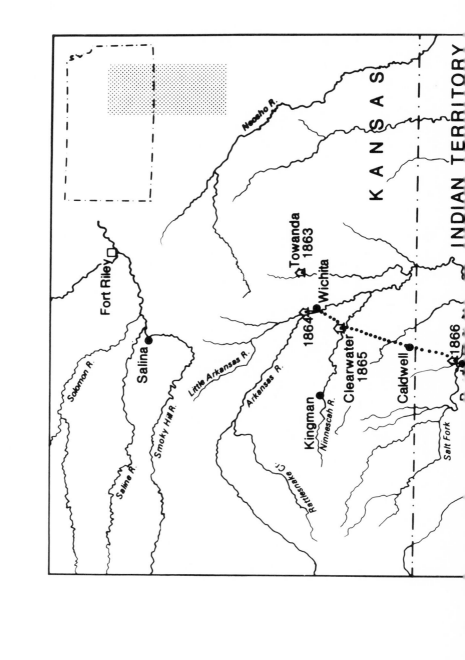

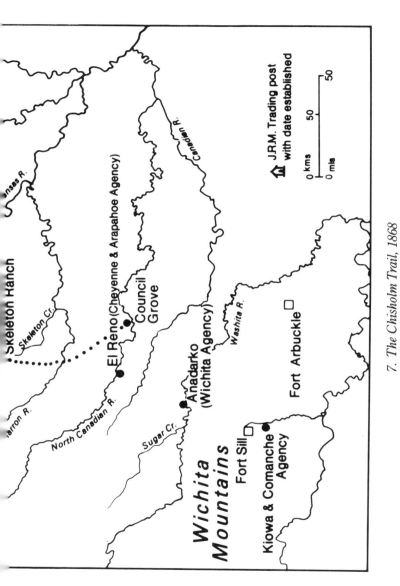

7. The Chisholm Trail, 1868

of his furs before I arrived. However, there was a big pile of buffalo robes under a walnut tree, which Chisholm asked me to buy. I looked them over and made an offer of $1,600 for the lot, which he accepted. None of us then knew the market value of such robes. On getting them to market I found they were worth double cost.

Mr. Chisholm first located at the ford of the Arkansas River where Mr. John Wilkin later made his farm. He then built some cabins, a trading house, and a strong corral at Walnut Grove, about 100 yards in front of the place where Mr. J. C. Davis now resides. On one occasion Chisholm brought up 400 head of cattle from his home place on the Canadian River. I bought them, paying $16 a head, and held them at the Walnut Grove, using the corral and buildings he had turned over to me.

About this time I had a stock of goods at an Indian village at Cowskin Grove, in charge of Davis Ballou, a Cherokee Indian. During June and July he collected for me 1,500 buffalo hides, but the Big Arkansas was such a great river that summer we could not cross, except by swimming on horseback, which we often did. Soon the moths commenced eating the hides. We moved them, beat them, put them on platforms with a big smoke underneath, yet still the moths ate them. Finally, towards the last of August, we got the running gear of a wagon across by men riding the horses and standing on the axles. We made a rack and hauled the hides to the bank of the river. Still it was impassable, and they lay on the banks for two weeks, waiting for the river to fall, which it failed to do. At last a party of thirty-five Kaw Indians came along, to whom I told my woes. They kindly offered to swim them over, so we built rafts of dry cottonwood logs, on which they would pile a lot of hides. Then one or two would swim ahead with a rope to a possible standing place and pull while others swam and pushed, sometimes landing a quarter of a mile below. They got them across finally, losing but a few hides. The great impassable river cost me in this instance $1,500, for on taking the hides to the market they were docked one dollar each for being moth-eaten.

In the early spring of 1865, Mr. John Stevens of Leavenworth loaded a number of teams with goods destined for the town of the Wichitas and placed them in the charge of Jesse Chisholm. He employed Indians (mostly Caddoes) to gather and drive up cattle from the territory, paying for them in goods. In the course of a summer they had collected a herd of over 3,000 head, which they held on the West Side, the Indians herding them over several miles of country between the rivers and the Cowskin. Their camp was about where the watch factory was later built on the West Side.[5] These cattle were first driven east, where Stevens was drowned crossing a river, and then driven to New Mexico on a government contract, as originally intended.

In December, 1865, Mr. Chisholm purchased goods from me, loaded a number of teams, and in January, 1866, started south across the country to his former trading post at the Council Grove on the north fork of the Canadian River. With him went Henry Donvell with several of my four mule teams. Donvell stopped at the Red Fork to trade with the Osages. On this trip Mr. Chisholm naturally selected the most direct and practicable route. This was the first wagon train to pass over the great trail which came to be called the Chisholm Trail.[6]

In the winter of 1865, I built a trading post in a bend of the Ninnescah River near the trail and near the present site of Clearwater. In April, 1866, Mr. Chisholm returned over the same route, bringing with him teams loaded with furs and robes, and 250 head of cattle. Now that the trail was open it became the most convenient route for traders and others having business in the territory. Among these were William Mathewson, William Greiffenstein,[7] and myself.

5. The Wichita Watch Factory never went into production. Work on the building was stopped in 1889, and the structure stood unoccupied for nearly 10 years before being demolished. The stones were hauled away by wagon teams and used to build the new Catholic Church at St. Mark, Kansas. See "West Side News," *Wichita Eagle*, March 31, 1889.

6. Originally the trail laid out by Jesse Chisholm extended from his trading post at the junction of the two Arkansas rivers to his post at Council Grove on the North Canadian River in Indian Territory. Later the name Chisholm Trail was applied to the entire route from the Rio Grande River in Texas to Abilene, Kansas, used by drovers taking cattle north to the railroad.

7. The following note from "Dutch Bill" Greiffenstein to JRM gives an indication of the ways in which traders cooperated and depended on each other: "Cowskin Grove, September 12th, 1866. Mr. James R. Mead, Dear Sir: I wish you would send me by the Bearer some fever & aigue Medicin & pills & 1 Gall of Whiskey & 1 padlock & 2 or 3 lb. of tobacco, & the first chance you get to send me 1 box of tobacco to the little Arkansas & also I would like to borrow 2 iron wedges, crosscut saw & if possible your grind stone. I have not been anywhere yet. The particulars you can hear of the bearer. Let him have some Mustard & 1 pr. of shoes No. 8. If you have time, come over, I am too bussy right now to leave. Yours respectfully, Wm. Greiffenstein." He then adds a

In the winter of 1866, I established a trading station at Round Pond Creek on the Chisholm Trail. Jack Lawton was in charge. That same year Grierson[8] and Custer, with the famous Seventh Cavalry, were stationed on the Little Arkansas at the Santa Fe crossing where there was a stone corral. They built a stockade. The crossing was a noted place on the trail, as running water was always present and timber for fuel abundant, as well as fine grass for grazing. Troops from St. Louis were scattered along the old Santa Fe Trail in small detachments because the wild tribes of the plains were at war. At least they were said to be on the warpath, but we travelled over the plains as usual, unmolested.

Early in July, 1867, William Mathewson went down over the Chisholm Trail, taking two boys whom he had rescued from the Comanches to the Commandant at Fort Arbuckle, to be returned to their parents in Texas. There he met Col. Dougherty of Texas on his way north with a herd of cattle. Mr. Mathewson directed him over the new trail and guided him as far as the North Canadian. This was the first herd of Texas cattle to pass over the trail and was followed in succeeding years by hundreds of thousands more.

In the latter part of August, 1867, Mr. Mathewson, returning from the Treaty of Medicine Lodge, crossed at the mouth of the Little River—the site of Wichita—with fourteen loaded teams for the new agency to be established at Eureka Valley on the Washita River. With him were his wife, Lizzie Mathewson, and her friend Miss Fanny Cox of St. Joseph. They were the first white women to go over the Chisholm Trail. On arriving at Red Fork, Mr. Mathewson left the trail, passing west of Kingfisher Creek, making a new trail through to the Washita.

In 1867 a detachment of Fifth United States infantry, under the command of Col. Thomas F. Barr,[9] was stationed near the mouth

postscript to order "1 doz. coarse Combs" and "4 papers small brass chain." Original letter in the Mead Collection, Wichita.

8. In 1908, George Martin of the Kansas State Historical Society exchanged letters with JRM about various points made by Mead in his article "The Little Arkansas." On Feb. 11, JRM wrote to say, "I never met 'Grierson of 7th Cavalry' at Santa Fe crossing, and know nothing of his history." Later Mr. Martin wrote again to pursue this point and on September 1, 1908, JRM replied: "I do not know which 'Grierson' was at the stone corral on Little Arkansas and I cannot now remember in what publication I found the account of it. I knew at the time of their being there." Original letters in the archives of the Kansas State Historical Society, Topeka.

9. The name and the year may be wrong here. Craig Miner records the name as

of the river by the Indian village where Wichita now stands.[10] This was an uncalled for and useless move. Why a company of infantry should be sent to this point we were never able to learn. In the previous years we had been coming and going over these plains with no protection whatever, and all had been peace and quiet in this part of the state. A company of infantry would not have been effective beyond a half-mile of their camp. None but well-mounted horsemen, trained to plains life, could have protected an extended frontier.

The troops brought the cholera with them, and it spread over the plains of Kansas and the Indian Territory. White men and Indians alike died. Among those who died in Butler County in the fall of 1867 was Sam Carter, my faithful clerk and all-round useful man. He died at my house in Towanda. Sam Fulton, Doc Shirley of the Washita,[11] who happened to be at my house, and I worked over him all night. Then, after his death, we washed and dressed the body and next day buried him.

The cholera spread all over the plains and soon commenced its deadly work among the Wichitas. Scattered over the northern part of the city of Wichita today are the graves of probably 100 Indians, including Owaha, hereditary war chief of the Wichitas; Sam Houston, a noted Indian; and many others. In the latter part of the summer orders came from Washington to remove the Indians to their old homes on the Washita, but no provision was made for their removal.[12] They refused to go until their crops were gathered and a supply of food prepared for the winter.

Captain Samuel Barr and states that the company of infantry arrived in May, 1868 (MINER, 35). In a letter to George Martin dated February 11, 1908, JRM writes: ". . . neither do I know any thing about Thos. F. Barr, only that he was in Command of a Co. of troops at Camp Beecher" (Kansas State Historical Society Archives, Topeka).

10. This camp was first known as the "camp at the mouth of the Little River." In June, 1868, it was known as Camp Davidson; in October, 1868, as Camp Butterfield; in November, 1868, as Camp Beecher. The site was abandoned as a military camp in October, 1869.

11. Doc John Shirley was a trader in Indian Territory. His trading post was about 80 miles from Fort Sill and two miles from Cherokee Town. His brother William was a trader at the Wichita Agency. NICHOLSON.

12. During the Civil War the U.S. Government had been too preoccupied to give much assistance to the Indians and the promised aid had not appeared. The crops which the Wichitas planted in 1865 and 1866 had been destroyed by floods along the Arkansas River. The game in the region was being hunted by both whites and other Indian tribes, and settlers were beginning to move into the area in anticipation that land would become

In the summer and fall of 1867 white horse thieves were engaged in running off the Indians' horses, going in the direction of Fall River and the Cottonwood. In retaliation, just before their departure, the Wichitas took some horses from those rivers. With the survey of the country in 1867, and its opening to settlement, there drifted into the country some of the most vicious and lawless characters to be found in the West. Very soon we found that it was necessary to lock our doors at night and take indoors any loose property we might have; something we were unaccustomed to do during the Indian occupation.

Along in the fall the Wichita Indians started down the old Chisholm Trail. Their first camp was on the Ninnescah, where misfortune again overtook them. They hobbled their horses one night in the tall grass in a bend of the river on the north side. During the night a norther set in, driving down upon them a furious prairie fire, burning eighty-five head of their best horses. This left a large number of the Wichitas afoot, as many of their other horses had been stolen and driven off by white outlaws, who had begun to infest the country that summer. The Indians were compelled to cache a large part of their provisions, which were afterwards stolen by white men, and proceeded on their journey, many of them afoot.

The cholera was still with them. They died all along the trail. Some were buried on the Ninnescah. At Skeleton Creek so many died that they lay on the ground unburied, and their bleaching skeletons gave the stream its name. Whole families died in the lodges after their arrival on the Washita, and the lodges were burned, with the bodies and all their belongings. From Skeleton Creek they scattered out in every direction. Some who had no horses stopped on the Red Fork of the Cimarron, subsisting on the black-jack acorns and wild turkeys, of which there were thousands.

Tawakoni Jim, now Chief of the Wichitas, with a band of mostly women and children afoot, camped at the mouth of Turkey Creek. Their food was what nature provided. From acorns they made palatable bread, by a process of their own. Nearly every evening they could be seen coming down the creek from the timber laden

---

available following treaties with the Osages. It was decided that the Wichitas should be returned to their former homes in Indian Territory, which was done between 1865 and 1868. MINER, 14–15.

United States surveyors at work in Sedgwick County, Kansas, in November, 1867. Mead Collection, Wichita.

with acorns, Jim usually bringing home four or five big turkeys he
had killed with bow and arrow. A blizzard, with severe cold and
deep snow, came along about that time. It was so cold a loaded
wagon could be driven across the streams on the ice, as I had occasion to find out. Big grey wolves and panthers came howling about
their camps.

Late one evening Jim came down the creek loaded with turkeys,
and straggling along were women and children with what acorns
they could carry, Jim's young wife among the number. She was
weak from lack of proper food. Darkness coming on, she became
separated from her companions among the sand-hills and brush,
and about a half a mile from camp she fell exhausted. She hung her
little shawl on a bush to aid her friends in finding her, drew a thin
blanket about her, and laid down to die with wild beasts howling
around. Jim and others hunted for her all night, and at daylight
found her, apparently dead. They carried her to camp and by careful attention revived the faint spark of life, and she recovered.

In January, 1868, during extreme cold and heavy snow, I was
camped near the mouth of Turkey Creek, on the Cimarron river.
About ten o'clock one night two panthers[13] came close to the
camp, less than 100 yards, and, lifting up their voices, let loose the
most unearthly, blood-curdling screams it was ever my good fortune to hear. Lobo, the big buffalo wolf, has a deep, profound, musical howl, which can be heard for miles over the silent, frozen
plains; and their music has lulled me to sleep as I lay wrapped in my
blankets in the snow; but the unearthly scream of a panther close
at hand will almost freeze the blood in one's veins, and for an instant paralyze almost any form of man or beast. My horses and
mules tied to the wagon usually paid no attention to wild animals;
but on this occasion they trembled like a leaf. Some Indian women
and children were sitting around their camp-fires. They screamed
and ran into their lodges. The few Indian men seized their weapons. I distinctly remember being astonished myself.

The next morning it was snowing. I took my trusty friend and
companion, my rifle, and waded through the snow to a dense body
of post-oak timber, half a mile distant. Underneath the interlocking

13. Panther, puma, catamount, and mountain lion were all terms which described
Felis concolor.

Wichita chief Tawakoni Jim and wives. Courtesy Wichita-Sedgwick County Historical Museum Association.

branches of the timber was a thicket of brush and greenbriers. I soon found the fresh tracks of two large panthers and followed their tracks through and under the brush and vines and between the tree trunks for an hour, always close to them, sometimes within two rods. I could not see them, as the falling snow covered the brush and vines, completely shutting out the sight of anything more than a rod distant. They could easily have sprung upon me from either side or behind. I failed to get sight of them.

CHAPTER 14

The Lone Horseman

In January, February, and March, 1868, I was closely associated with Jesse Chisholm, son of a Scottish Highlander and a Cherkoee mother, and a man of great influence among the Indians. He was trading that winter with the Kiowas and Comanches and the various bands comprising the Wichita tribes at a point about thirty or forty miles west of where El Reno is now situated, on the North Fork of the Canadian River. I was supplying him with goods from my ranch on the White River at Buffalo, Kansas.[1]

Along in the spring of 1868 I had occasion to go across country to the Washita River near the mouth of Sugar Creek. The Government had sent Col. J. M. Leavenworth, a man of great experience among the Indians and a trusted agent of the Government, to establish an agency on the Washita River in the Indian Territory at a place known as Anadarko. The object in establishing this agency was to make it a central point round which the Indians would gather, and thus the Government could get in communication with them and regain the influence and control which had been practically lost during the rebellion.[2]

1. This site has not been identified. An examination of "Extinct Geographical Locations," *KSHC* 12: 472–83, reveals that there were, between 1852 and 1912, several places called Buffalo in Kansas. As far as I am aware, there is only one at present, in northern Wilson County on East Buffalo Creek.
2. I.e., the Civil War.

Jesse Chisholm, "an honest and good man." From original print in Mead Collection, Wichita.

As I had business of importance with Col. Leavenworth, I drove down the North Fork of the Canadian River to a point some fifteen miles below Jesse Chisholm's camp, where there was good grass in the valley. Word had come to the Indians at Mr. Chisholm's camp regarding Col. Leavenworth's arrival in the country. So they held a council and sent a committee of some Caddo Indians to interview the Colonel and find out his object in coming into the country, the intentions of the Government, etc., and to report back to them.

I happened to be in the camp at the time these messengers returned, and by Mr. Chisholm's invitation went into his lodge, where were assembled the chiefs and principal men of several tribes. The lodge was about thirty feet in diameter, which afforded abundant room for the assembly, and a bright fire burning in the center made it almost as light as day. The assembled Indians spoke different languages, but among them were Indians who claimed they could speak all Indian languages, while others only understood one or two.

So when the Indian made his report, which he did sitting on an elevation at one side of the lodge, he proceeded in the Indian sign language to give all the particulars of his trip. He told what Col. Leavenworth had said to him, gave the number of wagons which he had loaded with Indian goods and presents, described the coffee, sugar, tobacco, calico, blankets, and various other things of use and ornament dear to the Indian heart—all of this he told in detail. He also related that two hundred head of cattle were on the route from Texas and would arrive within the week for their subsistence while visiting the agency.

Each Indian in that circle understood everything this messenger reported. During the entire conversation he was never interrupted nor asked to repeat a statement that he had made. At the end of every sentence all gave a grunt, signifying that they fully understood him. I also understood it as plainly as though it had been related in my own language.[3] The Indians were highly pleased with the report of the messenger and resolved that they would go down there at their earliest convenience and get a portion of the good things which their Great Father at Washington had sent them, and also to listen to any message which he had sent them through Col. Leavenworth.

While I was in Mr. Chisholm's camp on that trip, during the

3. For further information about sign language see MALLERY.

month of February, 1868, a very old Comanche Indian Chief named
Toshe and his wife came to visit Mr. Chisholm. Toshe had formerly
been a well-known Chieftain, but was now of such an advanced age
that he was incapacitated for active life. He was an intelligent man
of standing and character. I asked him, through Mr. Chisholm, how
old he supposed he was. He replied that he did not know. Mr.
Chisholm remarked that they were a hundred years old as near as
he could tell. Toshe said that when the stars fell—referring to the
great meteoric shower of 1833—he remembered that he had grown
sons at that time. He said it occurred in the fall of the year when
the leaves were falling from the trees. It was in the night and it
seemed as though all the stars were falling to the earth, in a blaze,
like a snow storm of fire. He said the Indians were stricken with
terror and supposed that they and all things on the earth were to
be destroyed for having offended the Great Spirit. None of them
were hurt, but the occurrence was so remarkable that the Indians
reckoned time from that event. Toshe said that the Meteor shower
was observed by Indians over all the country from the mountains
to the Gulf.[4] The hair of this Indian, as well as that of his wife, was
quite grey and had not been cut since their childhood days. Braided
into two long ropes, their hair dragged the ground as they walked.

One evening during my stay in Mr. Chisholm's camp at that time,
while we were sitting alone in his lodge, I called his attention to the
fact that he was getting to be an old man. In the natural course of
human events he must join his fathers in the Great Unknown beyond this life, and I asked him what his religious belief was and
what he thought of the future state.

"I don't know much about the Bible," he replied. "I don't take any
stock in preachers. But the Great Spirit has emplanted in my
breast and in that of every other man the knowledge of right and
wrong. I have never wronged any man in my life. I have been a
peacemaker all my life. I have all my life been engaged in making
peace between the tribes and settling difficulties between individuals. No man ever went from my camp hungry or barefooted, and if
not able to walk, I gave him a horse. And having done all my life
what my heart told me was right, I have no fear in going to meet

4. The Great Leonid Meteor Shower of November 13, 1833, was preceded by one in
1799 and followed by two others, one in 1866 and the second in 1966. The astronomer
Patrick Moore informed me (in a personal communication) that 1899 and 1933 "missed
out because of planetary perturbations." See MEAD [10].

the Great Spirit in the other world. Whenever he calls me, I am ready to go."

In setting out to meet Col. Leavenworth I left my men and teams in camp, taking with me an Indian boy to introduce me to any Indians I might chance to meet on the trip from the North Fork of the Canadian to the Washita—a distance of perhaps sixty miles. The country was unknown to me, as were the Indians we were liable to meet. We passed through a very rough country with some rivers to cross, the principal one being the Canadian. We found the country between the North Fork and the main Canadian sparsely covered with timber, very broken and full of ravines, and there was an abundance of deer and a few buffalo bulls. We came to the Canadian River, crossed it without difficulty, and found the land south of it level and abounding in deer. Bunches of from two up to ten were constantly in sight, and almost as tame as sheep. They would stand and look at us within a hundred yards without alarm. We also saw thousands and thousands of wild turkeys along the little branches and streams.

Just as it was getting dark we found ourselves on the high, sharp, precipitous divide between the Canadian and Washita Rivers. The gulches originating in this sandstone divide in places only left room for a trail along the summit. This was constantly used by wild animals, and in those narrow passages the rock was worn a foot deep by the countless multitudes of hoofs which had passed along it in past ages. We found it almost impossible to get down on the south side. At last I discovered a place where we could descend a steep gully, but not without difficulty. Our horses would place their feet together and slide down the smooth rock into a pot hole. Thus, sliding from pot hole to pot hole, we at length reached the bottom and found ourselves at the head of a little canyon. It was grown up with small cedar trees thirty feet in height and not larger than a man's arm, such as Indians use for lodge poles.

Here we camped beside a big log and made our supper of coffee and a little bacon. That night deer came within fifty yards of our camp, and we could hear other animals roaming about in the thick timber. In the morning after a hasty breakfast, we saddled up our ponies and continued on our journey. Soon we reached Sugar Creek, where we met a number of Comanche Indians; men, women, and children who had been down to see Col. Leavenworth and get some "tobac" and other presents. They were very friendly.

As we rode along I noticed a very peculiar bleached skull with long tushes. It was unlike anything I had seen before on the plains and I asked my Indian boy what it was. He looked at it for a moment and then exclaimed, "Cochenat!" which is the Indian word for hog. I then remembered that we had come into a country once inhabited by Indians who raised swine, and some of them, going wild in the woods, in time became as ferocious as the wild boars of Europe.

We arrived at the agency and stayed all night, having a very pleasant visit with Col. Leavenworth. Having completed our business, the next morning we started back to camp, taking our course without a trail, but very direct. The first night we camped on a branch of Sugar Creek, and soon after unsaddling, a bunch of 15 or 20 deer came out of the timber, feeding in the open ground near us, indifferent to our presence.

I had no weapon with me but a light .32 calibre gun, but in the course of the trip I shot some deer for food, and a number of turkeys. We saw abundant signs of bear and mountain lions and numerous carcasses of deer they had killed near a spring in the grove. I counted the bones of seven bucks. On our return trip we saw, I suppose, ten thousand wild turkeys. They were simply innumerable and subsisted in fall and winter on blackjack and white oak acorns, and became extremely fat. They were easy to approach as they had never been disturbed.

The most interesting incident on the trip occurred as I was approaching camp, about two miles distant. Looking back, I saw a lone mounted Indian following us at a distance, and after we reached camp, the Indian soon rode in. I asked him to get off, rest himself, have some supper and a talk. He threw his blankets and bows and arrows on the bank, turned his pony loose and, perfectly unconcerned as to his safety, sat down and ate a hearty supper with us. He was a jovial, pleasant man of about 30 years of age, and while I could not understand his spoken language, we readily conversed in the sign language.[5] After eating a hearty meal of bread, bacon, and coffee—the first he had tasted in two months—he lit his pipe and gave an account of himself and the expedition in which he had played a lone hand.

5. Unfortunately, JRM does not mention the name of this man's tribe, but from his accounts of similar horse-stealing expeditions, the man may have been Pawnee.

He said he had been out alone on a raid into Texas so that whatever he got would be his own. If he took anyone with him he would have to divide, and he concluded to take the chances by himself. He travelled mostly by night, for he said if the Osages should find him they would kill him for what he had. The Comanches and Kiowas would probably do the same. So he travelled as secretly as possible. He said that after a long journey through a country abounding in buffalo, and crossing Indian trails unobserved, he got down into the settled portion of Texas and there found a ranch where a man kept a bunch of horses and mules in a stockade. In the daytime this man had two herders, and one of them stayed with the animals constantly. The Indian lay in the brush watching them for several days, hoping they might leave them for a short time, but in this he was disappointed, for they never gave him an opportunity.

One night he crawled up to the stockade, which was close by the house. The gate leading into the stockade opened right in front of the house, and there was a fire in the house which made a bright light. And the man kept a cross dog. This gate was secured at night by a log-chain and padlock. The Indian worked for two or three nights, trying to pick that lock with a nail he had found, as he had no file with which to cut it. One night, while he was working at it, the chain rattled and the dog began barking savagely from the house. The Indian lay flat on the ground, perfectly still, while the man came out with his gun and sicked the dog on, but the dog seemed afraid and wouldn't go. The Indian then crawled away on his belly like a snake. He finally abandoned the idea of getting into the stockade at night, but waited in the vicinity, constantly watching for an opportunity.

Finally he noticed that in the mornings the herders would sometimes leave the animals for a few minutes on the prairie near the house while they were getting breakfast. So he concluded that his only chance was to run them off while the herders were eating their morning meal, and he made arrangements accordingly. His opportunity finally came one morning; he dashed in behind the horses, swinging his blanket, and stampeding them. Before the herders had discovered him, he was quite a distance away, rushing the horses and mules ahead.

The herders soon discovered that it was Indians that had stampeded their stock, and followed at a distance, shooting rapidly; but, thinking that there was a large party of Indians concealed in the timber, were afraid to follow far. The Indian wore a strange charm hung about his neck which was composed of claws, beaks, and bones of birds, besides sundry other things known only to the Indians. His enemies could not harm him, he said, while he wore that. The bullets of the herders had passed close by his head on either side but did not touch him, owing to his magic charm. At any rate he made his escape all right with his band of horses and mules, and he attributed it all to the charm he wore. I good-naturedly took up my trusty rifle and told him to get off a short distance on the prairie and let me try a shot at him to see if his charm would work all right. He laughed and said that the charm was made to protect him against his enemies, not against his friends, and that I could kill him easy enough if I wanted to. While the Indian had never seen us before, he placed the most implicit confidence in us and seemed perfectly unconcerned.

Then he went on to tell us his experiences in coming through the wild plains and mountains with his animals. He had travelled altogether during the night. During the daytime he would hide his horses in some secluded timbered gulch where there was grass and water for them. When it began to get dark he would start out again and drive on his course until morning. When he finally got back into his own country he did not know where his own people were. He could see smoke from Indian camps in every direction, but he did not dare show himself for fear he might get into some unfriendly band who would take his horses away from him.

He pointed out to me some ravines behind a hill about two or three miles from camp, where he had concealed his horses. He was going to keep them there until he could find somebody who knew where his people were so he could take them home. I asked him if he wasn't afraid that we would kill him and take his horses and mules, now that he had told where they were. He laughed and said that he was not, that he had heard of us before and knew that we would not harm him. He said he had ten head of horses and mules which he had confiscated from his old enemies, the Texans, and all good ones.

I told him that the bows and arrows he had were no account and that he ought to have a gun. He replied that his bow was light, easy to carry, and never missed fire. I pointed out a buffalo skull at a distance of 80 paces which I had been shooting at with my rifle.

The skull was turned face down, with the base towards us, so that the mark presented was quite small. I could hit it easily with my rifle as I was an expert rifle shot. Pointing out the mark, I told him that he could not hit it. He said he would show me and, reaching over his shoulder, he took out four or five arrows from his quiver and picked out one that had no barb on it. He brought it up before his eye, turning it in his fingers, and bending it a little to get it straight. Then he put it in his bow, drew it back to its head, and while sitting on his horse, let it fly with such force that it splintered the arrow in pieces when it struck the skull fairly in the center. Then he looked at me and laughed, asking if I did not think his bow was some account after all.

The remarkable thing about that Indian was his self-reliance, which enabled him to travel hundreds of miles alone through mountains and plains, far into Texas, and to outwit a skillful ranchman, secure his prize, and carry it through in safety; and the perfect confidence he placed in us, whom he had never seen before. He looked upon the dangers he had braved and the privations he had endured in much the same manner as a hunter looks upon a successful hunt. During the entire trip he had subsisted upon the natural products of the country—the game that he killed with his bow and arrow. He appeared to be in perfect health, without any indication of having gone through hardships or privations. His clothing consisted of a light blanket, a pair of moccasins, buckskin leggings, and a breech clout, besides his magic charm which he claimed prevented his enemies from killing him. His only weapons were a bow, two dozen arrows, and a knife, which all Indians carry.

After our pleasant visit, and getting the information he desired, for which he seemed to be very grateful and pleased, he rode off in the direction of his horses and I never saw him again. His manner was as charming and his conversation as pleasing as any person I ever met; I regret that I never met him again.

We came from this camp directly home, travelling upon the old Chisholm Trail. Crossing the Arkansas about where Wichita now stands, we continued on to the Whitewater to "Mead's Ranch," the present site of Towanda in Butler County Kansas, between which place and the settled portion of Texas there was no human habitation—a distance of about 500 miles.

CHAPTER 15

Captured by a Cheyenne War Party

AFTER my arrival home from that trip I loaded my wagons and immediately started back to Mr. Chisholm's camp on the North Fork of the Canadian. I had five four-mule teams loaded with goods consisting largely of sugar, coffee, flour, and tobacco, besides saddles and blankets and other Indian goods of various sorts.

In the meanwhile the Cheyenne Indians on the plains had gone to war, and a few days after I crossed the Arkansas River, where Wichita is now situated, and started South on the Chisholm Trail, a war party of about two hundred Cheyennes came to the mouth of the Little Arkansas River and talked about following us and capturing us. But as the traders of this portion of Kansas at that time had a good understanding with all the Indians of the plains—a sort of understanding that neither we nor the border settlements were to be disturbed—traders felt tolerably secure. At any rate the Indians did not follow me, so far as I know.

When we had got several days' journey down the trail from the Arkansas I noticed the buffalo were travelling with rapidity and acting as though they had been disturbed. I knew then that somewhere ahead of us there were Indians not far away. What Indians they were I could not tell, but they were likely to be war parties. So I drove as rapidly as possible and camped late one night about ten miles North of Pond Creek on a partially concealed little spring branch.

212

All night the buffalo were travelling past us, going North. They had evidently been disturbed by someone, and I felt considerable uneasiness. At daylight the next morning we hitched up our train and started, intending to drive to Pond Creek, and there to camp and cook our breakfast. When we were within four miles of Pond Creek I saw a war party of Cheyenne Indians, about 75 altogether, galloping down a slope toward us in plain view, probably a mile away. Every man was coming as fast as his horse could carry him, and each was leading an extra horse, which is their customary way of going into battle. I could see their long, glittering lances in the sunlight as they rode. Each Indian had on his war bonnet, adding to their hideous appearance.

I immediately stopped the teams and directed each man to stand at the head of his lead animals to prevent their stampeding. I told them not to be scared, but to keep cool and do nothing but attend to their teams. Being the only extra man, I rode out in front, got off my horse and stood facing the Indians who were rapidly approaching. While they were still a quarter of a mile off I saw a big, fat Indian who, from his appearance, I believed to be the chief of the party, making every effort to reach us as soon as the rest. But being so heavy, his pony could not make quite as good time as his fellows, and there were a number of young men in advance of him. They were spread out in the shape of a fan, perhaps two hundred yards across. One of the foremost Indians was a young fellow with long black hair, streaming in the wind, his eyes shining like black snakes, riding a very fleet black pony. In his hand he carried a long lance with a steel point, poised ready to strike, and coming directly towards me. I could easily have killed him, but I knew that if I did we would all be dead ourselves inside of two minutes. As he rushed by me, he gave his wrist a quick twist, turning the butt end of the lance and striking me in the breast. He was evidently waiting for the chief to give the word to begin the attack.[1]

1. The young Cheyenne was counting coup, that is, scoring points in the complicated system of reckoning warrior status. He was, moreover, counting coup in front of witnesses. G. B. Grinnell explains: ". . . to touch an enemy with something held in the hand, with the bare hand, or with any part of the body, was a proof of bravery—a feat which entitled the man or boy who did it to the greatest credit. . . . In Indian estimation the bravest act that could be performed was to count coup on—to touch or strike—a living, unhurt man and to leave him alive, and this was frequently done. . . . It was regarded as an evidence of bravery for a man to go into battle carrying no weapon that would do harm at a distance. It was more creditable to carry a lance than a bow and arrows." GRINNELL [2], 29–30.

In the meanwhile this chief of the party, as I had supposed, had got to within about two hundred yards. At that distance I told him in sign language that we were Indian traders and were going to their friends at Ten Bear's Comanche camp.[2] He recognized my signal instantly, threw up his hand in answer, and commenced yelling at the top of his voice to his warriors to hold on and not commence proceedings. In the meanwhile they were riding around our wagons in a circle at full speed, waiting for him to give the word to slaughter us.

The chief rode up to me at full speed and jerked his horse back on his haunches and ordered his men to stop their riding until we had had a talk. I then told him that we were Indian traders, and explained to him where we were going. He then explained this to his warriors and told them that they must not disturb us as we were their friends and were going to trade with their friends. Most of the young fellows were not satisfied. They said that they were out for hair and plunder, that they now had a splendid opportunity, that there were things in that train which they needed, and that they ought not to allow this chance to slip. After parleying for awhile I finally proposed that we go on to their camp at Pond Creek and talk to their head chief and see what he would do with us. This was finally agreed to, much to my relief, as I could easily carry my point with Indians if I could get them in a parley.

So the chief told us to get on our wagons and drive ahead. A lot of the Indians climbed on the wagon seats and crowded the drivers out, and they got on the wheel horses. When the Indians thought the train was not moving fast enough, they would prod the horses with their lances, and amused themselves in various ways. I rode in front of the train with the chief and some of his warriors, trying to entertain them to the best of my ability, and get into their good graces as much as possible.

When we got down to Pond Creek I found that their camp was in a narrow neck of land made by a sharp bend in the creek, through which the trail passed. They were camped in that narrow point on each side of the trail. There were probably a hundred warriors in the party. They had a picket guard of about a dozen Indians stretched out in a line across the road in front of us. They were

2. Chief Ten Bear is mentioned by James Mooney in his *"Calendar History"* (MOONEY [2]), but no biographical details are given.

dressed in cast-off soldiers' clothes and each one was armed with some old discarded firearm, ranging all the way from an army carbine to a shot gun. One bow-legged Indian who evidently thought he was a first lieutenant was standing in front trying to keep the others in line. When we drove up they told us to halt.

The head chief of the party, who had not gone out on the prairie, was sitting on some buffalo robes under a large oak tree. He was a fine-looking man with a good countenance and quite intelligent. He had on a beautiful head-dress made of eagle's feathers covering his forehead. He motioned me to come and sit down beside him and have a talk, so I got off my horse and went and sat down beside him. He asked me a great many questions, where I was going, etc. I told him all in sign language; where we were going, where we were from, how many days we had been on the road, and what we were loaded with. He then said that he knew where we lived. When I told him that I was going to the Comanches and mentioned where they were camped, he said that he knew they were camped there.

About this time some of my men told me that the Indians were stealing goods out of the wagons. I called the chief's attention to the fact that his men were getting into the wagons and taking our goods. He shouted out something in Indian language, and instantly about a dozen of his men jumped on their horses bareback and rode around the wagons like lightning, prodding the offending Indians with their lances. I never saw such getting into the brush in my life. One fellow ran so fast (he was looking over his shoulder to see where the Indian was that was after him) that he ran over a supple young tree. It bent over and in some way caught his feet, throwing him into the air and causing him to turn a summersault in the air. The Indians all laughed and shouted and thought it was great fun. We didn't feel very funny ourselves.

After asking us numerous questions the Chief told me he would be glad if he could find the Osages, as he wanted to clean the whole tribe out. I thought this was a rash statement as they could turn out about a thousand warriors as good as his and better armed. After asking some further questions, he told me that he had never had the pleasure of seeing me before, but that he had often heard of me through other Indians and had always heard a good report of me; how I always gave them something to eat when they came to my camp to trade, and treated them well in every way. That being the case, he considered that I was his friend and he was not going to disturb us—a conclusion which was quite gratifying to myself and the parties with me. He stated furthermore that he had been out on the war-path for a long time and that he and his men had had nothing to eat but buffalo meat, and that they wanted some coffee, sugar, and flour. I told him that was all right; I always gave my Indian friends something to eat when I met them. So I had my men set out four or five sacks of flour, probably fifty pounds of sugar, and about the same amount of coffee, as well as a lot of tobacco. This seemed to please them very much.

Then the Chief told me they had no ammunition and he wanted all I had. I happened to have about half a keg of powder, some twenty-five pounds of lead, and a dozen boxes of caps—our usual supply while on such an expedition. I set it all down on the ground beside us, and then told the Chief that it would not be fair for him to take it all. We might get into trouble with the Osages and need it, and we had to kill buffalo for meat and, besides, Chief Ten Bear might also want some ammunition.

"Oh yes, I hadn't thought of that," the Chief replied.

I suggested that we divide it into two equal parts. He said that would be about the fair thing. So we divided it, pouring the powder out on a blanket and dividing it as nearly as we could into two equal parts; likewise the lead and the caps. The Chief said that was all right, so I took my half and put it back in the wagon and one of his men took charge of his share.

In the meantime some of his men wanted to trade their scrubby little ponies for our large fat horses and mules, and they were quite persistent in their demands. I knew enough of Indian character to know that if I refused them point-blank, they would get mad and take them anyway. So I explained to them that our wagons were heavily loaded, that we had a long way to go, and that their little animals couldn't pull them at all. We would never get to Ten Bear's camp and Ten Bear would hear about it and be mad at them. The Chief seemed to take the same view of the case and told his men to let us alone, that we had to have those horses to pull the wagons. He then told us that we could go on about our business, as he was through with us and didn't want to delay us any longer.

About this time I noticed a great commotion in the rank and file of the soldiers. They seemed to be excited and all were talking at once. I asked the Chief what was the matter with them. He said that those were soldiers of his who had been on guard across the road and they thought they ought to have something for their trouble. I told the Chief that was all right and ordered the men to set out a couple of sacks of flour. This appeared to be satisfactory to the soldiers who laughed and joked. Evidently they were having lots of fun playing soldiers.

I should say something more about the dress of the war party. Some of them had scalps and strips of red cloth tied onto their horses' manes and tails. Nearly all of them had on their war bonnets. This most singular dress is made of the long tail feathers of eagles and turkeys. They stand out at right angles over the head and down each arm and also down the back. They wave back and forth in the breeze, so that when an Indian was riding rapidly it gave him the appearance of being larger than his horse. Altogether it produces a most terrifying effect on men who are not used to seeing Indians in their war costume. This peculiar dress has the effect of making an Indian resemble a huge flying monster and an inexperienced person would hardly know where to shoot to hit the Indian, if he had nerve enough left to attempt it. All this happened on a Sunday morning, and my men remarked that they never wanted to see the Indians again with their Sunday clothes on.

We then drove across the creek, a very difficult stream to ford, and on out into the bottom about a quarter of a mile to a little spring branch. Here we turned our horses and mules loose on the prairie, made a fire, and cooked our breakfast. We sat and ate it in plain sight of the Indian camp and not one of them came near us.

If I had been inexperienced in life on the plains and in dealing with Indians, our train would unquestionably have been captured, and probably we would have been killed. In any event, when the Indians made their first charge, if by any accident a gun had been fired, we would have been dead in two minutes.

CHAPTER 16

Jesse Chisholm

AFTER eating our breakfast and grazing our horses for an hour or so, we proceeded on our journey without further mishaps. At the end of three or four days, about noon, we arrived at our destination, which was Chisholm's camp on the North Fork of the Canadian.[1] Here, two or three weeks previous, I had left Mr. Chisholm and his trading outfit surrounded by a great number of Indians of various tribes who looked to him as their father, counsellor, and friend, as well as a trader.

Near this camp ground, a few miles to the North midway between the North Fork of the Canadian and the Cimarron, there is a large salt spring gushing out at the base of a high cliff covered with cedar timber.[2] Here the Cherokees and other semi-civilized Indians resort every year to boil down salt and where, previous to the rebellion, Mr. Chisholm had taken a number of large iron kettles for use in manufacturing salt. This salt he sent by ox train into Texas, as well as supplying the semi-civilized Indians of the Eastern part of the Territory. While he was in camp trading with the Indians, he would have some of his men at the spring making salt. The water of that spring is so thoroughly saturated that a handful of salt thrown in a bucket of water would not dissolve over night. The quantity of

1. Present-day Watonga in Blaine County, Oklahoma, is near the site of Chisholm's camp.
2. The town of Hitchcock is near this site.

the water is practically unlimited. This was another reason why the camp at which Mr. Chisholm was located was a central and well-known point, and where he and the Indians expected to remain for quite a length of time. The buffalo were also in reach, supplying them with meat.

When I arrived at the camp, to my utter astonishment I discovered it was abandoned. There was not a human being remaining in the country, and on the camp site there were about a thousand wild geese feeding. I was the more surprised as I knew the Indians were at peace and that it was Mr. Chisholm's intention to remain there for a considerable length of time. Also, I had arranged to meet him there with my train load of goods. So I knew that something extraordinary had happened, but what it was I could not imagine and had no possible source of information.

A rain storm which had fallen quite recently had nearly obliterated all tracks and trails. As near as I could discover the Indians had scattered in every direction. The next question that presented itself to my mind was what was I going to do? There I was out in a wild Indian country with a train load of valuable goods to be delivered at a certain place and behold! there was not a human being in the country!

We drove down to the bank of the river, turned our animals out to graze, and got our dinner. I concluded that the only thing to do was to drive on down the river in the direction where I knew the semi-civilized Indians lived, and where I was acquainted. This, however, was a long distance away. There was no use to seek the wild Indians. I did not know where they had gone, perhaps a hundred miles away for all I knew. After resting our animals we hitched up and started down the trail, which followed along the North bank of the river.

In about ten miles we came to a prominent point or bluff against the river. This was known among the Indians as "Little Mountain" and was the place where Mr. Chisholm and other representatives of the semi-civilized tribes of the Territory were accustomed to meet the chiefs of the wild Indians of the plains every summer. Here they talked over their affairs and arranged any differences that might have occurred between them, and also arranged with Mr. Chisholm where he would meet them during the following Autumn or Winter for purposes of trade.

Immediately at that point the river turns South until it strikes the bluffs on the South, leaving a beautiful valley on the North side of the river looking East. Here I noticed just round the point of the timber a small covered pen made of notched logs recently constructed. This I very well knew indicated a recent grave and burial. I immediately rode down to it and saw a board stuck into the ground on which were carved the words:

Jesse Chisholm
Died March 4th, 1868

I then knew the cause of the sudden breaking up of the camp and the departure of the Indians.[3]

The very scant information conveyed by that sign board, while it satisfied my mind as to the reason for the scattering of the Indians, left me entirely in the dark as to its cause. The probability seemed to be that there had been a disturbance of some kind among the Indians in which Mr. Chisholm was killed, as I had left him in good health a short time before. Yet I could not imagine how such a thing could have occurred, unless by accident, for no living Indian would have harmed him.

Mr. Chisholm had a ranch thirty or forty miles down the river from that point, where years before he had constructed buildings and corrals and for many years had kept a trading establishment.[4] Knowing that there were always some Indians at that point, I thought that would be the nearest place to get information. Accordingly, we drove down the river and in due time arrived at Mr. Chisholm's ranch. There, to my surprise and gratification, we found two other trading outfits with whom I was acquainted and on intimate terms. One was owned by William Greiffenstein ("Dutch Bill"), and the other by Dr. Greenway, an Osage Indian trader.[5] Mr. Chisholm's own outfit of wagons and men was also there and I got the full particulars of Mr. Chisholm's death.

It seems that along during the Spring the Indians had entirely consumed their supply of fat buffalo meat, and they had nothing to eat except lean meat and flour. The small supply of bacon that the

---

3. This site, now farmland, is approximately six miles northwest of present-day Geary, Oklahoma, and not far from Greenfield.

4. This was at Council Grove, now Oklahoma City.

5. A. F. Greenway was later among the early settlers on the Wichita site. See ANDREAS, 1385.

*Trader William Greiffenstein. Courtesy William C. Ellington, Jr.,
Wichita.*

traders had taken down was entirely consumed and Mr. Chisholm was complaining because he had no fat meat. One Indian woman remembered that she had a small brass kettle partly filled with bear's grease, which she brought and gave to Mr. Chisholm, and he ate quite heartily of it. It is possible that the bear's grease, having remained in that kettle since the previous Autumn, had become poisonous by contact with the metal, for what he ate of it threw him into a very violent attack of *Cholera morbus*, which caused his death in the course of twenty-four hours.

At the time of his death the Indians were thrown into the most profound grief. He was like a father to many of the Indians of the Territory, as well as those of the plains. They loved him more than any other man, for he was a friend and never misled nor deceived them. Large numbers of Indians were present at his burial. Ten Bear, Chief of the Comanches, took off the bronze medal which had been presented to him by the Government and which he had worn for many years, and laid it on the breast of his departed friend, weeping like a child as he did so, and it was buried with him.

It was customary when traders met on the plains to camp together if possible and narrate the incidents of their various journeyings and impart to one another all the information and news they had. On this special occasion as four trading outfits had met, with also quite a number of Indians and half-breeds who lived in the vicinity present—all friends of our deceased comrade—we thought something more than ordinary should be done. So out of the center of a barrel of sugar was exhumed a five gallon keg of Kentucky's best. Contrary to all regulations of the Government and the bonds which we licensed traders had given, somebody had taken this along to have on hand in case of sickness or accident and up to that time it had not been tampered with. It was unanimously decided that we hold a wake over the demise of our friend. So a faucet was inserted and a tin cup or two was brought into service. The contents of the keg was very highly appreciated by all, especially by Mr. Greiffenstein and Mr. Greenway, who for many years had been cultivating a taste for that kind of beverage. While the writer never indulged in such things at home, under the peculiar circumstances of the occasion he also endeavored to do his best.

After we had all got into a very happy frame of mind, it was proposed that we get up a shooting match, which was one of the common methods of entertaining where frontiersmen had come together for a little recreation. Mr. Greiffenstein, who on account of his weak eyes couldn't tell a man from a horse at a distance of a hundred yards, undertook to distinguish himself in shooting at the mark. On discovering this, all the Indians who were standing around retreated to the rear in good order and as rapidly as possible. Mr. Greiffenstein certainly did some remarkable shooting, but so far as we could ascertain, with no harm to the target. The rest of us attempted, in various amusements of a perfectly harmless nature, to confer honor upon the memory of our deceased friend.

That night I deliberated about what to do with the goods I had on hand, and also how to get a settlement from the heirs of Mr. Chisholm for about $3,000 worth of goods which I had previously furnished him. I concluded that it was necessary to go sixty miles in a South-easterly direction down into a timbered portion of the Indian Territory where Mr. Chisholm's home ranch was situated, to see his wife and foreman. So the next morning I mounted a saddle mule and, taking with me a half-breed named "Californy," who had been raised by Mr. Chisholm, I started out at a rapid rate, following the divide between the North Fork of the Canadian and the main river, finally reaching the North Fork of the Canadian at a point known as "Shoto," or Chouteau. Here, where a creek emptied into the river, there was located many years ago a French trading post run by traders from St. Louis, nearly opposite the present site of Dennison, Texas.[6] From there the trail led through timber

6. There seems to be an error in the manuscript here. We have just been told that JRM followed ". . . the divide between the north fork of the Canadian and the main river, finally reaching *the North Fork of the Canadian* [my italics] at a point known as 'Shoto' or Chouteau." A careful examination of maps, JRM's text, and other historical sources clearly shows that the above quote should read ". . . the divide between the North Fork of the Canadian and the main river, finally reaching the Canadian at a point known as 'Shoto' or Chouteau." Thus JRM travelled southeast from what is present-day Oklahoma City, passing east of Norman, and reaching "Shoto," which is about five miles northeast of present-day Purcell, Oklahoma. From there he turned approximately due east and proceeded to Chisholm's "home ranch," also known as "Edwards' Store" after James Edwards. This was located on the north bank of the Canadian River in what is now Hughes County, Oklahoma, roughly five miles east of present-day Sasakwa and five miles south of present-day Spaulding. The Chouteau dynasty was founded by Auguste Chouteau (1739–1829), who was born in New Orleans. With his younger brother Pierre (1758–1849) he was founder of St. Louis, Missouri, site of a winter camp established in 1763–64 while the brothers were engaged in the fur trade. Auguste's son Pierre devel-

the entire distance, and my guide became lost owing to the numerous trails running in all directions. It was only through my knowledge of woodcraft and the general direction that enabled me finally after dark to find the ranch.

After my business there had been completed, I concluded that the only way to dispose of my goods was to go about one hundred miles through to the Washita River near Col. Leavenworth's camp.[7] There Mr. Greiffenstein (known in those days by all the traders on the plains as "Dutch Bill") had an Indian wife named Jennie. She was the sister of a noted Cheyenne Chief and a woman of great ability, and was engaged in trading with the Indians.[8] I made the trip alone, saw Jennie, and made arrangements with her to take all my goods and pay me, so far as she was able in such robes and furs as she had on hand. I then rode back across the country, over what was to me an unknown route, to where I had left my teams in camp on the North Fork of the Canadian at Chisholm's trading post. I took them across country to the Washita, delivered my goods and, taking what robes and other things Jennie had on hand, I started back through the Western part of the territory towards home. I feared, and in fact it was reported, that the Cheyenne Indians were on the war path. I had met them on my trip down, and I didn't care to chance it with them on my return.

We followed what was known as the old Delaware trail by the Seminole Agency and through a country covered with timber full of game and wild horses. After more than a week's travel we reached the Arkansas River about ten miles below the mouth of the Cimar-

---

oped the fur trade into a vast business empire, and in turn, his son, Auguste Pierre Chouteau travelled widely in the West in the early nineteenth century, buying furs and trading with the Indians. Many trading posts established by the Chouteau family were known locally as "Shoto." STRATFORD, 6–7, and MAYHALL, 86.

7. Anadarko.

8. Greiffenstein's wife was known everywhere on the plains as Cheyenne Jennie. She died in 1868. In a letter dated October 10, 1868, S. F. Wikley, acting Indian agent at the Kiowa and Comanche Agency wrote to Gen. W. B. Hazen: "Too much cannot be said in praise of Cheyenne Jennie for the interest she took and exertions she made in recovering the captive children from the Comanches, visiting their camps, invalid as she was, riding in her ambulance when she was not able to sit up, giving her own horses for the captive McElroy children that they might go home with their father. She also had great influence with all the wild Indians, which she used in trying to have them keep in the straight road. 'Her work is done; she has gone to her happy hunting grounds.'" See Box 76, Philip Sheridan Collection, Manuscript Division, Library of Congress, Washington, D.C.

ron or Red Fork, as it is known in the Territory. We found the river to be at that point a quarter of a mile in width, and the water was just over the backs of our tallest horses. We had to raise the beds of our wagons up on top of the standards and lash them securely there. We then partly loaded them with our robes and camp equipage and, putting a man on the back of each horse and mule to prevent the current sweeping them away, we finally crossed with much difficulty. Everything arrived safely on the other bank. Our loose stock, a number of which we usually took along in case of accident or loss, we swam across.

We then followed a trail running in a Northerly direction for a number of days until we finally struck the old California Trail, then abandoned, over which the Forty-Niners and later gold miners travelled from Arkansas on their route towards California. This trail we followed for several days until we finally reached the Walnut River in Butler County, Kansas, two miles below the present site of El Dorado, and only eight miles from my home.

I reached home in safety and found that I had been reported killed by Indians, and that my family and friends had given me up as lost. There I was content to remain, enjoying the society of a beloved wife and children.[9]

9. JRM occasionally made brief diary entries in his trading post ledgers. After returning from this journey, he wrote, "Jessee Chisholm Died Mar. 4th 1868 on North Fork of Canadian River, I.T. An honest and good man." Original document in Mead Collection, Wichita.

CHAPTER 17

A Kansas Blizzard and Other Storms on the Plains

GENERAL Sheridan came out and organized a winter campaign in October, 1868. The Nineteenth Kansas Cavalry was ordered to proceed across the country to the junction of Beaver Creek and the North Fork of the Canadian, via Camp Beecher at the mouth of the Little Arkansas.[1] They left Topeka on November 5th and arrived at the mouth of the Little Arkansas on November 12th, 1868. By chance, I met the command going into camp on the South Fork of the Cottonwood on November 9th. They were a splendid body of men and horses, under an able and honored commander whom I well knew,[2] and was invited into his tent.

On asking the Colonel where he was going, he replied that he was not allowed to say, but from inquiries he made as to the country beyond, I soon learned his destination.

"Colonel, you cannot get through that country at this season of the year unless you know just where to go; it is exceedingly broken and difficult." I asked to see his guides.

He sent an orderly out who brought in two young men, neither of

1. Governor Samuel J. Crawford of Kansas issued a proclamation calling for the formation of the Nineteenth Kansas Cavalry Regiment at Topeka on October 11, 1868. HADLEY.

2. The commander was Samuel J. Crawford. He had resigned as governor of Kansas in order to take command of this regiment.

Texas cattle fording the Arkansas River at Wichita in July, 1869. Mead Collection, Wichita.

whom I had seen before. I knew they were never in that part of the country or I should have known them. They were absolutely ignorant of the country they were attempting to guide a regiment through. One of them was Jack Stillwell,[3] who knew the country north of the Arkansas well enough.[4] They soon went out.

When I told the Colonel that he would never get through with those men as guides, and offered to furnish him with guides who knew the country, as for several years we had sent teams over that same route in winter and summer, trading with the Comanches, who wintered in the vicinity of his destination, our outfits always returning safely, he replied in language too forcible to repeat that Sheridan had furnished him these guides, and they had to take him through, and he had no authority or money to employ other guides.

On November 10th they camped in the timber north of El Dorado, on the Walnut. On the 11th they camped on the west bank of the Whitewater. The Command passed along the road 100 yards north of my place and Governor Crawford kindly placed a guard about my buildings and property. My foreman sold them a rick of hay and other supplies. I was away.

At 3 p.m. on the afternoon of November 12th they arrived at Camp Beecher at the mouth of the Little Arkansas. The roads from Topeka to Camp Beecher were very muddy and heavy. Short marches were necessary. All camp sites were well chosen. The country was open and unfenced. Horses and men were in fine condition. There was no grain or hay along the road in any quantity. No one had been sent ahead to provide feed at the camping places.

The trail ran west from Camp Beecher, where Wichita now is, to Cowskin Grove, seven miles. The Caddos were camped there and "Dutch Bill" was trading with them. The Command camped there the first night after leaving Camp Beecher, probably getting a late start. From there they followed our trail to Ninnescah, just below the Junction—a plain trail. Here they naturally camped, distance about eighteen miles over a level plain. From there to the Chikaskia

3. "Jack Stillwell was alright in his place, but he outrageously imposed on Sheridan and Crawford when he represented himself as able to guide 1,200 men through a difficult country *he had never seen.*"—JRM.

4. The other young man was Apache Bill Simmons, though his name is given as Apache Bill Sampson in *KSHC* 17:362, and as Apache Bill Simpson on p. 873 of that same volume. James A. Hadley confirms that neither Stillwell nor Simmons had ever been south of the Arkansas River. HADLEY, 435.

there was a plain trail, twenty-five miles, one day's march. Here they made camp, no timber.

From there on the trail was scattering, indistinct; known only to ourselves. They camped next on a branch of the headwaters of Bluff Creek. From then on *they were lost*, travelling at random. They camped on Medicine Lodge, several miles above its mouth. Their proper route was by the junction of Medicine and Salt Fork, where there was an abundance of timber, thence southwest to Eagle Chief, where there was plenty of timber. Instead, they reached the Salt Fork some miles above its junction, where there was no timber and a difficult crossing. Camp Supply was only three days' march beyond, over a good route, if one knew where to go. It was a six day trip from the Little Arkansas to Camp Supply; a good horseman could ride it in three days with ease.[5]

The Command left Camp Beecher on November 14th and reached Camp Supply on November 28th. They should have arrived safely at their destination two days before the terrible snow storm of the afternoon of the 22nd, which came near destroying the command and caused untold suffering and loss. A competent guide could have avoided most of their woes, but the stampede on Medicine Lodge was one of those unforseen accidents which will sometimes overtake the most experienced and careful plainsmen.[6]

In the winter of 1867–68 I made three trips with loaded teams from Towanda to the North Fork of the Canadian, below where Camp Supply was afterwards built, always returning safe and sound without the loss of a man or animal, or suffering any hardship, and we could have taken the Nineteenth Cavalry through just as easily. My only apology for writing of this stupendous blunder is that it is properly a part of the history of the Little Arkansas.

In the summer of 1868 I took a claim on the Wichita site. It was bounded by what is now Lawrence [Broadway], Central, Washing-

5. Camp Supply actually did not exist in early November, 1868; one of the Nineteenth Kansas Cavalry's duties was to go down and establish it. In this context, by "Camp Supply," JRM means the junction of Beaver and Wolf creeks.

6. The newly formed regiment consisted of 50 officers, 1,300 men, 1,150 horses, and 110 mules. The stampede at Medicine Lodge occurred on November 18 and was caused by a mount that bolted while being unsaddled. Altogether, the regiment made a 24-day march on 9 days' rations and 7 days' forage. As horses and mules died of exhaustion, exposure, and starvation, they were eaten by the troopers. For a full account written by a man who was there, see HADLEY.

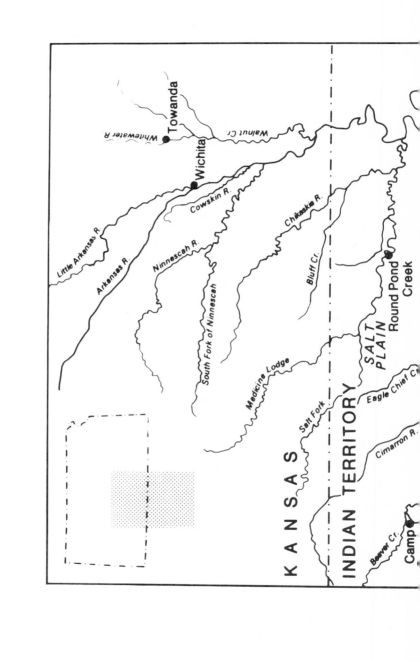

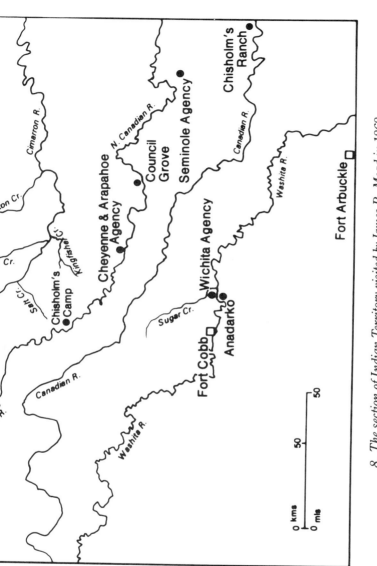

8. *The section of Indian Territory visited by James R. Mead in 1868*

ton, and Douglas Avenues. It was a piece of wild, unoccupied prairie. No man had ever claimed it or drove a stake in it, unless it was to picket a pony; not a dozen claims had been taken in the County at that time, and those were along the River where was wood and water. No one wanted a piece of open prairie.

Cities are not the result of chance, nor do they make themselves. Their prosperity and greatness are in large measure due to the sagacity and enterprise of their founders and early settlers in reaching out and drawing to them the channels of trade and commerce. Our city of Wichita is an illustration of what may be accomplished by making the most of opportunities.

One of the incidents of our early history, when Wichita was about in the condition of a chicken just emerged from its shell, and which perhaps was the turning point in our career, has never appeared in print.[7]

'Twas the spring of 1871. The Texas cattle drive of the previous year had passed east of our city along the bluff, and north to Abilene, on the Kansas Pacific road. In the meanwhile, the A. T. & S. F. road had crept along until it had reached a point north of Wichita and laid out a town called Newton, and there paused. Their object was to secure and control the Texas cattle shipments. Their rival—the K. P. road—did not propose thus to be robbed of what they considered to be one of their things, and a prominent item of their business. So they held council and decided upon a scheme to hold the cattle trade, and incidentally kill Wichita and build up Park City, at that time a flourishing town and no mean competitor of our own banting.

In pursuance of their plan, they built stock yards at Ellsworth—a point forty miles further west than Wichita—and employed Major Henry Shanklin, late agent of the Wichita Indians, who was familiar with the country, to locate and stake a new trail from the Ninnescah to Ellsworth, leaving Wichita far to the east. Maj. Shanklin was provided with an ambulance, mules, and saddle horse, with an African acting in the double capacity of driver and cook. He quietly proceeded to stake out a trail, as instructed, the good people of Park City seconding the scheme. This new trail intersected the

7. This account appeared under the title of "The Four Horsemen" in the *Wichita Eagle* on February 28, 1884.

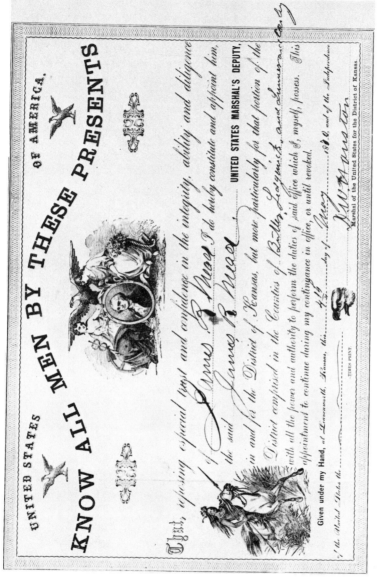

James R. Mead's certificate of appointment as a United States marshall's deputy, May 4, 1870. Mead Collection, Wichita.

Chisholm trail at McLain's Ranch[8]—now Clearwater—down which trail he travelled, meeting the Texas herds at Red River on their annual pilgrimage to Kansas and a market. To them he explained that the old trail was closed, and he, as the agent of the great Kansas Pacific road, had come to see them safely over the new. Accompanying them leisurely up the trail, nailing up at each creek and camping ground a printed notice of the new route, one sunny afternoon they reached the Ninnescah River. Our friends of the ranch immediately dispatched a messenger to Wichita, bringing us the astonishing intelligence that our rivals had outmaneuvered and flanked us, and were about to get away with the baggage. A council of war was called which decided to send a committee forthwith down the trail, to turn, if possible, this living river of life and wealth through our embryo town. The parties selected were N. A. English,[9] Mike Meagher,[10] J. M. Steele,[11] and the writer.

It was evening. The sun had gone down behind the tall cottonwoods which fringed the classic banks of the "Nile of America," the lengthened shadows extended over the luxuriant grass on Main Street and Douglas Avenue. No time was to be lost; in haste we saddled our fleet-footed, long-winded mustangs, buckled on spurs and revolvers—our saddle pockets provided by friends with other things considered necessary—and mounting, we rode forth into the placid waters of the river on a mission which might decide for weal or woe the destiny of a city. Across the river safely, we galloped down the trail, over where Robert Lawrence's house now stands, straight across the valley to the Cowskin, crossing where Cartwright now resides. Impressed with the momentous import of our errand, we galloped on in silence into the darkness, over the

8. A much-used halting place on the Chisholm Trail south of Wichita on the Ninnescah River. More than the name "ranch" suggests, this was a small settlement near present-day Clearwater and boasted a store and a saloon.

9. Nathanial A. English was an early settler in Wichita and pioneer businessman. He dealt in real estate, was chairman of the Board of County Commissioners, and active in the grain market. He died in 1892.

10. Mike Meagher was marshal of Wichita from 1871 to 1874 and from 1875 to 1877. He was elected mayor of Caldwell, Kansas, in April, 1880, but was arrested only four months later for running a keno game. He was killed in December, 1881, in a gun battle. CUNNINGHAM.

11. James M. Steele arrived in Wichita in 1869. Together with H. G. Smith, he ran an office in the Buckhorn Tavern (Henry Vigus, proprietor) as agent of the Great American Wire Fence Company. He was active in church affairs. After some years in Wichita he moved to Washington state. LONG, 21.

Main Street, Wichita, 1870. The view north from where Douglas Avenue was later built. Mead Collection, Wichita.

prairie, with no sound breaking the stillness of the night but the clatter of our horses hoofs.

The twenty miles were quickly left behind, and drawing rein at the friendly ranch, we learned that the advance of the cattle drive—four large herds—had crossed the river in the afternoon and, guided by Major S., had hurried past on the new trail. Things looked gloomy for the four horsemen and Wichita. The night was cloudy and dark; the herds could not be followed over the prairie grass in the darkness; so we picketed our horses, spread our saddle blankets on the dirt floor of the ranch with our saddles for pillows and laid down, but not to sleep. Our minds were too full of what the morrow would bring forth. Long before the morning dawned, we saddled our horses and with the first light struck out on the trail to the North-west. After two hours of hard riding, we saw ahead of us the herds, already strung out and on the move. Maj. Shanklin's outfit was just starting from the campfire. As we rode up he saluted us with, "This is a Wichita delegation, I presume. You are too late." We only stopped a moment, but noticed a tent and bedding tied on behind the ambulance, frying pans, bake oven, coffee pots, tin cups, guns, etc. tied on every available point, and a sack of flour and a side of bacon under the seat. Also what appeared to be sundry boxes of cigars and kegs wherewith to beguile the artless Texan.

We rode on to the leading herd and called a halt. They halted; the cattle men gathered round us. We told them they were misled and off the trail, liable to get lost, miss the best market and a paradise of a town, and much more to the same effect. Major Shanklin, coming up, replied that the old trail was closed up by settlers who would stampede or shoot their cattle, that Chisholm Creek was an impassable quagmire, that the only way they could get through was to follow him. And so we argued hot and fast. The cattlemen hesitated; they were already some ten miles west of Wichita; the prairie was fresh burned east of them; the stubs would hurt the cattle's feet they said; they feared trouble and loss.

We guaranteed them safe escort and payment for all losses, but to no purpose, when a happy thought occurred to one of our party. Taking the leader of the cattlemen to one side, he used an argument in the way of a handsome consideration which proved more potent than words. He won our case; the word of command was

McLain's Ranch

McLain's ranch trading post on the Ninnescah River was the chief halting place on the Chisholm Trail south of Wichita. It was located close to modern-day Clearwater, Kansas. In 1870, Harper's Weekly *sent a writer-artist team to report on Wichita and the cattle trade. This woodcut of McLain's, showing a saloon and a grocery store appeared in the May 2, 1874, issue of the magazine.*

given. The great herds of cattle swung around to the right and headed for Wichita, leaving Major S. alone on the prairie with his sable John.

In due time we arrived in town triumphant and exultant, and the drovers literally had the "freedom of the city." The cattle forded the river just below the present bridge; thence along Douglas Avenue over the ground where Eagle block stands; thence across Smythe and Sons corner; thence over where J. H. Todd and J. W. Hinton reside, crossing Chisholm Creek below the Hoover bridge. We accompanied the herds on their way; paid for one beef $15, as agreed, that unfortunately broke its neck in crossing Chisholm Creek; again met and discomforted Maj. Shanklin, who had taken a wide circuit and met the herds with a fresh installment of bugaboo stories; and on a grassy bank a few miles north of town we alighted, drew up a paper which all the drovers signed, in substance stating the route by Wichita was the shortest, best, safest, and only practicable route, and the Wichita folks the cleverest people they had ever met, and advising all Texas herds to drive to Wichita, the first, best, and only supply point on the route. We then returned to town.

Not yet had the *Eagle* plumed its pinions,[12] or the *Beacon*'s light shone forth,[13] but "Hutch" and Fred Sowers of the *Vidette*[14] printed a lot of circulars containing the statement of our Texas friends, which were at once sent down the trail and posted as far as Red River.

On the day we turned the herds toward Wichita, Park City learned of their approach on the new trail, and foresighted matters a little by sending a dispatch to the daily papers of the State, announcing that the first herds, numbering fifteen thousand, had arrived at their town on the new trail, which guaranteed them the Texas cattle trade and the supremacy of the Arkansas Valley.

Alas for their fond anticipations, no herds passed that way. The four horsemen had killed their town. Today, and for many years past, the fine farm of our friend W. T. Jewett has occupied their town site.

All that summer and the next the stream of cattle and trade and traffic flowed in and through the streets of Wichita. Of the four horsemen, one has gone to his rest, slain by the assassin's bullet

12. JRM persuaded Col. Marshall Murdock to sell his newspaper publishing business in Burlingame, Kansas, and move to Wichita. The *Wichita City Eagle* was first published in 1872.

13. The *Weekly Beacon* was founded in 1872 with Fred A. Sowers as editor and publisher. As a daily the *Beacon* dates from September 1, 1884, with Henry J. Allen as editor and publisher. CONNELLEY [4].

14. William Bloomfield Hutchinson (known as "Hutch") and Fred Sowers published and edited the *Wichita Vidette* from August 25, 1870, until sometimes in 1871. See the "The Mystic Emblem '30,'" *Wichita Daily Eagle*, June 21, 1894.

while in discharge of official duty on the same old Chisholm Trail.[15] One resides on the shores of far-off Puget Sound,[16] but the man who made the argument which won is with us here to-day, an honored member of our city government.[17]

In 1871 the Santa Fe Railroad sent a corps of surveyors to Wichita to run a line of preliminary survey to the Southwest. As they knew nothing of the country, I went with them as guide at their request. I also acted as hunter for the party and killed all the antelope and buffalo required for their use, which they all enjoyed and pronounced excellent.

We surveyed a very excellent route until we came to the Medicine Lodge River about twelve miles below the present town of Medicine Lodge. On the trip down we found an abundance of game and must have seen half a million buffalo. We struck the Medicine Lodge River where there was a high bluff on the opposite side. The engineers were afraid of the wild Indians and declined to go further, so we made a detour down to the salt plain just below the junction of the Medicine Lodge and the Salt Fork rivers, and then came home.

At that time there was on the plains a noted frontiersman and hunter named Mosley.[18] He was the most perfect specimen of physical manhood I ever saw. He was not as strong as Sandow, but nearly so; had immense locks of raven hair hanging down about his shoulders. His eyes were as blue as the sky on a clear day, and his cheeks were as rosy as a girl's. He had the strength of an ox and a heart as big in proportion. Hearing of our surveying trip down into that region, he thought it a good place to establish a hunting outfit. For this purpose he built on the East side of the Medicine Lodge River a log house and enclosed it within a stockade. He also took with him a tall, lean, lank Tennesseean; so tall, so lank, so lean, so bony—and his wife, an exact counterpart. Each of them was over six feet in height, I should judge.

After Mosley had been there a year or two, a party of Black Dog's band of Osages,[19] and some Cheyennes who had had some

---

15. Mike Meagher.
16. James M. Steele.
17. Nathaniel A. English.
18. Ed S. Mosley. See note 28 in Chapter 9.
19. Black Dog's portrait appears opposite p. 62 in the *Twenty-seventh Annual Report of the Bureau of American Ethnology*, (Washington, D.C.: Government Printing Office,

Mike Meagher. Courtesy
Kansas State Historical Society

Nathaniel A. English. Courtesy
William C. Ellington, Jr.

James M. Steele. Courtesy
William C. Ellington, Jr.

James R. Mead. Mead Collection, Wichita.

fights with Mosley in years past, resolved to chase him out as they
did not want any white man to settle there among the buffalo. So a

_____

1911), and as an informant, he provided numerous oral traditions which are published in
other *Annual Reports* of the Bureau; but no biographical details are given.

party of thirty or forty of these Indians prepared themselves and arrived near his ranch in the evening.

About daylight the next morning they came and surrounded his stockade. Mosley, who was a man utterly without fear, very rashly went out to bring in his horses, which were picketed just in front of his house. The Indians commenced shouting out something at him, which he answered back. They then began firing on him, to which he paid no attention until one of them shot his thumb off. He proceeded, however, after his horses. But one Indian, who had hidden behind a sand hill some 50 yards distant, shot him in the back, causing a dangerous wound which eventually proved fatal.[20]

The Tennesseean and his wife, and possibly another man, who were inside the stockade, claimed that they kept up a fight with the Indians for an hour, shooting from port holes. The Tennesseean told me that whenever an Indian showed his head above a sand hill he would immediately shoot the top of his head off, throwing his brains in the air, and that he had killed fifteen Indians that he knew of. At any rate, the Indians went away without dislodging Mosley or disturbing his ranch any further.

In the Winter of 1874–1875 I was holding a large herd of cattle on the Medicine Lodge River and had working for me a short, heavy-set fellow named Johnny Martin who used to get drunk whenever he had an opportunity. In the meantime the Tennesseean and his wife had built a cabin and a stockade and had some horses on the east side of the river where Mosley's camp was situated.

In the course of the winter I discharged this man Martin, who went down and made his home with the Tennesseean and his wife. About two weeks thereafter, I had occasion to go down myself. When I came to the river I found it was covered with a coat of ice two-thirds of the way across, but it was thawing and somewhat rotten. It looked as though it would be impossible to cross it, but I happened to be riding an excellent long-legged horse. I rode him into the river until he came to the ice, when he climbed up with his front feet until it broke down, then he would climb up again until he broke through. He seemed to understand perfectly what I wanted of him. Finally he broke a road clear through the ice so that I was

20. "His bones are buried on the east bank of the Medicine River near Kiowa. I named a street of our city [Wichita] for him."—JRM.

New York, March 26th, 1874.

GENTS: We solicit from Trappers, and shippers of Furs and Skins, their consignments, and would here say we are prepared to receive for sale on Commission large lots (as well as small) of Furs and Skins, as we reserve an entire floor in our Store building for this part of our business. An experience of several years, and a large acquaintance with first-class buyers, both Manufacturers and Agents of the London and Leipsic markets, enable us to feel confident we can give entire satisfaction to those who favor us with their consignments. Below we give you quotations to date, revised from the latest London sales. Since our last issue (18th) Skunk have advanced still higher.

Yours respectfully, DODD & JONES.

Reference, New York National Exchange Bank.

We will remit to shippers by Post Office money order when preferred to check.

Established 1865.

PRICE LIST
OF
DODD & JONES,
333 WASHINGTON STREET,
NEW YORK,
COMMISSION MERCHANTS
FOR THE SALE OF
RAW FURS AND SKINS.
March 26th, 1874.

Item		Low		High
BADGER		$0 25	@	$0 50
BEAR, Black, Northern and Eastern		12 00	@	15 00
" " Western		8 00	@	10 00
BEAVER, per skin, Canada		2 00	@	3 00
" " Lake Superior		2 00	@	3 00
" " Western		1 50	@	2 00
CAT, Wild, Northern and Eastern, csd		25	@	50
" " Southern and Western		15	@	25
" House, ordinary		8	@	12
" Black furred		20	@	35
DEER SKINS, Summer and Fall, per lb.				45
" " Winter				30
" " Indian tanned				1 75
FISHER, Northern and Eastern		9 00	@	10 00
" North-western		7 00	@	8 00
FOX, Silver, according to size and color		20 00	@	75 00
" Cross, Northern and Eastern		3 00	@	8 00
" Penn., N. J. & O.		2 00	@	5 00
" Red, Northern and Eastern		1 75	@	1 87
" " Western		1 50	@	1 75
" Gray, Northern and Eastern		60	@	70
" " Southern		40	@	45
LYNX, according to size		1 50	@	4 00
MARTIN, N. Y. State and Eastern			@	2 00
" Lake Superior			@	3 00
MINK, N. Y. State and Eastern, large 1, very dark		4 00	@	4 50
" " ordinary		2 00	@	3 00
" Minnesota and Canada East		2 00	@	3 50
" Michigan and Wisconsin		2 00	@	3 00
MINK, N. J., Penn. & Ohio		2 00	@	2 50
" Md., Va., Mo., Ills., S. Iowa & Ky.		1 00	@	2 50
" North Carolina, Tenn. and all Southern.		1 50	@	2 50
MUSKRATS, Northern and Eastern, Spring		30	@	32
" " " Winter		24	@	26
" " " Fall		20	@	22
" North. Ohio & Mich., Spring		28	@	30
" " " Winter		23	@	25
" " " Fall		18	@	20
" Common Western, Spring		26	@	28
" " " Winter		21	@	23
" " " Fall		16	@	18
" Kitts		5	@	6
OTTER, Northern and Eastern		9 00	@	10 00
" Western		7 00	@	8 00
" South-Western		6 00	@	7 00
" Southern		6 00	@	7 00
OPOSSUM, Northern, cased		15	@	20
" Southern and open Northern		6	@	10
RACCOON, North. Ohio & Mich		70	@	75
" Western		50	@	60
" South-Western		35	@	40
" Southern		25	@	30
SKUNK, Prime Black; No. 1, cased		1 25	@	1 75
" Half striped		65	@	1 00
" Striped		25	@	30
" White		12	@	15
WOLF SKINS, large Mountain			@	3 00
" " Prairie			@	1 00

The above quotations are for prime Skins, excepting Muskrats. Other qualities in the usual proportion.

Price list of Dodd and Jones, New York, for the sale of raw furs and skins, March 26, 1874. Mead Collection, Wichita.

enabled to cross to the road leading up to the stockade, which was about one hundred and fifty yards distant and in plain sight.

I rode along quite leisurely and as I approached saw a man get up out of a turret in the corner of the stockade. He was armed with a long Kentucky squirrel rifle, the hammer of which he let down, and walked into the house. On my riding up to the gate, the Tennesseean came out of his house with a wild look in his eyes and spoke to me. When I told him who I was he made me heartily welcome and invited me to get off and come in. He made me some coffee and set out what he had to eat. He then told me that he had come within a hair's breadth of shooting me by mistake; that I was wearing the same kind of a hat and coat and was riding the same kind of a horse that Johnnie Martin did; and when he saw me coming he intended to shoot me.

I asked what was the matter with Johnnie Martin and him.

"Don't you think that Johnnie Martin has been staying around here and has been making his home at my house for I don't know how long?" he asked. "He is a lazy old hound, always getting full of whiskey and meddling with other people's affairs. Don't you think that when he came down from your ranch to my house that I took him in and treated him white? Then one morning the rascal got full of whiskey and when I came back from looking after my ponies I found him making love to my wife! I made for my rifle to shoot him, but it was gone and while I was searching for it, he went out, and so did my wife, and I have not seen her since. And that goldarn Martin stole my best horse, and I said I would kill him on sight."

He then told me of the fight in which Mosley was mortally wounded; of the great number of Indians which he had killed, all of which I took in with some grains of allowance. Whether the Tennesseean, Johnnie Martin, and the old woman ever made up, I never learned.

In that same winter [1874–1875] there was a tragic occurrence in which my knowledge of plainscraft saved me, but it did not save some other parties. I was wintering a herd of beeves at a ranch on Elm Creek, a branch above Medicine Lodge, when there came a fall of snow about two feet in depth, damp and soft. Soon after this I started home to Wichita, setting out one beautiful, warm, melting day, taking the trail to Kingman. There was a ranch on the head of

Chilasly[21] where I got my dinner. There I found the mail carrier, also on horseback, going to Kingman, and he proposed that we travel in company during the afternoon over the remaining twenty-five miles.[22] So we struck out together and kept together for two or three hours. But as he had a much poorer horse than I, he could not keep up, and told me to go ahead; that he knew the trail very well and that he would make it through all right, so I rode on alone.

Not long after, I saw a dense bank of fog coming rolling down from the North and in fifteen minutes one of the fiercest blizzards struck me that I ever experienced. In a short time the trail was utterly obliterated and the sharp driving snow carried by the wind cut my face so that I could hardly face it and could not see any distance. But I kept my course until dark. There I was out on the wild prairie, the air filled with sharp driving snow and ice, and but one human habitation within fifty miles. I must either find that or lie out all night in that terrible storm.

I kept my course as well as I could, riding through hills and hollows, and had been riding an hour or two in the dark when suddenly I caught the smell of buffalo chips burning, which might have been quite a distance away. I knew that I must be due South of the two or three houses there were at Kingman, so I turned my horse and rode directly against the wind and sleet, not daring to turn to the right or the left for ravines, hills, or anything. I presume I rode some three or four miles, when I came down into a level valley, and shortly found myself on the bank of the river which I knew to be the Ninnescah. The question then arose, which way was Kingman? If I went up the river to the left and missed it, there would be no other house between me and the mountains. The buildings were on the other side of the river, and I could not see a hundred yards.

I sat there on my horse quite awhile, thinking what was the best thing to do, when I thought I could see a dark object a short dis-

21. So it appears in the manuscript, but "Chilasly" is clearly intended to be Chikaskia. JRM stopped for dinner at the Reed Ranch.
22. The mail carrier was G. D. Mounts. The date was January 1, 1875. Mr. Mounts had never carried the mail before. He was substituting for the regular carrier, Barney O'Connor. See the *Wichita Eagle*, Thursday, August 8, 1929. The trail followed by JRM ran from Elm Creek in Barber County to the northeast, crossing Sand Creek and proceeding to the head of Chikaskia, then on to the northeast, passing near present-day St. Leo in Kingman County. From a point near present-day Cleveland JRM turned north toward Kingman.

tance up the river. I rode up about one hundred yards and there came to a wooden bridge across the river, and on the opposite side were the houses. I rode over and woke up my friend Ball, got my horses into a dugout, ate some supper, and told them about the mail carrier who was behind and unquestionably lost. They put a light in the upstairs window facing South, but said it was utterly impossible to go out that night and hunt him.

The next morning I got all the men in town on horses, with blankets and stimulants, and we started out to find him. After several hours riding we found him exhausted and bewildered, but still alive, leading his pony into the hills in the opposite direction from what he should have been going. It froze so hard during that night that horses could cross the river on the ice, while at noon the day before it was as warm as a day in Spring.

Toward morning of that same night, my men back at camp heard someone calling from up the creek. On searching, they found two men who had been caught with their teams on the high prairie. They had made the best windbreak they could out of their wagon bed and other things, and wrapped themselves up in their blankets, trying to keep warm, until they found they were about to freeze to death and would perish before morning. So, wrapping themselves up the best they were able, they rode South until they got down into the creek on which my camp was situated. Near the camp the snow had drifted so deep that their horses fell, floundering, and could go no further. My men found them almost frozen to death. They brought them to camp and put their frozen legs and hands into a tub of cold water. They were frozen so badly that a thick coat of ice gathered on their feet and hands in the water. The result was that one man lost both of his legs and possibly his hands—I don't remember—and the other man was frozen so badly that I think he died. That was only one of the contingencies that a plainsman might expect to encounter at any time on the plains.

I was once travelling alone with a team in Kansas and made camp by the side of the road at Sycamore Springs in Butler County. The place is so named from the large spring boiling up from the rocks under the roots of an immense sycamore tree. In the night there came up a terrible thunder storm. The flashes of lightning and the peals of thunder followed each other incessantly and appeared to be striking all round me. I became so alarmed that I took a blanket and went down into a ravine, on the sides of which I found a patch of grass that raised me up above the surrounding ground and kept me from the torrents of water running everywhere. Putting my blanket under and drawing a buffalo robe over me, with the skin side out, of course, I curled up in a little circle like a cat going to sleep, and lay there until morning.

On another occasion, when I was holding a herd of cattle on the Ninnescah, there came up a thunder storm in the night. One bolt of lightning killed six beeves within fifty yards of where I was on my horse, trying to hold the cattle. This I found to be impossible to do, so the cowboys and I drifted with those cattle all night, keeping them together as much as possible, and in the morning we found ourselves six or eight miles from camp. But we had our cattle all right.

Once I was riding through in the night from the Chikaskia to the Ninnescah, and as I approached the divide there came up a furious thunder storm, which was one continual roar of thunder and flash of lightning. Points of light shot up from the ears of my horse and also from the frayed edge of my broad-brimmed hat. I was riding as rapidly as I dared through the storm when my horse, a very tall animal, stumbled and fell, turning a summersault. As he fell I sprang forward on my hands and knees, and running forward, thus got out of his way. As he was a very wild animal, I thought I would be left afoot fifteen miles from my home in a terrible storm. But when my horse got up he seemed so under the influence of fear that I walked up to him and caught him readily. Then I rode on until I came to a deserted ranch built of sod that used to be occupied by Billy Polk.[23] There I found a bunk and some rotting blankets that were steaming with moisture. I was wet to the skin myself, with no means of making a fire. But I picketed my horse on the grass and lay down and slept till morning without light or fire, and at daylight went on my way rejoicing.

In all my experience on the plains in thunder storms, when the country was covered thickly with buffalo, and bolts of lightning were striking the ground in every direction, I never saw or heard of a buffalo being killed by lightning.

Two or three days before Christmas, while at my cattle camp, I

23. William Polk arrived in Wichita in the spring of 1870. ANDREAS, 1385.

took my rifle and went up the creek to kill a wild turkey or two. Within an hour I had shot three fine fat gobblers that would weigh probably fifteen pounds apiece. I was beside the trail which led to Wichita, where my family was living. As I was resting, along came a man in a light spring wagon.

I asked him where he was going and he said, "to Wichita, and going through in a hurry."

Says I, "Mister, I'll tell you what I'll do. You are going to Wichita. I have three turkeys here. Now if you will take two of them to my family, you may keep the other one for yourself."

He said that he would do it. So my family had two fat turkeys for Christmas, but I was not there to help eat them.

While I had never seen that man before, I had not the slightest doubt that he would take those turkeys to my family. It was a fact that in the early days on the plains, there was the strictest honesty between men. There was no law to enforce the collection of debts, and yet I have trusted men some of whom were supposed to be outlaws and thieves engaged in running off government mules from trains and stealing Indian ponies. I have trusted that class of men time and again to the amount of hundreds of dollars, with no possible security or recourse excepting their honor, and never lost a dollar by one of them. Such a thing as a man not paying a debt that he had contracted with another plainsman, if it was in his power to do so, was unknown. The Indians themselves frequently got credit at my trading post, and I also trusted the wild Indians on the plains to quite large amounts, and they invariably paid me according to agreement. Sometimes I would not see them for six months.

In those years there were no courts, no officers, no law but the law of the plains: "Do as you would be done by." Yet life and property were as safe as they are today, and a man could ride all over the country, camping alone at night without the slightest apprehension of danger.

CHAPTER 18

The Indians Have Melted Away: Looking Back Across Thirty Years

THE changes that have taken place in central Kansas since the days when I roamed among the buffalo and Indians are so wonderful that it is almost impossible for any person not familiar with the facts to believe them. Where I used to hunt buffalo, elk, and deer, and where Indian villages were located, are now found commercial cities with railroads branching in every direction. A good illustration of this is the city of Wichita with 24,000 inhabitants and four or five trunk lines of railroads, paved streets, electric lights, electric railways, colleges, and universities, all situated where for years I hunted buffalo and traded with Indians. Prior to the coming of the white men I saw the place occupied by two different tribes of Indians successively,[1] and I am still, so far as my feelings and activity are concerned, a young man.

I was forcibly impressed with these changes when, after an absence of twenty-five years, I revisited the cave on Smoky Hill River which I had discovered in 1862, and where, among the multitude of Indian hieroglyphics, I found the name *Trudo, 1786*. The romance which lingers round that spot and other localities along the Smoky Hill River induced me to revisit it, but instead of going as in former days with my team and wagon, I rode there in a Pullman railway car. And instead of camping out on the river bank and cooking my

1. The Osages and the Wichitas.

248

own supper, I stopped at a fine hotel in the flourishing town of Wilson, two or three miles from the caves.[2]

In starting out to revisit my camp, I found it a very difficult matter to locate it, as the timber along the river had all been cut down and groves of trees had been planted in the adjoining prairies. The entire country was enclosed by wire fences surrounding cultivated fields or pastures and, but for some prominent natural landmarks, I might have found great difficulty in locating the spot.

On arriving at the cave I found that it was embraced within the enclosure of a farm. About a hundred yards from it was a commodious farmhouse with orchard and outbuildings, and the cave itself was used for a corral and shelter for stock. Most of the rocks on which were carved the Indian hieroglyphics had been broken down to build fences, but the name and date which were of particular interest to me, with my own name which I had carved underneath, had fortunately escaped destruction, and were as plainly to be read as they were in 1862.

On that same trip I also rode along up the Saline River on the railway to visit my old ranch. There I found the entire valley of the river, which was the scene of so many of my hunting adventures and adventures with Indians, converted into corn fields—not a vestige of my ranch or buildings remaining. The fine groves of immense cottonwood and oak timber which grew on three sides of my ranch were entirely gone, and nothing but a scrubby growth of brush along the river marked its course. But the rocky buttes and the hills and the ravines, every one of which were as familiar to me as the cow-paths of my father's farm, were there unchanged. In place of buffalo there were cattle; in place of antelope there were sheep; the flocks of glossy bronze wild turkeys had disappeared, and in their place were chickens, ducks, and geese. The beautiful clear water of the river had, from the constant washing of the cultivated lands and numerous pens of cattle and hogs along its banks, become very much like a sewer.

---

2. "The cave is 2½ miles S.W. of Wilson's Station on the Union Pacific Railroad. Four miles N.W. of this station is a cliff of sandstone rock, from which flows a fine spring. This was a favorite camping place of the Indians."—JRM. JRM returned to the Wilson area on at least two occasions to revisit the scenes of his youthful adventures and to copy petroglyphs: once in May, 1887, and again in July, 1892. "Trudeau, 1786," was inscribed by fur trader Jean Baptiste Trudeau, who left Montreal for St. Louis in 1777.

The Banner County of the Great Arkansas Valley.

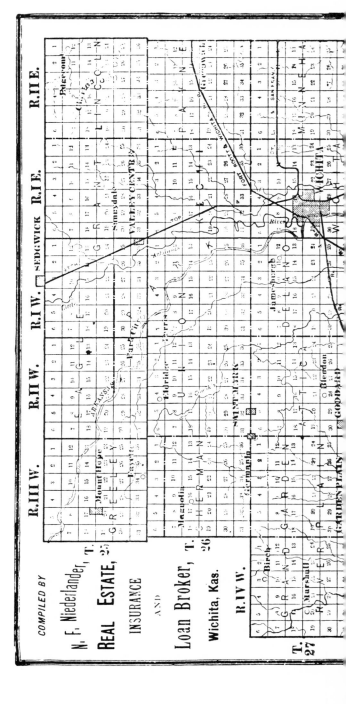

COMPILED BY

N. F. Niederlander, T.

REAL ESTATE,

INSURANCE

AND

Loan Broker,

Wichita, Kas.

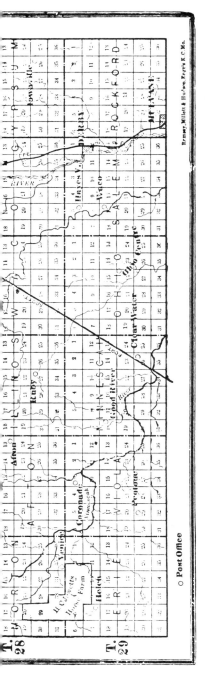

○ Post Office

READ THE OFFICIAL RETURNS FOR THE YEAR 1884.

Acres of Wheat	79,612
Acres of Rye	2,701
Acres of Corn	129,707
Acres of Oats	23,020
Acres of Potatoes	1,481
Acres of Millet and Hungarian	9,325
Acres of Timothy	1,611
No. of Horses	9,352
No. of Mules	2,036
No. of Cows	10,172
No. of other Cattle	28,829
No. of Sheep	23,610

No. of Hogs	61,611
No. of bearing Apple Trees	47,123
No. of bearing Peach Trees	310,688
No. of acres in Cultivation	285,081
No. of acres Uninproved	311,931
Value of Taxable Lands	$3,958,280
Value of Town Lots	1,270,275
Value of Personal Property	1,419,536
Value of Railroad Property	489,686
Total Value	7,137,777
Population of Wichita and suburbs	13,299
Population of Sedgwick County	29,829

9. *Map of Sedgwick County, Kansas, with agricultural, demographic, and property statistics for the year 1884*

In the early winter of 1894 I passed down the old Chisholm Trail again, but this time on the Rock Island Railway instead of by the slower, but not less pleasant, trip with freight wagons. The Rock Island Railroad follows South from Wichita almost exactly on the old Chisholm Trail, and every river and creek and camping ground was perfectly familiar to me as we rode along. On arriving at Pond Creek, where I was captured by the Cheyennes, I found in place of the Indian and the buffalo a flourishing young city.[3] And here would be a suitable place to give the history of the name attached to that locality.

Mr. Chisholm's teams and my own were the first which ever passed over that route, and we marked out what afterward became the celebrated Chisholm Trail. On arriving at what is known as Pond Creek, where we selected a crossing, we found a circular bayou filled with water, surrounding an island of some ten acres in extent on which grew considerable timber. This bayou was the old creek bed, which ran round in a circle until it nearly met itself again. In the course of time, during some flood, the waters had cut across the little neck of land, forming an island and a circular lake. The water took a straight cut instead of going round the circle, and the annual overflow soon filled up the entrance and outlet to this old channel. To this peculiar circular body of water we gave the name of Round Pond as most appropriate, and called the creek Round Pond Creek, as it had no other name to our knowledge.

Soon after, I established a trading post there for the Winter and built a log cabin and sent Jack Lawton[4] and a couple of other men out to trade with the Indians. This was known as Round Pond Ranch. Afterwards, when the Chisholm Trail became a great highway for Texas cattle passing North, as well as a great interstate commercial highway, there was an extensive trading establishment and ranch maintained at that place, which continued down to the opening of the Cherokee Strip for settlement. Then a town was located at that point, and it has grown into considerable prominence

3. Pond Creek in Grant County, Oklahoma.
4. "Jack Lawton was later in charge of my trading post between the rivers where Wichita has since been built. He was killed by a renegade white man in 1866 while sitting on the counter in the store—the only crime committed in the country during the five years that the Wichita Indians were there. In the first five or six years *after* the Indians left I have a record of some twenty men who came to a sudden and violent death. Most of these were no special loss to the country."—JRM.

The home that James R. Mead built in 1872 at 307 East Central in Wichita. Standing from right to left are James L. ("Bunnie") Mead, James R. Mead, and Lucy Inman Mead. The other persons have not been identified. Later the rectory and school of Saint Mary's Cathedral were built on the site. Mead Collection, Wichita.

and has lately occupied much space in the Associated Press dispatches, owing to a rival town and trouble with the railroads.

On proceeding down the road I found at Skeleton Creek the flourishing city of Enid growing up. Skeleton Creek was named from the fact that in 1867 a large number of Wichita Indians died there of the cholera and their unburied bodies lay scattered about on the surface of the ground. Further along, down on Turkey Creek, where I once wintered and spent the time in hunting and trading with the Indians, I found a settled country with wheat and corn fields and thriving farms.

On arriving at the North Fork of the Canadian, I could scarcely recognize the river. The luxuriant timber which once fringed its banks was almost entirely gone. On the South bank of the river was built a city,[5] while a few miles West was the large military establishment of Ft. Reno. The smooth, beautiful valley, which once was covered with a velvety carpet of buffalo grass, on which grazed thousands of buffalo and other game, was partially ploughed up and in places covered with an unsightly growth of sand burrs and sunflowers. And the river, which formerly flowed with an ample volume of pure water, clear as crystal, had almost dried up, so that the river bed was utilized for miles as a pleasant carriage drive.

Once the North Fork of the Canadian was the most beautiful river in the Indian Territory, with the purest, sweetest water. Its Indian name was Co-co-ha-ca-yo, which means in the Caddo language "White Water." This name is derived from the pure white sand which composes the bed of the river, which made the river look white in looking down from the bank through its crystal waters. Scattered along the river to the West were the Cheyenne and Arapaho Indians, still there under the allotment system adopted by the Government. The Cheyennes and Arapahoes had taken up the entire valley of the river for thirty miles West of El Reno, and were still camped along the river much to their fashion. But instead of buffalo, they subsisted on Texas beef and Government rations, and lived in teepees made of cotton cloth instead of dressed buffalo skins.

On visiting the Indian camp, I found them to be but the dejected, miserable remnants of a former proud and haughty race. The entire destruction of the game on which they formerly subsisted had broken up their methods and customs of life which they had practiced from time immemorial. Their change of food and enforced sedentary habits, together with the vices they had acquired from their so-called civilized and Christian neighbors had brought to them a train of sickness, disease, and death. Their proud and haughty spirit was broken, and life apparently afforded them no pleasure for the present or hope for the future, excepting possibly their annual medicine dance, where they revived the customs and the traditions of their ancestors. The attempts of the Government to change them into farmers were evidently a failure. They seemed

5. El Reno in Oklahoma's Canadian County.

James R. Mead, about 1898. Mead Collection, Wichita.

to be about as spiritless and worthless as a lot of wild animals brought from the wilderness of Africa and confined in cages for purposes of exhibition.

The Indian was fashioned and given his intended faculties by the Great Creator of the universe, who placed him here to subsist upon the natural products of the earth. He gave them cattle in unlimited numbers for their subsistence, and these furnished them with everything necessary for their mode of life. The robe of the buffalo furnished them with clothing, bedding, and shelter. Their flesh was the Indians' food. From his skin they made their lodges, covered their saddles, made ropes and moccasins, carpets, and bedding. From their sinews they made thread and bowstrings. From their long hair they made lariats, from their horns they made spoons, and from their bones they made quirt handles, and various other implements of use. The trees of the forest afforded them shade and shelter in summer, and wild fruits and nuts, and the many roots which they utilized furnished them all the vegetable food which they required—all the free products of nature, without great labor on their part. And the attempt to change their life has, in a great majority of instances, proven an entire failure. Following the destruction of their buffalo and other game, the Indians have melted away like snow before a summer's sun. For instance, the Kansas or Kaw tribe of Indians, who numbered fifteen hundred when I first went among them, have now less than a hundred members alive, and other tribes have decreased in like proportion.

The beauties and blessings of civilization are very largely a myth. In a majority of instances it is but a daily round of ceaseless toil. The freedom and the beauty and the chivalry of the plains are a thing of the past; nothing now remains but dull, plodding labor, and many thousands of settlers are now squatted down on a little circumscribed piece of prairie land, trying to eke out an existence by constant toil and privation where once roamed the Indian, free and unfettered, a stranger to fear or care, with thousands of fat cattle on every hand to supply his wants, living a life of ease, happiness and pleasure unknown to his white successor.

All these changes which have taken place during the last thirty years seem like a dream as my mind travels back over the events that have occurred during this period of my life. While surrounded by all the comforts and conveniences of modern civilization, I long

for the good old times of entire personal freedom which I once enjoyed on the plains; where there were no laws or customs or hin-
drances to the enjoyment of our own sweet will; where the earth
and all it produced were as free as the air or sunshine; where life
was not a daily struggle for existence as it now is with so many
thousands of people; where the tax-gatherer came not and mort-
gages were unknown; where the nearest route between two points
was our road, unobstructed by wire fences or cultivated fields.

In those happy days the plains rejoiced in their pristine beauty,
unmarred by civilization, which first destroys so far as is possible
whatever Providence placed here for man's use, and then commences the slow process of reproducing what it has destroyed.
Then these plains were covered with unnumbered myriads of buffalo, sufficient to supply the nation with meat. The wanton greed of
the white man has slaughtered the last one. The elk, the deer, and
the antelope have likewise disappeared. Our rivers and streams
once swarmed with fish, now the State Fish Commission is seek-
ing to restock them. In my recollection our water courses were
skirted with noble groves of cottonwood, walnut, hackberry, oak,
and elm. They are gone, and the men who now occupy the land are
planting trees. Verily, in some respects, to quote a remark by my
Indian friend Not-ta-tunka, the white man is "heap no good." And,
as another old Indian Chief once remarked in my hearing:

"The sun does not shine as bright, the grass is not as green, the
air is not as pure, and the water is not as sweet as it was before the
white men came."

Bibliography

SOURCES CITED AND CONSULTED BY THE EDITOR

ANDREAS   Andreas, A. T. *History of the State of Kansas.* 2 vols. 1883.

AUSTIN   Austin, O. L. *Birds of the World.* London: Paul Hamlyn, 1961.

BARRY   Barry, L. *The Beginning of the West: Annals of the Kansas Gateway to the American West, 1540–1854.* Topeka, Kans.

BENTLEY   Bentley, O. H., ed. *History of Wichita and Sedgwick County, Kansas, Past and Present, Including an Account of the Cities, Towns, and Villages of the County.* 2 vols. Chicago: C. F. Cooper and Co., 1910.

BLACKMAR   Blackmar, F. W., ed. *Kansas: A Cyclopedia of State History, Embracing Events, Institutions, Industries, Counties, Cities, Towns, Prominent Persons, etc.* 2 vols. Chicago: Standard Publishing Co., 1912.

BOLTON   Bolton, H. E. *Tawakoni.* In HODGE, F. W.

BRAMWELL   Bramwell, R. P. *City on the Move.* Salina, Kans.: Survey Press.

BURT AND   Burt, W. H., and R. P. Grossenheimer. *A Field Guide*
GROSSENHEIMER *to Mammals.* Boston: 1952 and 1964.

CAMPBELL   Campbell, H. B. "Camp Beecher." *Kansas Historical Quarterly* 3 (1934): 172–85.

CONNELLEY [1]   Connelley, W. E. "Indian Treaties and Councils Affecting Kansas: Dates and Places, Where Held, Names of Tribes, Commissioners and Indians Concluding Same."

Kansas State Historical Society Collections 16 (1925): 746–69.

CONNELLEY [2] ———. "Notes on the Early Indian Occupancy of the Great Plains." Kansas State Historical Society Collections 14 (1918).

CONNELLEY [3] ———. "The Lane Trail." Kansas State Historical Society Collections 13 (1914).

CONNELLEY [4] ———. History of Kansas Newspapers; A History of the Newspapers & Magazines Published in Kansas from the Organization of Kansas Territory, 1854, to January 1st, 1916, etc. Topeka: Kansas State Historical Society and Department of Archives, 1916.

CUNNINGHAM Cunningham, G. L. "Gambling in the Kansas Cattle Towns: A Prominent and Somewhat Honorable Profession." Kansas History: A Journal of the Central Plains 5, no. 1 (1982): 2–22.

DRIVER Driver, H. E. Indians of North America. Chicago: University of Chicago Press, 1961.

EDWARDS Edwards, J. P. Historical Atlas of Sedgwick County, Kansas, Compiled, Drawn, and Published from Personal Examination and Surveys. Philadelphia, 1882. Reprint. Mid-West Historical and Genealogical Society, Sedgwick County, Kansas, 1982.

EMMERT Emmert, D. B. "History of Sedgwick County." In EDWARDS.

EWERS Ewers, J. C. "Hair Pipes in Indian Adornment; A Study in Indian and White Ingenuity." Anthropological Paper no. 50. Smithsonian Institution, Bureau of American Ethnology, Bulletin, no. 164, Washington, D.C.: 1957.

FRONVAL AND Fronval, G., and D. DuBois. Indian Signs and Symbols.
DUBOIS New York: Sterling Publishing Co., 1978.

GEOG. "Extinct Geographical Locations: A List of 'lost' Towns, Post-Offices, Overland Stations, Missions, Settlements, & Trading Posts in Kansas, 1852 to 1912." Kansas State Historical Society Collections 12 (1912): 472–83.

GOSS Goss, N. S. History of the Birds of Kansas. Topeka: G. W. Crane and Co., 1891.

GREEN [1] Green, C. R. Early Days in Kansas Along the Santa Fe Trail; Council City 1854–5; Superior 1856, & Burlingame 1856–1864. Green's Historical Series, no. 2. Olathe, Kans, Charles R. Green, n.d.

GREEN [2] ———. Early Days in Kansas, Along the Santa Fe and Lawrence Trails. Green's Historical Series, no. 3. Olathe, Kans.; Charles R. Green, 1913.

GRINNELL [1]   Grinnell, George Bird. "Bent's Old Fort & Its Builders." *Kansas State Historical Society Collections* 15 (1922): 28–91.

GRINNELL [2]   ———. *The Fighting Cheyennes*, Charles Scribner's Sons, 1915. Reprint. Norman: University of Oklahoma Press, 1956.

GRINNELL [3]   ———. *The Cheyenne Indians: Their History and Ways of Life*. 2 vols. New York: Cooper Square, 1962.

HADLEY   Hadley, J. A. "The Nineteenth Kansas Cavalry and the Conquest of the Plains Indians." *Kansas State Historical Society Collections* 10 (1908): 428–456.

HAINES   Haines, E. "Early Days in Ottawa County." *Kansas State Historical Society Collections* 10 (1908).

HISTORY   *History of Scott County, Iowa*. Chicago: Inter-State Publishing Co., 1882.

HODGE   Hodge, F. W., *Handbook of American Indians North of Mexico*. Smithsonian Institution, Bureau of American Ethnology, *Bulletin*, no. 30. 2 vols. Washington, D.C., 1910.

HOWES   Howes, C. C. *This Place Called Kansas*. Norman: University of Oklahoma Press, 1952.

JOHNSTON   Johnston, J. H. *Early Leavenworth and Fort Leavenworth: A Photographic History*. Leavenworth, Kans.: J. H. Johnston, 1977.

KAPPLER   Kappler, C. J. *Indian Treaties, 1778–1883*. New York: Interland Publishing Co.

KSHC   Kansas State Historical Collections (Topeka).

LONG   Long, R. M. *Wichita Century: A Pictorial History of Wichita, Kansas*. Wichita: Wichita Historical Museum Association, Inc., 1969.

MALLERY   Mallery, Garrick. "Sign Language Among North American Indians. . . ." *First Annual Report of the Bureau of Ethnology*. Washington, D.C.: 1881.

MAYHALL   Mayhall, M. P. *The Kiowas*, Norman: University of Oklahoma Press, 1971.

MEAD, F.   Mead, Fern. *James R. Mead*. In BENTLEY 2: 534–38.

MEAD   Mead, James R. "Journal of Incidents and Events Occurring During an Excursion to the Rocky Mountains." Manuscript, 1859. Mead Collection, Wichita.

MEAD [2]   ———. "Reminiscences of Frontier Life." Manuscript dated (probably incorrectly) 1888. Mead Collection, Wichita.

MEAD [3]   "Hon. J. R. Mead's Address at the Old Settlers." *Wichita Weekly Beacon*, February 28, 1883.

MEAD [4]   ———. "The Four Horsemen and the Cattle Trail." *Wichita Eagle*, February 28, 1884.

MEAD [5]   ———. "The Chisholm Trail." *Wichita Eagle*, March 1, 1890.

MEAD [6]   ———. "Early Days in Butler County." *Walnut Valley Times* (El Dorado, Kans.), February 19, 1892.

MEAD [7]   ———. "Trails in Southern Kansas." *Kansas State Historical Society Collections* 5 (1896): 88–93.

MEAD [8]   ———. "Felis concolor." *Transactions of the Kansas Academy of Science* 16 (1898): 278–79.

MEAD [9]   ———. "Were Quails Native to Kansas?" *Transactions of the Kansas Academy of Science* 16 (1898): 277–78.

MEAD [10]   ———. "The Leonid Meteors of 1833 as Observed on the Plains by a Native Kansan." Paper read at the 32d Annual Meeting of the Kansas Academy of Science, McPherson, Kansas, December 28, 29, and 30, 1899.

MEAD [11]   ———. "The Wichita Indians in Kansas." *Kansas State Historical Society Collections* 8 (1904): ;171–77.

MEAD [12]   ———. "In the Beginning." *Wichita Eagle*, February 12. 1905.

MEAD [13]   ———. "Notes on the Archaeology of Butler County." *Transactions of the Kansas State Academy of Science* 9 (1905): 329–30.

MEAD [14]   ———. "The Saline River Country in 1859." *Kansas State Historical Society Collections* 9 (1906): 8–19.

MEAD [15]   ———. "The Little Arkansas." *Kansas State Historical Society Collections* 10 (1908): 7–14.

MEAD [16]   ———. "The Pawnees as I Knew Them." *Kansas State Historical Society Collections* 10 (1908): 106–111.

MEAD [17]   ———. "Addendum to the 19th Kansas Cavalry and the Conquest of the Plains Indians by J. A. Hadley." *Kansas State Historical Society Collections* 10 (1908): 664–65.

MEAD [18]   ———. "Addendum to Diary of Luther A. Thrasher." *Kansas State Historical Society Collections* 10 (1908): 663–64.

MILLER   Miller, N. H. *The Thirty-Fourth Star*. Topeka: Kansas State Historical Society, 1976.

MILLISON   Millison, D. G. "The Founding of the Beacon." In BENTLEY 2: 468–77.

MINER   Miner, C. *Wichita, The Early Years, 1865–1880*. Omaha: University of Nebraska Press, 1982.

MOONEY [1]   Mooney, J. "The Ghost Dance Religion and the Sioux Outbreak of 1890." *Fourteenth Annual Report of the Bu-*

reau of American Ethnology. Pt. 2. Washington, D.C., 1896.

MOONEY [2]   ———. "Calendar History of the Kiowa Indians. *Seventeenth Annual Report of the Bureau of American Ethnology.* Washington, D.C., 1898.

MOONEY, V.P.   Mooney, V. P. *History of Butler County, Kansas.* Lawrence, Kans.: Standard Publishing Co., 1916.

MORGAN   Morgan, Lewis Henry. *The Indian Journals, 1859–62.* Ann Arbor: University of Michigan Press, 1959.

MURDOCK   "Mead Tells Murdock About the Walnut." *Wichita Eagle,* April 30, 1909.

NEVINS   Nevins, A. *Frémont, The West's Greatest Adventurer.* 2 vols. New York: 1928.

NICHOLSON   Nicholson, W. "Tour of the Agencies in Kansas and the Indian Territory in 1870." *Kansas Historical Quarterly,* 3 (1934): 355.

PHILLIPS   Phillips Petroleum Company. *Pasture and Range Plants.* Bartlesville, Okla., 1963.

RYDJORD   Rydjord, J. *Indian Place Names: Their Origin, Evolution & Meanings, Collected in Kansas from the Siouan, Algonquian, Shoshonean, Caddoan, Iroquoian, & Other Tongues.* Norman: University of Oklahoma Press, 1968.

SHERIDAN   Philip Sheridan. Box 76, Correspondence. Manuscript Division, Library of Congress, Washington, D.C.

SOCOLOFSKY   Socolofsky, Homer E., and Huber Self. *Historical Atlas*
AND SELF   *of Kansas.*

SOWERS   Sowers, F. A. *Early History of Wichita* In BENTLEY 2:6–14.

STARR   Starr, D. *The Mooney Memorial Christian Church.* North Newton, Kans.: Mennonite Press, Inc., 1978.

STRATFORD   Stratford, J. P. *Butler County's Eighty Years, 1855–1935.*

STRIBLING   Stribling, M. L. *Crafts from North American Indian Arts.* New York: Crown Publishing Company, Inc. 1975.

THRASHER   Thrasher, L. A. "Copy of Diary of Luther A. Thrasher, Quartermaster, Nineteenth Kansas Cavalry, October 15 to December 31, 1968." *Kansas State Historical Society Collections* 10 (1908): 660–63.

VAUGHT   Vaught, M. "Chelsea Township." In STRATFORD.

WEICHSELBAUM   Weichselbaum, T. "Statement of Theodore Weichselbaum, of Ogden, Riley County, July 17th, 1908." *Kansas State Historical Society Collections* 11 (1910): 561–71, Topeka.

WILSON AND   Wilson, J. G., and J. Fiske, eds. *Appleton's Cyclopedia*
FISKE   *of American Biography.* New York: Appleton and Co., 1888.

WITAKER   Witaker, J. O. *The Audubon Society Field Guide to North American Mammals.* New York: Chanticleer Press, 1980.

WYNDHAM-   Wyndham-Quin, W. T., Fourth Earl of Dunraven. *Canadian Nights.* London: Smith, Elder and Co., 1914.
QUIN

YOUNG AND   Young, S. P., and E. A. Goldman. *The Wolves of North America.* 1944.
GOLDMAN

ZORNOW   Zornow, W. F. *Kansas: A History of the Jayhawk State.* Norman: University of Oklahoma Press, 1957.

OTHER ARTICLES, ADDRESSES, AND PAPERS BY JAMES R. MEAD

1880   "Hon. J. R. Mead's Address," Old Settlers' Annual Reunion, Wichita, February 19.

1883   "Times Before Old Settlers." *Wichita Eagle*, March 1.

1883   "Primeval Kansas." An Address given in Wichita at the Old Settlers' Meeting. *Topeka Capital*, March 3.

1885   "Results of Some Explorations Among the Pueblo Ruins in New Mexico." *Transactions of the Kansas Academy of Science* 10: 73–77.

1890   "Notes on the Occurrence of Gold in Montana." *Transactions of the Kansas Academy of Science* 12: 5–6.

1890   "From Wichita to Helena." *Wichita Eagle*, April 16 (pt. 1) and April 20 (pt. 2).

1890   "Reminiscent." *Wichita Eagle*, July 15.

1892   "A Hunt in the Cheyenne Country." *Okarche* (Okla. Terr.) *Advocate.* May 28.

1892   "Towanda." *Walnut Valley* (El Dorado, Kans.) *Times*, April 8. Also in STRATFORD.

1893   "How the Pheasant 'Drums.'" *Transactions of the Kansas Academy of Science* 14: 113–14.

1894   "A Dying River." *Transactions of the Kansas Academy of Science* 14: 111–12.

1896   "The Drill Hole at Wichita." *Transactions of the Kansas Academy of Science* 15: 20–22. Also in BENTLEY 1: 113–14.

1897   "Some Notes on the Birds of Southern Kansas." *Transactions of the Kansas Academy of Science* 16: 216–17.

1898   "Some Natural History Notes of 1859." *Transactions of the Kansas Academy of Science* 16: 280–81.

1899   "Notes of a Trip Through Western Wyoming." Paper read at the 32d Annual Meeting of the Kansas Academy of Science, McPherson, Kansas, December.

1900   "Archaeology of Catalina Island." *Transactions of the Kansas Academy of Science* 17: 215–16.

1900   "The Flint Hills of Kansas." *Transactions of the Kansas Academy of Science* 17: 207–208.
1902   "Origin of Names of Kansas Streams." *Transactions of the Kansas Academy of Science* 18: 215–16.
1903   "In the Fall of 1859." *Wichita Eagle*, October 18.
1903   "Where Wichita Got Its Name." *Wichita Beacon*, December 5.
1904   "Reminiscences of Prairie Life." *Wichita Eagle*, December 11.
1905   "Native Wild Fruits of Kansas." *Kansas State Horticultural Society Transactions* 28: 144–49.
1907   "History of the Little Arkansas River & Sedgwick County." *Wichita Beacon*, December 6.
1907   "Church History." *Topeka Journal*, February 23.
1907   "Of Chisholm and His Trail." *Wichita Eagle*, October 27.
1910   "The Meaning of the Word Wichita." Attributed to JRM but probably written by O. H. Bentley for BENTLEY 1: 111–12.
1910   "The Indians in Kansas." In BENTLEY 2: 525–34.

Index

267